# Scott
# Hamilton

# SCOTT HAMILTON

A Behind-the-Scenes Look at the
Life and Competitive Times
of America's Favorite Figure Skater

An Unauthorized Biography

## MICHAEL STEERE

ST. MARTIN'S PRESS
NEW YORK

B
Hamilton

Editor: Barbara Anderson
Copyeditor: Fred Goss
Design by Kingsley Parker

Library of Congress Cataloging in Publication Data
Steere, Michael.
  Scott Hamilton.
  l. Hamilton, Scott, 1958–  . 2. Skaters—United States—Biography. I. Title.
GV850.H34S72 1985     796.91′092′4[B]     85–11753
ISBN 0-312-70449-6

First Edition

10 9 8 7 6 5 4 3 2 1

To Dolores Sylvia Zajicek Steere

# Acknowledgments

Virtually everyone the author encountered in the last thirty months has done something for this book. It might not have been written at all without Susan Dovichi, who brightened an otherwise dark year. And Helen, who sent sustenance at the critical moments. My father, who told me to go to Colorado to see Scott. My uncle, Lowell Steere, who gave me a place to stay and a Dodge to drive when I got there. My grandparents, who fed me in Wisconsin, and Barbara Anderson, an editor who is a saint, and a telephone-crisis genius. Sharon Jadin, who typed, and Danielle, who drew on her mother's typing. And Stuart Moore, for additional typing. Too many people to mention gave to this project. Thanks to Don Laws, to Scott's family and his "Scott people," and to the skaters and officials of the United States Figure Skating Association. The skating people made the ice warm and welcoming, always.

# Author's Note

The largest part of this book is an intensely close look at Scott Hamilton in the 1982 competitive season, the season in which he successfully defended the World Championship he first won in 1981.

This second World Championship, in Copenhagen, was not Scott's most celebrated win. But it played an important part in his gold-medal victory at the 1984 Winter Olympics in Sarajevo, and in Scott's spectacular preeminence in skating in 1984. At the 1982 Copenhagen World Championships, Scott's skating turned a corner.

The year 1982 was a turbulent one for Scott. He was bedeviled by all the brain demons that come to athletes who must defend a title, any title, for the first time. His most potent adversaries that year weren't other skaters, but foes that lived in his head.

The scenes from 1982 are not always picturesque: Scott calls it the worst skating year of his life. But the difficulties of 1982 are instructive. Scott's competitive letdown in Copenhagen foreshadowed his supremely difficult moments in Sarajevo. Victory at Sarajevo became a matter of inner winning, just as it had been in 1982.

The following narrative is based primarily on Scott's running commentary on events during the 1982 season, taped and transcribed, and augmented by the author's observations. Most of these interviews have been edited, but convey the essential flavor and information of the original. Materials for the life history included taped interviews with Scott, and with his family, friends, and acquaintances. School records and news stories were also consulted, but few of the relevant medical records were available. An understanding of Scott's perplexing childhood difficulties is owed almost entirely to Dr. Harry Shwachman.

This book has not been authorized by Scott Hamilton.

—Michael Steere
Toledo, Ohio

# Contents

*Photo sections follow pages 96 and 204.*

# The Formative Years

*1958 to 1981*

# 1

# The Hamiltons' Special Boy

Dorothy McIntosh was born on September 2, 1928. She was the first child of Everett and Helen McIntosh, both schoolteachers, who lived in Weymouth, Massachusetts, a suburb of Boston about twelve miles south along the seashore from the city. Everett taught high school industrial arts, and Helen taught first grade. Dorothy represented the convergence of several old and distinguished New England bloodlines. Her father's family had prospered in the quarrying and cutting of stone at Quincy. Her mother's family, the Prays, were eighteenth-century pioneers, with a homestead near Weymouth. Helen was also directly descended from the presidential Adams family.

Dorothy's mother, who still lives in the house where Dorothy was raised, recalls that Dorothy was, from infancy, a model child. She was quiet, agreeable, and well behaved, a contrast to her little sister Marjorie, who was headstrong and flamboyant. Helen says that her girls' contrary temperaments show through in the musical instruments they chose to play when they were adolescents. Dorothy played the pipe organ; Marjorie took up the saxophone.

Dorothy, in many respects, was cast in the mold of her father. Chief among the similarities was an inexhaustible willingness to do for others. Everett, a stocky man (Dorothy also inherited the body type), was an indefatigable joiner and leader of voluntary organizations. He served as president of the Massachusetts Teachers Association, chaired a committee of the National Education Association, and directed that association's state unit. He was a leader in the local Masonic lodge, and chairman of the park board in Weymouth.

By the time she was a teenager, Dorothy was giving many hours to volunteer work. She devoted herself very actively to the Camp Fire Girls, and played organ for the Rainbow Girls, a Masonic group. When she reached dating age, Dorothy formed serious, long attachments with boys. Her mother remembers prodding her a little to let go of that emotional fixity and socialize more actively. Dorothy grew into a petite young woman, given to the plumpness that one day would swell into vexatious adult weight problems. She stood five feet three inches tall. Her eyes were bluish-green, lively and bright; her forehead high and her hair dark blond. Pictures of Dorothy in young womanhood show a very likely mother for Scott Hamilton. Indeed, acquaintances often tell Helen how much Scott looks like his mother. And Helen has an explanation: "They say that kids grow to be like the ones who love 'em."

Dorothy and Marjorie initially regarded the idea of following in their parents' professional footsteps, becoming teachers, with horror. Both, as it turned out, did become teachers. Dorothy attended the Massachusetts State Teachers College at Framingham for two years, and then transferred to the University of Massachusetts at Amherst to complete a bachelor's degree in home economics. In her first year at the university Dorothy went out on a blind date with a slight, studious-looking sophomore named Ernest Hamilton—Ernie to family and friends.

Ernie, who declared a major in botany the year he and Dorothy started dating, was born in Greenfield, about twenty miles north of Amherst. For much of his childhood Ernie and his parents—he was an only child—had migrated from western Massachusetts to Florida every year, wintering in St. Petersburg or Orlando. This annual migration was occasioned by the trade of the elder Ernest Hamilton: sign painting. The family, whose surname points to kinship with Alexander Hamilton, settled in Greenfield during the war years, and remained in the area while Ernie was in college.

Ernie and Dorothy's dating quickly became serious. Dorothy was a frequent weekend visitor at the Hamiltons' home in Greenfield, and Ernie's parents were delighted with her. While Ernie completed his senior year, Dorothy taught home economics at South Hadley High School, not far from Amherst. Ernie graduated in the spring of 1951, and the young couple was married that summer.

That fall they moved south to New Brunswick, New Jersey, and Rutgers University, where Ernie began work on a master's degree in botany. Dorothy taught high school home economics for two years at a school near Rutgers. Just as Ernie was about to finish his degree work, he found himself facing the draft. He won a short extension that gave him time to earn his master's, and, just as it looked as if Ernie might go to Korea, he was transferred into the signal corps and stationed, as a meteorologist, in New Jersey. Later in his twenty-one-month army stint, Ernie was stationed in Maryland, where his first child, Susan, was born. When he was mustered out of the service he returned to Rutgers, where he began work toward a doctoral degree. Dorothy taught second grade.

Ernie received his Ph.D. in botany in 1956, and that fall he began teaching at Bowling Green State University, in Ohio.

Susan was meant to be the start of a large family, but Dorothy and Ernie found themselves unable to have more children. Time and again Dorothy miscarried. She was pregnant once again when the Hamiltons moved to Bowling Green. A doctor in New Jersey had given her hormone treatments to ensure that this baby would not be lost. In the middle of the school year, Dorothy gave birth to a boy. Had he lived, the boy would have been named Donald. But because of numerous internal defects, he died eight hours after birth. Dorothy was shattered, because the doctor had told her that Donald should be her last attempt to have a baby.

Dorothy was teaching again in 1957, in charge of a second-grade class in nearby Haskins, Ohio. That year, she and Ernie began a long relationship with the Lucas County Child and Family Services agency in Toledo, which would result in their adoption of Scott.

By this time the Hamiltons were living in a new three-bedroom ranch house at 257 State Street, just south of the university, on the eastern fringes of Bowling Green. All around the Hamiltons lived young faculty families and professionals who would remain their friends for decades. Dorothy and Ernie were not at all distressed to be so far from their native New England. Bowling Green, situated in the featureless flatlands of northwestern Ohio, made up for its lack of scenic charm with the warm human companionship it provided. The Hamiltons were delighted by the friendliness of the university and the town itself.

As 1957 became 1958, another event occurred, probably in Toledo. What happened exactly, and to whom it happened, will probably never be known, unless Scott Hamilton changes his mind and decides to trace his biological parentage. While Dorothy and Ernie, who couldn't conceive a child but desperately wanted one, were waiting, another man and woman inadvertently and unwillingly conceived Scott Hamilton.

At one time Dorothy and Ernie knew a great deal about those mystery parents of Scott Hamilton. But what they knew has long since been lost. The whole story is told in Scott's adoption records in Toledo, but it seems very likely that Scott will never open those records. Once, when he was a boy, he wondered out loud who his biological parents might have been. Dorothy was so hurt that Scott forswore such speculation forever.

These few facts were released by the agency that handled Scott's adoption: He was born on August 28, 1958, in Toledo. At birth he weighed five pounds and seven ounces, and measured nineteen and one half inches. No medical problems in his mother's family were indicated. His father's family medical history included asthma, tuberculosis, heart condition, and cystic fibrosis. It seems that Scott was a full-term baby, because the record does not indicate otherwise. Doctors who examined Scott at birth indicated that celiac malabsorption was a concern, probably because of his relatively light weight.

Those are the only facts available. Unsubstantiated family recollections say that Scott was premature, but there is no reason to suppose he was. There was, for that matter, no reason to suppose that anything at all was wrong with the infant adopted by the Hamiltons. The Toledo agency indicated to the Hamiltons that they were getting a healthy baby boy.

Scott's later medical problems, which have played such a large part in all tellings of his life story, make speculation about his scanty birth records irresistible. The weight, for instance, seems low. But without a great deal of supporting information, no judgments can be made.

But there was no hint of future troubles when Ernie and Dorothy drove the twenty miles north to Toledo, to a former mansion in the city's old West End that housed the Lucas County Child and Family Services agency. They saw a skinny baby boy, but they couldn't take him home that day. Regulations said they had to look, go home and think about the adoption one last time, and then pick up their baby the next day. Of course the Hamiltons had no second thoughts. They took home the baby, who would be named Scott Scovell Hamilton, in October 1958. Scott started to squall on the way back to Bowling Green, so Ernie turned on the car radio, and Scott became quiet. Twenty-two years later Scott Hamilton would still be finding comfort in music.

Susan, who was five and a half years old, had been prepared for the new arrival with books designed to help children adjust to adopted siblings. The idea of a baby brother delighted the little girl, but she was let down by Scott in the flesh. He was thin and wrinkled, with huge eyes. He alternately looked like a wizened old man or a frog. Sue, who was a warm and motherly child, was quick to accept the new arrival, once she got over his looks. She took him to school, for show and tell, that first year.

Scott was not cute in the traditional chubby-baby sense, but he was, unconventionally, an irresistible child. From the beginning he worked a personal charm on his adoptive mother and her friends, a charm that he would work on motherly women for the rest of his life. The Hamiltons rebuilt their family around Scott. Dorothy was highly protective of her new baby. Neighbors would offer to baby-sit Sue and Scott so Ernie and Dorothy could get away, but Dorothy didn't want to leave Scott.

Scott was installed in his own room, in an enormous crib built by Dorothy's father. The huge crib, which would have held most infants, quickly proved inadequate for Scott. He was a climber, clambering like a monkey over the crib's sides. Ernie built a lid on the crib, turning it into a cage, to contain this active and agile little boy.

Corralling Scott was a perpetual difficulty through his first years. He never toddled, or walked, Ernie recalls. He got up and ran, and kept running until sickness slowed him down. He remained an escape artist, disdaining restraints such as a backyard playpen and most other devices meant to keep him in one place. And he kept climbing. One summer's day Ernie was working on the roof. He left the ladder next to the house and went to a neighbor's home. When he got back, two-year-old Scott was trotting along the roof's edge. Scott liked to nest in a kitchen cabinet over the refrigerator. Seeing that cabinet, a good six feet off the floor, it's hard to believe that such a little boy could contrive to reach it.

Motherhood and household duties rested very lightly on Dorothy. Neighbors remember a busy, but orderly, home at 257 State Street, run with great expertise by Dorothy. And it seemed as if two children weren't enough for the familial warmth of the Hamilton household. Ernie took an interest in foreign students' activities at the university, which brought to him and Dorothy a parental connection with dozens of students from overseas. There were dogs in Scott's childhood home, and a series of cats named Puffy Buttons. In those early years Scott enjoyed an idyllic childhood, with all the advantages and love and attention a little boy could want. His world was bounded by the property limits of a very happy and lively household.

# 2

# The Shadow Years

Scott Hamilton enjoyed a normal early childhood. It may be that his first five years were somewhat happier than normal, as Scott was particularly cheerful, and the undisputed apple of his mother's eye. Even the arrival of his adopted brother, Steve, who is roughly three years younger than Scott, did not dim the spotlight of motherly attention that shone on him.

Scott was tiny and spindly, but he was surprisingly strong and agile, always wanting to do what the older kids were doing. One neighbor has a picture of Scott in a ridiculously large baseball cap that belonged to an older boy who played in a league. Scott, the woman recalls, showed a great deal of coordination with bat and ball for a boy so young.

Among the scraps of early memory that survive is the day Scott Hamilton first stood on ice skates, an event that gave absolutely no hint of Scott's great future on the ice. His first rink was a flooded and frozen driveway across State Street from the Hamiltons' house. Other children were skating, and somebody had put skates on little Scotty. "We were holding on to a car, and we were skating around a car," he recalls. "I fell off my skates and landed on my head and cried for two hours. I just wanted those things off my feet. I said I'd never put them on again. . . . I never wanted to skate again." Scott was about four when he had this inauspicious introduction to his sport. Five years would pass before he skated again.

Scott was enrolled in kindergarten at the nearby Crim School immediately after he turned five, in August 1963. Dorothy, encouraged by Jane Hallberg, a neighbor who would teach Scott's kindergarten class, gave some thought to waiting another year before sending him to school. It would be better, Mrs. Hallberg believed, to delay and avoid the disadvantage of being the youngest in class. But Dorothy decided to have Scott start in September 1963. He was, Mrs. Hallberg recalls, anxious to go to school, perhaps because he had been so well prepared by his mother, who was experienced in primary education. And, of course, he knew Mrs. Hallberg.

Scott was an average kindergartner. His teacher thought his age might have made progress somewhat more difficult for him than it was for the older children. But he kept up well. And the same star quality that made Scott the center of attention at home also prevailed in school. Mrs. Hallberg and later grade-school teachers have all recalled that Scott, by virtue of his size and charm, attracted attention. This standout quality shows in the kindergarten class picture, where Scott is immediately noticeable, partly because of his small stature, but mostly because of his evident personality and grooming, which were a cut above the other children. That the boy was the best dressed in class was, of course, Dorothy's work. Her special pride in Scott was always obvious, Mrs. Hallberg recalls. The teacher tried to persuade the Hamiltons to allow Scott to repeat his kindergarten year, but they decided to let him go on. The idea was not fostered by poor performance, or any other problems, but by concern that his age, coupled with his smallness, would put him at a disadvantage.

Dorothy began teaching again in 1964, when Scott went into the first grade. She taught second grade in nearby Haskins, Ohio.

Scott's first-grade year started normally. His first-grade teacher, Grace Bell, recalls that he showed a special aptitude for rhythmic action games with music, like "The Farmer in the Dell." He was also particularly adept at drawing, paying attention to details, showing signs of the perfectionism that later took him to the pinnacle of the figure-skating world. And Scott got along well with his classmates. But by the end of that school year, Scott's bright early childhood had darkened.

The first shadow had appeared a few years earlier, when Scott was three. Dorothy and Ernie Hamilton had noticed that Scott, who had been slight and small for his age to begin with, had stopped growing. They had taken Scott to local doctors, then to specialists in a larger city, and finally to a university hospital.

During that first-grade year, a restricted diet became part of Scott's existence. His mother came to school and told Mrs. Bell about the special food that doctors had prescribed for Scott, and from then on he nibbled things prepared for him by his mother while his classmates had milk and cookies and the sorts of lunches that children relish. Mrs. Bell recalls that Scott didn't like his snacks and lunches. He'd toy with the food at lunch hour, trying to make jokes to distract his teacher from noticing that he wasn't eating. As the year wore on, Scott became increasingly thin and fragile and weak. But his good cheer shone through the shadows, and he tried to be dutiful about eating his miserable food.

The medical particulars of this period have not been accessible, so a certain amount of guesswork, based on family recollections and the material provided by Dr. Harry Shwachman at the Boston Children's Hospital, must suffice for the missing details. The diet on which Scott was put when he was in the first grade was probably a gluten-free diet, still the standard treatment for celiac malabsorption. It can be said with certainty that he was later on the gluten-free regimen, which involves eating nothing with wheat or wheat products. The diet is particular torture for children, whose favorite treats are virtually all made from flour. Cookies and cake were out of Scott's reach from then on, except for special occasions with a special dispensation from the doctor.

At this point Scott's sickness became the family's—particularly

Dorothy's—preoccupation. Scott's life was far from normal, isolated as he was from his peers by illness and the increasing amount of time taken up by visits to doctors and, finally, extended stays in hospitals. It seems likely that Scott was already under the care of specialists when he was in the first grade. Doctors did indicate at some early point that Scott was the victim of a malabsorption syndrome. The diagnosis was refined to celiac disease, a congenital condition that called for the gluten-free diet. Scott's apparent digestive difficulties, which may have been the result of the purported dietary cure, failed to clear up. But he was kept on his difficult and restrictive diet for the next few years.

Early in 1965, when Scott was still in the first grade, the Hamiltons moved from State Street to a house built for them in the new Westgate development, on Brownwood Drive. The opening of the development across town from the university caused a group migration from State Street. The Hallbergs were among the friends and neighbors of State Street who lived near the Hamiltons in Westgate. The house on Brownwood was large, with a separate apartment over the garage that was meant to be occupied by Ernie's parents. It remains an imposing specimen of a modern bi-level home, commanding a low rise on a wooded corner lot.

Scott's second-grade year began at Kenwood School, near the new house. By this time, he and his mother were making frequent trips to the hospital for tests and evaluation. Virginia Draney, his teacher, has vivid memories of a listless boy with dark circles under his eyes, a boy so small that he couldn't work comfortably at a second-grader's desk. His teacher got him a desk and chair from a first-grade classroom. The desk contained, in addition to sandwiches made from rice bread and other gluten-free items, a bottle of pink liquid medicine. The boy's treatment, the teacher recalls, included large doses of antihistamines, which increased Scott's torpor. Scott made valiant efforts to keep up with his lessons, but sometimes he couldn't finish his work. Mrs. Draney didn't push him to keep up: it was obvious that he was doing the best he could.

Rough-and-tumble outside play was out of the question, particularly in the winter, so Scott often spent recesses by himself, in quiet play with toys. His disposition struck Mrs. Draney as marvelous. In spite of his miserable circumstances, Scott never demanded special attention. He didn't feel sorry for himself or throw tantrums. Seven-year-old Scott was quite stoic about the burden he had to bear. He remained very popular with his classmates, becoming something of a pet. He got motherly fussing from the girls, and help from everyone when he needed it.

Dorothy was a frequent visitor to Mrs. Draney, as she was to all of Scott's elementary school teachers. The teachers and others who knew the family report that she was completely absorbed in her son's difficult case. Dorothy was constantly hopeful that the special food and continuing attention of doctors would bring about a breakthrough, but she was deeply worried that Scott might die. Scott was virtually Dorothy's only topic of conversation in this period.

The shadows were very dark around Scott in the third grade. His head was skull-like, with sunken cheeks and a bluish cast to his complexion. Diane Hunter, his teacher, worried that he might not live through the school year. Ms. Hunter wondered what on earth Scott would do with his life if he did live. She worried that he'd be some kind of a freak, and gave extra effort to teaching Scott his multiplication tables. She reasoned that he might, if he lived to adulthood, make a living as an accountant or a bookkeeper. It seemed out of the question that his future vocation would involve any great physical activity or public contact.

Dorothy's reports to the third-grade teacher changed through the year. At times she relayed news from the doctors that Scott was going to die. At other times the news was more encouraging. There seems to have been a great deal of confusion as to what,

14

exactly, might be wrong with the boy. New diets were introduced and abandoned. One aspect of the special diet that must have brought a good deal of envy from other children was Scott's Coca-Cola. He was allowed to drink Coke to keep up his energy. Scott brought the Coke to school, and in cold months his teacher put the cans of soda on the classroom's windowsill to chill.

As Scott's case deteriorated, he spent more time in hospitals. He was an inpatient for relatively short stretches, mostly during school vacations. But the illness dominated Scott's consciousness. Scott's memories from those dark years are like those of an enemy of a harsh regime—stretches of lone confinement broken by torture. Even today he detests hospitals; the smell of hospital disinfectant is enough to upset him.

Scott, like most sick children, was overindulged. He got toys every time his parents came to the hospital, and tended to get his way at home. Dorothy visited every day when Scott was in the hospital. Scott habitually made a loud demonstration when his mother went home. When Dorothy left, he would go into a men's room on his floor and howl, "I want my mommy!" Often he'd get another little boy to howl with him, doubling the din, which reverberated very nicely in a big tile bathroom.

Late in that third-grade year, Scott wore a lurid emblem of illness that he would continue to wear until after he started skating. A small-gauge plastic tube wandered out of his right nostril and up across his left cheek to his ear. The tube curved up over his ear and trailed free about three inches, with a small nylon coupling on its end. The tube was taped to his face.

The nose tube was part of a torturous daily medical therapy meant to counteract Scott's malnutrition. Every day Scott's tube was connected to a bottle of chalky nutrition concentrate. A valve in the tube system was meant to squeeze the flow of liquid into a slow drip. But Scott hated being tethered by his nose. If nobody was looking, he would open the valve full-bore for an uncomfortable quick fill-up that sometimes made him sick. But fast misery was better than slow misery. Dorothy and Ernie caught on to Scott's fast-feeding trick, but they let him get away with it. They were tired of seeing their boy in torment.

While Scott suffered through his third-grade year, Dorothy had intimations of her own future health problems. She was almost constantly debilitated by infections picked up from her second-grade pupils. Her poor resistance to the children's colds and flu showed no signs of strengthening, and she was forced to give up grade-school teaching. She left the Haskins district in 1966. In 1967, she enrolled as a graduate student at Bowling Green State University, and in the second semester of 1967 she was appointed a part-time instructor in the university's home economics department.

During the summer of 1966, between Scott's third and fourth grades, Dr. Andrew Klepner made a critical intercession on the boy's behalf. Dr. Klepner—Andy to the adult Hamiltons—lived down the block and across the street from the Hamiltons' house. The Klepners, who had two daughters, one of whom was about Scott's age, were dear family friends. Dorothy and Andy were particularly close. Andy was, moreover, the Hamiltons' family physician, who watched Scott's progress under the care of the specialists with increasing alarm. That summer the jolly, heavyset doctor, a native of New Jersey trained in Switzerland, gave the first of several invaluable boosts to Scott's recovery and subsequent career.

Dr. Klepner, who viewed the findings of the specialists with increasing disbelief, became positive that Scott was not a victim of celiac disease, and, consequently, that the elaborate diet was completely unnecessary. Scott, he was sure, could eat anything he wanted. He showed the Hamiltons that his hunch was correct one summer weekend when the families were staying together at a cottage on Lake Erie. Adults and children sat down to a huge vacation meal, and Andy told Scott to eat whatever he wanted, to forget about the special food, that he had medicines to take

16

care of him should anything happen. Scott was stunned, but with encouragement he took cautious bites of the food that everyone else was eating. Absolutely nothing happened.

Dr. Klepner's demonstration helped to overturn the celiac diagnosis. This incident might have removed the shadows, but Scott went back into the hospital for a long in-patient evaluation. In the autumn of 1967, when Scott was in the fourth grade, the Hamiltons heard Scott's physicians give the boy a death sentence. Dot and Ernie were told that Scott had cystic fibrosis, a fatal congenital disease. Scott, the doctors said, seemed to be nearing the end. Scott remembers a very somber visit from his family during this last stay in the hospital. Even his little brother came. His years of contact with medicine had made him sensitive to what scenes like this meant. And, by that time, he was in the habit of sneaking looks at the medical charts at the nurses' station. Nobody spelled it out to Scott, but he knew that everyone thought he was going to die. Ernie remembers Scott succumbing to an almost paralyzing depression at this point.

But once again Andy Klepner interceded on Scott's behalf. He was incensed by the latest medical opinions. He told the Hamiltons that he didn't believe Scott had cystic fibrosis, and that they should take him to the Children's Hospital in Boston—the world's preeminent pediatric hospital—as soon as possible. The Hamiltons made the trip during Christmas vacation. Scott went into the hospital, and the Hamiltons stayed with Dorothy's sister.

In Scott's four days of hospitalization, Dr. Harry Shwachman, a Harvard Medical School professor who was in charge of the chronic nutrition diseases department and who specialized in cystic fibrosis and gastrointestinal difficulties, lifted the shadows once and for all. He found that Scott did not have the characteristic symptoms of cystic fibrosis, and suggested that Scott's failure to thrive was secondary, not based on a primary disorder of the intestinal tract. During his hospitalization, Scott was seen by a psychologist, who noted that Scott was unusually anxious, that he seemed constantly to be anticipating attack, and that he was concerned about his illness and illness in his parents. Dr. Shwachman concluded that psychological care would be the best route to pursue, combined with improved eating habits.

The Hamiltons went home to Bowling Green. In January, Dorothy wrote to Dr. Shwachman. She thanked him for getting to the root of Scott's problem and letting the family know, after all those years of diets and treatment and medication, that Scott did not have a serious medical condition. Scott was about to begin seeing a child psychiatrist, she wrote, and his appetite had doubled.

And so the shadows vanished.

Family recollections of Scott's childhood illness have followed quite a different line than that given by the record. The shadow years are clouded over by analgesic forgetfulness, in Scott's case further clouded by the fact that he was a little boy when the illness came. In addition to the forgetful clouding, the family's facts have been somewhat rearranged to agree with a version of Scott's early life that began to be told the year he came out of the shadows. This account was repeated in virtually every long press article about Scott in connection with his participation in the 1984 Winter Olympic Games.

The account says that a dangerous illness almost killed Scott just before he started skating. The dangerous illness was an intestinal paralysis that kept Scott from absorbing his food. The alimentary disorder that kept Scott from thriving is called, in many of the recent accounts, Shwachman's Syndrome, an extremely rare condition first identified by Dr. Shwachman. Virtually every retelling includes phrases about how doctors said Scott had less than a year to live, and how Scott proved them wrong, and how, moreover, skating seemed to give him the weapons he needed to fight for his imperiled life.

But now that version of Scott's life history must be let go. The medical record and the testimony of Dr. Shwachman show that it is wrong. Many of the particulars are factual, but the wrongness of the legend lies in its emphasis on the physical causes of Scott's afflictions. Dr. Shwachman believed that Scott did not have Shwachman's Syndrome when he was examined at the Boston Children's Hospital in December 1967.

The fabrications and omissions that were built into the popular version of Scott's childhood were never deliberate misstatements; nobody lied. Dishonesty, major or minor, is not part of the fabric of Scott Hamilton, or Ernie. The story that has been told has been the truest and most merciful way of accounting for the awful things that happened to Scott when he was a little boy. All families have legends. But most do not become public property, as Scott's has. And most are never weighed against the record for their literal truth.

One series of events in Scott's early years is absolutely verifiable, however. It began with a decision on the part of Bowling Green State University, which would prove to be momentous. During Scott's shadow years, the university decided to build an ice arena, which was opened in 1967, as if to accommodate the town's secret, suffering ice genius. The coincidence was perfect. Scott's ice was ready just as he was ready for the ice. The millions spent by the university on its new ice have yielded a good deal of Olympic gold. Besides becoming a seedbed for Scott's skating, the Bowling Green ice became, a decade later, the competitive proving ground for two players who would be instrumental in the U.S. hockey team's stunning Olympic gold-medal victory at the 1980 Lake Placid games. And by the late 1970s, Bowling Green would have a nationally ranked college hockey team.

But for our purposes, we must return to November of 1967, the month before Dr. Shwachman lifted Scott's erroneous death sentence: Scott went skating one Saturday morning at the ice arena. His debut on the ice is owed in large part to Dr. Klepner, who had already played a hero's role in this dark chapter of Scott's life story. Dr. Klepner's children, Pam and Sandy, were attending Saturday-morning club skating sessions at the new arena, and Scott wanted to go, too. Andy pushed the idea, thinking exercise and activity with other children might be good for Scott. Dorothy thought skating might be beneficial, but the idea of Scott skating scared her. She wanted him to go, but she didn't want to see her sick little boy on the ice. It would be some time before she would have anything to do with Scott's skating.

So, on a Saturday morning, Scott went to the rink with Pam and Sandy Klepner and his big sister, Susan. He went one or two —possibly three—times; the memory is not clear. That November he went as a guest of the Klepners, without joining the Bowling Green Skating Club, or making a commitment to lessons. There was, after all, a strong belief that Scott was about to die. The idea was to bring a little fun into his sad existence.

Scott says he fell and cried the first time he stepped onto the arena's ice. Others say he was an instant skater. What happened that Saturday morning is not clear, but it seems certain that the ice appealed to Scott. After Dr. Shwachman lifted the death sentence and banished the shadows, Scott went back to the ice and never left it. In early 1968 he enrolled in Saturday-morning group classes at the arena, beginning the career that would take him to the gold medal in Sarajevo.

# 3

# Ice

Rita Lowery gave Scott his first lesson. She remembers a pale, skinny boy with big, staring eyes who said very little. Rita knew Scott was getting over a serious illness, but she extended no special consideration to him. In her class on the ice, Scott was a child among a dozen others. He had come to a place where sickness and the nose tube did not make him special.

Within a few Saturdays, the nose tube was trailing horizontally behind a kid who was born to go fast on skates. Scott was fearless and adept, learning everything Rita taught, always ready for more. In his first five-week series of lessons, Scott showed a talent for skating that Rita and her husband, David Lowery, also an ice professional at Bowling Green, knew was worth developing.

Scott Hamilton, even at age nine, looked at the world with an adult's sense of irony. He thought the Lowerys were conning Dot and Ernie when they talked about his special gift for skating. But he loved to skate. When the Hamiltons paid for thirty minutes of daily private instruction from Rita, Scott threw himself into the new work as he had thrown himself into group lessons.

That winter Scott's deathlike pallor went away. The body parts that hadn't worked started working. The tube was gone. The sweet, sleepy little boy who had been the object of so much concern in the first, second, and third grades, also left the scene. Scott the fourth-grader was a wound-up kid, sometimes a smart-aleck. He was given to teasing other kids, particularly girls, a

21

pastime that he has yet to give up. Scott in the fourth grade was not a discipline problem, but rather a kid with an excess of energy and wit. Now and again the teacher had to, as teachers say, sit on him. Scott's fourth-grade picture shows an entirely new Scott sitting Indian-style next to the "Kenwood School—1968—Grade 4" sign, looking quite pleased with himself, eyes leveled at the camera, and with a relaxed semi-smile that might be the expression of a grown man in a television commercial. This is unusual confidence in a boy so young, particularly so young-looking. Scott was still dwarfed by his classmates, but the size disparity no longer implied a tragic difference.

Scott's transformation accelerated through his ninth year. The ice seemed to be the boy's particular elixir of life. The more he skated, the less he was sick. Scott skated in Bowling Green's first "Ice Horizons" show in the spring of 1968 (as of 1985, he has yet to miss one of his home rink's annual shows). In the premier show Scott played a rival of Hans Brinker in a reenactment of the "Silver Skates" race. Scott had to fall down so the hero would win.

In summer of 1968 Scott placed second in a Sub-Juvenile event at an invitational competition in Bowling Green. By that summer Scott was no longer a sick boy. The Hamiltons, quite naturally, saw a cause-and-effect linkage between Scott's recovery and his skating. The ice had killed whatever had tried to kill him. The family legend is that skating turned out to be the perfect therapy for the bodily things wrong with Scott. The cool, moist air, apparently, was perfect for Scott's problem lungs, and other qualities of ice were also just right. Dr. Shwachman, in a follow-up conversation with the family, found out Scott was skating and averred that it was, medically speaking, a great idea. The doctor's encouragement seems to have reinforced the family's belief that skating was Scott's miracle cure. This is, however, a mysterious validation. Since no one knows what was wrong with Scott, no one knows why skating was so right for him. It may be that other activities would have done as much. Maybe only skating would have been so miraculously right for Scott. No one can know.

Correct or incorrect, the fervent belief that Scott was in danger and that skating helped remove him from danger is critically important in what followed. It gave the family a motive for contributing time and money to skating. There are no skating stories without parental motives. A child's talent and love for skating are not enough. Skating costs too much money and takes too much time and energy for a child, unassisted, to do anything at all in the sport. If parents don't buy into the skating dream, the dream does not come true. The Hamiltons were prepared to give Scott's skating whatever it demanded because they felt themselves to be under the heaviest possible obligation to skating: they owed Scott's life to it. It was some time before Scott's progress at skating overshadowed the belief that skating was good for Scott. By then the Hamiltons were skating parents, bought in too far to buy out.

Without delving into the mysteries of his early life, it is possible to see some of skating's patent rightness for Scott Hamilton in November 1967. When Scott put steel on ice that Saturday morning, he stood for the first time on an equal footing with children his own age in a sport. He didn't have to catch up, because all the children in Rita Lowery's class were new to the ice. Size and strength didn't count. After his sickly years, it must have been fabulous to leave other boys and girls behind him, to earn attention with speed and physical cleverness. It is easy to imagine that Scott formed a gratitude to skating that was akin to his parents'.

The timing of Scott's first skating was just right. The ninth year is a good year for boys to begin. Scott's first lessons were particularly timely because they came just as the veil of illness was lifting, before he had a chance to let his boyish interests run in a dozen directions.

Rita Lowery was in her mid-thirties then. She taught with a ladylike iron hand, and spoke with an accent reminiscent of her native Scotland. She was the first of five foreign-born coaches to train Scott. A former dancer, Rita had been hired away from a starring role in a Paris show to join "Holiday on Ice." On the ice she performed the adagio, a commercial species of pairs skating. Her husband, David, was a former Canadian National Champion pairs skater. The Lowerys were Bowling Green's first ice professionals, in charge of setting up all figure skating training at the new rink. The university president had gone to the rink at Troy, Ohio, where the Lowerys worked before coming to Bowling Green, to lure them to his brand-new ice.

In Scott's first lessons, Rita saw in extremely rough, miniature form, Scott skating as he skates today. His moves were quick, with sureness and economy of motion. He had, as she put it, "neat feet." He also had a natural understanding of what needed to be done. "You didn't have to put him in positions," Rita said.

Scott had natural ability, but he was less than a prodigy. Rita had seen children who picked up harder tricks faster than Scott. This was not blindingly bright talent, but a mind-and-body rightness that Rita liked better than too much, too easy. Scott had a head for skating. He took his time on the ice seriously, applying himself to each lesson, accepting and working on each new challenge. "He loved what he was doing," Rita recalls. "Loved it to the point that it didn't matter if it went bad one day, because he'd keep after it."

Scott started coming to extra open sessions at the rink, to skate for the fun of skating. His first private lessons with Rita were two daily sessions totaling thirty minutes, fifteen minutes for school figures, fifteen minutes for freeskating. Scott's natural bent was for freeskating. Indeed, he seems to have had only a dim conception that there was anything but freeskating when he went to his first figures session. Scott remembers skating blithely across the other skaters' patches. "Patch" is skaterese for an area of ice allotted for practicing compulsory figures. Skaters work at figures like gardeners, each keeping to his own plot, with a strong sense of propriety. All the big kids yelled "Stupid!" and Scott quickly found out what a patch was. Even after he learned the rudiments of edge control and went to work on the figure eights and three-circle figures that are skating's barre and chromatic scale and primary color palette, all in his own patch, freeskating caused trouble for Scott. He wanted to swoop through his figures, much too fast for proper control. Rita had to scold Scott to slow down.

Figure skating resembles schoolwork as much as it does other sports. A child might rise in a team sport, or track and field, simply by being good. Skaters have to take tests. Tests move a skater up the competitive ladder: Sub-Juvenile, Juvenile, Intermediate, Novice, Junior, and Senior. The names imply age level, but admission to each higher classification is controlled primarily by tests administered by officials credentialed by the United States Figure Skating Association. Tests are not competition, but one cannot compete without taking tests. When Scott reached Senior-level competition in 1976, he had passed nine figures and six free-skating tests. Every step of his progress had been rigorously policed by the USFSA. Name one of his coaches and Scott can instantly recall which tests he went through with that coach. Scott passed his preliminary tests under Rita.

Under Rita, Scott's skating was allowed to grow freely, with no great expectations on the part of Scott or his family and friends. Rita believed that big ambitions and commitment at that early stage did no good. The idea was to let the skating gift reveal itself, and decide what to do with it later. Scott learned edge control, and began pushing himself through his room-sized figure eights, daily exercises for the next seventeen years. And he learned one-rotation jumps. Flight is an incremental process in the USFSA training regimen: first the bunny hop; then the waltz jump, forward on the left foot, to backward on the right foot; then the full-turning Salchows, loops, and Lutzes. Early experience showed that Scott jumped "regular," turning counterclockwise in the air. Now and again a skater begins with the habit of turning the other way, a contrariness that generally continues. Scott learned a few of the jumps in class, and the rest of his initial repertoire in private lessons. Scott, Rita recalls, had a natural spring and uprightness in the air. He turned very quickly. The blurring speed of Scott's jumps are still a Hamilton hallmark.

The gold ore in Scott's skating was most apparent to those, like Rita, who knew the sport. At least one witness, a schoolteacher, was unimpressed. She saw a little stick figure throwing himself around the ice and thought to herself that poor Scott wasn't going to go far.

But Scott, virtually as soon as he started skating, began to gather a loyal audience at Bowling Green. He attracted attention because he was so small, a mighty atom on the ice. He was very likable when he skated, radiating the smiley good cheer that he still throws off in performance. Scott wanted to be funny on the ice. He was enthralled by a young skater who learned comedy tricks from the Lowerys. Scott would follow the older boy, mimicking what he did. "You saw an actor in Scott," recalls Rita.

And so the Hamiltons' focus shifted to the ice rink. Dorothy became enthusiastic about her son's new pastime. Ernie built props for the first "Ice Horizons," as he has done every year thereafter. Sue was learning to skate, but her little brother far outdistanced her on the ice. During that first year, she broke an arm trying to do a jump that Scott demonstrated for her.

The Lowerys came to barbecues at the house on Brownwood. Rita was very taken with Scott's mother, "a bubbly, delightful woman." Her observations about Dorothy are echoed by most of those who remember her—Dorothy was keenly interested in Scott and his skating, but she was not a "skating mother." A skating mother is a species of stage mother, a pushing, psychologically ruinous character. Dorothy's investment of attention rested lightly on her boy. She seemed to be good for him.

After two years at Bowling Green, the Lowerys moved on. They were committed to training advanced skaters, and the rink at Bowling Green, tied up with its many university and community programs, couldn't give them the time they wanted for advanced training. They went to Buffalo, leaving a coaching vacuum at Bowling Green. An unsettled, somewhat unhappy period in Scott's training ensued. He was coached first by a very young woman who was something of a martinet. Scott needed a softer touch; he rebelled. He was also taught during this period by a college man who had been a student of the Lowerys.

Scott couldn't pass his First Figure test. His interests wandered from skating. "I'm not going to figure skate unless I play hockey because all of my friends play hockey and they think I'm a sissy because I figure skate!" he announced to his parents. They let him play hockey, but only if he kept up his figure skating. So, his already long hours at the rink were augmented by hockey practice.

A new coach seemed to offer some hope of moving Scott onward in figure skating. Scott was placed under the tutelage of Giuliano Grassi, an Italian-born professional based in Fort Wayne, who went to Bowling Green regularly to teach. Scott's lessons with Grassi were a back-and-forth affair, a weekend at Bowling Green and a weekend at Fort Wayne, with Scott staying at the home of another skater. Grassi seemed to be what Scott needed. Under the new coach, Scott passed the First Figure test the first time he took it.

Meanwhile, Scott had his first spate of national press attention. A local news story, written as an advance story for "Ice Horizons— 1969," told how "An ice skating rink has replaced a hospital room for a Bowling Green boy who was told last spring he had less than a month to live." The story was picked up by wire services and run nationally. BOY BEATS DEATH PREDICTION, headlines said. ICE SKATING UPLIFTS LIFE OF 'MIRACLE CHILD.' The picture showed Scott in harlequin costume for his role as a jack-in-the-box, a solo with "Ice Horizons."

Dorothy told the newspaper reporter, "Actually, both my husband and I have to pinch ourselves every once in a while just to prove everything is real. . . . He's not supposed to be here, you know."

The youngest and smallest "Ice Horizons" soloist, who was ten in 1969, stood forty-nine inches at the end of the fifth grade, up a half inch from the beginning of the year. He weighed fifty-one pounds, according to school records. Scott did fine in the fifth grade, his first year of really intensive skating, "Satisfactory" in all subjects. By spring, 1969, he was skating every day, a total of more than twenty hours on the ice weekly.

About three weeks before "Ice Horizons—1969," Scott placed first in a Sub-Juvenile competition, his first taste of gold.

Scott's relationship with Giuliano Grassi deteriorated. The coach failed to hit it off with the Hamiltons, who thought he was hotheaded. They didn't like his noisy remonstrations with skaters. Grassi was also teaching a boy who turned out to be Scott's chief competitor in the area, which added tension to an already unhappy situation. The trouble anticipated another break Scott would make with an Italian-born coach, in 1979, when he left Carlo Fassi primarily because Fassi had begun to teach Scott's particular rival in Senior Men's competition.

The Hamiltons switched coaches in mid-competition, after figures, during a meet in the 1970 season. Their new coach was Herb Plata, a ruggedly good-looking German, a former Junior National Champion in his home country, who had begun to teach at Bowling Green. "Herb was like the new guy coming in on his white horse," Scott recalls. The German was very appealing to Scott. Herb was a former "Holiday on Ice" star, a very flashy free skater.

With Herb Plata, Scott's skating took off again. Scott acquired a complete set of double jumps, Salchow, loop, toe loop, flip, and Lutz. Herb laid down sound jumping technique, which served Scott for the rest of his career. Herb was a good figures coach, but figures failed to hold Scott's attention. He wanted to go fast and to jump.

At the close of 1969, when Scott was eleven years old and a sixth-grader, he placed first among Juvenile Men in the 1970 Eastern Great Lakes Regional Championships. Regionals are the first of three annual ranking competitions that culminate with the United States National Championships. The seven-state Eastern Great Lakes Region belongs to the twenty-four-state Midwestern Section. Winners of the three U.S. Sectionals—Eastern, Midwestern, and Pacific Coast—compete at Nationals. Nationals competition includes only Novice, Junior, and Senior skaters, so the highest honors won by low-level skaters are at Regionals and Sectionals.

In the summer of 1970, skating took Scott to the Golden West Championships in Culver City, California, his first long-distance trip to compete. He was second in Pre-Bronze Freestyle and—this is very odd for contemporary Scott Hamilton fans to contemplate —third in Bronze Free Dance. Scott's early training included a very brief career as an ice dancer. His partner at the 1970 Golden West, was about the right height for Scott, but a good deal more robust than he.

A newspaper report from about this time notes that the Hamiltons bought two pairs of skates for Scott every year. Skates are what most of us would call blades, the metal arangements that are screwed to the bottom of the skater's boot. The skates cost eighty dollars apiece, not enough to cause a family like the Hamiltons hardship, but certainly an expense that would have been noticed. Those skates were the very least of the expenses connected to Scott's skating. Everything in skating costs money—coaching, ice time, costumes, travel and expenses at competitions for skater, family, and coach, and on and on.

No one without direct experience can conceive of the burden, financial and otherwise, carried by a family with a child in competitive skating. The business of paying for the country's future Olympic glory always sounds ennobling on television, when the screen takes us back to the champions' childhoods and dwells briefly on what it took to get to today's big win. And it seems so patently worthwhile, because we are looking at the stories of family sacrifices that paid off big. But the down payments on gold medals are made in obscurity, without cameras and lights, and they are made blind. No eleven-year-old's parents can see what all that skating money will buy. They can only hope that something beneficial will come of it and, meanwhile, that skating does the child good. Banking on future championship at that stage—at any stage—is vain, probably heartbreaking. Skating has to be worth what is paid for it. Of course parents regularly spend money on improvements for children that may lead to nothing. They buy French horns and ballet lessons and home computers. Next to skating, though, such things are trifles.

By 1971, skating may have been the Hamiltons' greatest expense, more than mortgage and utilities combined. What, exactly, they gave to the ice back then cannot be known. Ernie says he doesn't want to know. Contemporary estimates of what it costs to train a child for the ice run to $16,000 a year, and upward. Deflate that amount to 1970 dollars, and you may have something like what the Hamiltons were spending. What Dorothy earned in her instructorship at the university was going straight to Scott's skating. And the Hamiltons felt a general pinch. "We didn't go out much," says Ernie.

The ice had been good to Scott in 1970. The 1971 season, which began in late 1970, was better. Initially, though, the Third Figure test threatened to wreck the 1971 season. Scott failed it four times. Twice Scott's attempts were so botched that the judges stopped the proceedings. He finally passed the Third test, which moved him from Juvenile to Intermediate class, a week before the 1971 Eastern Great Lakes Regionals. Scott won figures at Eastern Great Lakes, a notable feat considering the trouble he had doing the figures that qualified him to compete. He went on to win overall, impressive again, because that competition was his first as an Intermediate man. Winning Regionals earned Scott a berth at Midwesterns. He finished third. Still skating under Herb Plata, Scott finished his seventh-grade school year and went into a busy summer of competitions. He garnered wins at competitions in Port Huron, Michigan; Lake Placid; and Toronto. His medals included a gold and a silver in Interpretive Skating, an event in which competitors listened three times to music provided by the judges and then skated to that music.

By this time skating occupied the position once held by Scott's affliction. The family was mobilized around Scott, with Dorothy, as she had earlier, leading the efforts on Scott's behalf. Skating took Scott out of the company of other children to the point that he remained somewhat remote from everyday-kid life. His existence was immeasurably better, but it was as abnormal as it had been when his world was peopled by adults who thought he was going to die. A woman who taught him in grade school observed, when he was reaching for Olympic gold, that Scott probably has no idea about life as most of us know it. He never lived such a life.

Dorothy, who had once told Bowling Green about Scott's illnesses, now told about his skating. Before anyone else, she dreamed the championship dream, knowing from the first that the ice would take Scott to wonderful places. The family friends listened with some amusement, sharing the mother's joy and pride, but less sure about Scott's golden prospects.

Skating was chiefly a partnership between Dorothy and Scott. For financial and logistical reasons, Ernie generally stayed home while mother and son went to competitions. The disproportionate amount of money and mothering going to Scott rankled slightly, but Ernie could not forget his wife's loss of Donald and the near-loss of Scott. Sue and Steve were less understanding. The inequalities of having a star in the family seemed to give a theme to their domestic bickering and fighting.

Scott and Steve fought, as all brothers fight. Steve had been bigger than Scott since his fourth year, but age and wiry strength won out. Scott never lost. Sue protested and argued with her mother over what Scott got—and what she didn't get. Later, in her senior year of high school, when Scott was in the seventh grade, Sue had a French-horn solo in a pops orchestra concert. Dorothy and Ernie watched Scott practice skating during her first performance. Sue refused to play a second performance unless her mother went to the concert. Her boyfriend, later her husband, compelled Sue to play, and, in mid-concert, Dorothy came to listen. The young Hamiltons—Steve, Scott, and Sue—have long since discussed, and forgiven, the seeming injustices in their upbringings. Sue had time to find harmony with her mother after those sometimes rancorous high school years.

The facts at this stage suggest an unattractive picture of Scott: a spoiled mama's boy, Little Lord Figure Skater. But the circumstances that might have ruined another child did not ruin Scott Hamilton. The unattractive picture does not fit him at all. Those who remember his boyhood are unanimous in saying that Scott, at any age, was not spoiled. For all the attention he got, he never seemed to demand it. He was polite, pleasant, cheery, kind—as if by virtue of an indestructible good character. Dorothy should probably be credited with the preservation of Scott. Her preoccupation with him was not blind. She knew, everyone who was there agrees, how to keep him in line.

And for all his attractiveness to adults, Scott was no goody-two-shoes, a type as repugnant as the spoiled brat. Scott's tastes in fun ran the right ways for a boy from Ohio. He threw firecrackers at his sister, or off the roof of the skating arena. An incident involving fireworks and the skating arena roof showed that young Scott Hamilton had a certain amount of nerve. It also shows that his likability—next to skating, his greatest gift—never let him down. The policeman trying to catch the kid throwing firecrackers would go to one side of the building, and Scott would go to the other. Then he'd shoot off more firecrackers, to keep the policeman's attention. The cat-and-mouse was fun while it lasted, but

Scott got caught. Annoying the police with illegal fireworks, having fireworks at all for that matter, could have been big trouble, with a phone call to Scott's parents, maybe even a fine. But Scott charmed the officers out of doing anything at all. They didn't even take away his firecrackers.

The time had come to bury Scott's hockey career. Considering his size, Scott had done well. Clippings from the *Daily Sentinel-Tribune* tell of Scott Hamilton of the BG Squirts contributing a goal in a 5–2 win over the visiting Lima Squirts. He had an assist in a Youth game. And, in an amazing dual performance, Scott played in a Pee Wee League exhibition match and put on a three-minute figure skating performance during the same Youth Hockey Night. "It was a Jekyll-Hyde thing," Scott says. The activities don't blend easily. Ernie and Dorothy wanted Scott to give up hockey because they thought figure skating deserved all his attention. And they worried about him. Most of the time his lightning skating kept Scott out of the other kids' ways. But hard hits on a few occasions knocked Scott cold. The Hamiltons didn't like to see their son carried off the ice. With his parents' encouragement, Scott hung up his hockey skates forever.

The 1972 season began at home. The Bowling Green Skating Club hosted its first Regionals competition in December 1971. Scott, who had moved up to Novice level, was pictured among the local skaters with high hopes for Regionals in the *Sentinel-Tribune*'s extensive advance coverage of the event. Scott told the *Toledo Blade* that he wanted someday to teach skating, or join an ice show. But a long *Sentinel-Tribune* story trumpeting Scott's win at Regionals mentioned, for the first time, higher ambitions:

> His goal isn't to stop with a national title, however, as he has his sights set on a world title and "then to the Olympics."
>
> "That's my big dream, but I don't think I'll get there. Oh,

33

I might get there but probably won't place first," Scottie says, trying to mix reality with humility.

"It takes time to get things you work for."

In the same story, thirteen-year-old Scott gave a very practical account of why a skater ought to smile. "I think smiling helps. I think your marks come easier. If you're smiling, it looks like you're not working as hard and things are coming natural to you." That might have been the Scott of 1984 talking.

That feature story marked a turning point in Scott's press coverage. The illness-and-recovery legend was there, but the meat of the story had to do with Scott's skating, in particular the thrilling freeskating that won him the Regional title. From then on skating overshadowed sickness.

That 1972 Regionals performance featured a small act of defiance against his coach. Herb had told Scott to leave the double loop out of his freeskating. Scott didn't need the jump in his program to get to Midwesterns, so why risk it? Scott did the double loop anyway, raising his eyebrows and grinning broadly at his coach when he landed it.

Monday morning after Regionals, Scott and Herb were off for Midwesterns in Minneapolis. Scott placed third in figures at Midwesterns, which opened up a thrilling possibility. It looked as if he might qualify for Nationals, which were to be in Long Beach that year. The hope stayed alive when Scott placed third in the long program. But he finished fourth overall, missing his first chance to go to Nationals.

The letdown in Minneapolis effectively ended Scott's connection with Herb Plata. The Hamiltons wanted a new coach for their son. But the 1972 Midwesterns brought them to a much larger crisis. The judges and important skating people told Scott's parents what the crisis was. They said that Scott had enormous potential in skating, that he might well have the stuff of an international champion. But to develop that potential Scott was going to have to look beyond Bowling Green for coaching. The Hamiltons went home mulling over their next move. Something, Dorothy knew, had to be done.

It should be recognized that Scott's long skate for an Olympic gold medal could have stopped here. His progress might have been stalled by his parents, had they decided that his skating had gone far enough, or decided against sending him away from home. His destiny seems manifest now, but back then he was one of a dozen Novices who finished fourth or above in Sectional competition. There were Juveniles and Intermediates coming up behind and Juniors ahead of him. Some of those boys appeared to be quite as talented as Scott. In 1972, Scott hardly had a lock on a brilliant skating future.

The Hamiltons decided that his future on the ice was worth more of their money, and worth sending Scott away from home. Dorothy phoned Nancy Meiss, a judge from Cincinnati who had taken an early interest in Scott's skating. Dorothy asked the judge to contact Slavka Kohout, who was head coach at a rink in Rockton, Illinois. Slavka's most celebrated skater, Janet Lynn, had just won her fourth consecutive National Championship, and other skaters were doing well under Slavka. Dorothy wanted Slavka to accept Scott as a student. The Hamiltons, Dorothy told Nancy Meiss, had decided to do whatever they could to support their son's skating. They would sell their home, if the need arose.

Nancy said she would call Slavka, but only on the condition that Dorothy forget about selling her house. Skating, Nancy told Dorothy, was not worth such a sacrifice.

Slavka told the Hamiltons to come to Rockton. Ostensibly the trip was for Scott to audition to skate under Slavka herself, but Janet Lynn's coach had something else in mind. She had an idea that Pierre Brunet, who also taught at Rockton, might accept Scott. And so the Hamiltons made a trip to the ice at the Wagon

Wheel. They had been to Rockton once before, at the 1971 Midwestern Sectional Championships.

In 1984 it seems incredible that Rockton was once one of the skating world's capitals. The last rink at the Wagon Wheel was closed in 1980, and the place had lost its preeminence before then. Even at the height of the Wagon Wheel's prestige, Rockton seemed a very unlikely locale for a global sports center.

Rockton, home to fewer than three thousand people in 1972, lies about a hundred miles northwest of Chicago. To the north of Rockton is Beloit, Wisconsin, and to the south, Rockford. The countryside belongs, in spirit, more to Wisconsin than to Illinois, particularly Chicago's part of Illinois. The land rolls, broken into holdings more wooded and picturesque than the prairie farms farther south. In 1972, A Rockford businessman operated a resort at a bend in U.S. Route 2, just south of Rockton. The place was called the Wagon Wheel, and bore a rustic American motif. The Wagon Wheel had a chapel for marrying, and all the facilities for recreational weekends away from the city—horses, golf, tennis, swimming, and a good dining room. After the owner acquired some used refrigeration machinery, it also had year-round indoor ice skating.

The Wagon Wheel owner hired a then little-known skating professional to teach on his ice. That woman, Slavka Kohout, founded an empire. She gave all she had to her pupils, who began to shine in competition, which in turn brought better skaters. The brightest star in Slavka's constellation was Janet Lynn, a freeskating genius who won her first Senior National Championship in 1969. Slavka was joined at Rockton by Pierre Brunet, a French-born skating legend who was then almost seventy years old. Pierre had coached in New York for about twenty-five years, working with skating greats such as Olympic and World Champion Carol Heiss, and Canada's International Champion Donald Jackson. "Monsieur Brunet" was Pierre's title of respect in the skating community, and Slavka was "Miss Kohout." Monsieur Brunet brought with him a promising skater named Gordie McKellen, who was on the verge of National Championship. With Miss Kohout and Monsieur Brunet, the Wagon Wheel ripened into a nationally important training center, with a reputation for discipline, excellence, and spirit. It boded well for Scott's future that he was accepted as a student of Monsieur Brunet's. In summer, 1972, at age thirteen, Scott moved into a room in the dormitory across a parking lot from the Wagon Wheel's ice rink. From then on his life would be gypsyish, following skating, with all things ordered to the demands of skating. Family life and school were filled in on a catch-as-catch-can basis. Scott went to Rockton for a summer session in 1972, then made preparations in the fall for the 1973 season. He went back home after the season. Rockton took more of his time each year. He was virtually a year-round resident by 1974 and 1975.

Scott settled into a two-dollars-and-ten-cents-a-day dorm in Illinois, and left local-level skating forever behind him. For the first time he was among champions. The following three and a half years at Rockton would be a period of intensive maturation, both on and off the ice. At the end of the Rockton experience, Scott would be a facsimile of the Scott of the 1980s—young and unfinished, of course, but still recognizably the Scott of Sarajevo.

The agent of change in Scott's skating, molding the gifted boy into a national-level competitor, can be counted among the gifts of fortune to Scott's career. Monsieur Brunet seems to have been just what Scott needed, the perfect master-worker to develop Scott's potential.

The first session was a cautious exploration. The elegant gentleman, who looked like a Gallic Fred Astaire and spoke like Maurice Chevalier, asked Scott to review what he knew. He asked the boy what he wanted to learn, and how he thought further work should proceed. Monsieur Brunet sensed immediately that Scott had a mind for skating, an ability to know what made sense on the ice. Beyond the obvious talent for performing, Scott could understand what he did. Dorothy cautioned Monsieur Brunet that Scott might miss a lesson or two because of his condition. But she told the coach to give her boy the same discipline as other skaters, and to expect as much from him.

The coach was pleased with his new charge. Together they proceeded to dismantle everything Scott knew, working on the simplest moves until they were rock-solid. Before a brilliant career that included singles competition and pairs skating with his wife, Andrée Joly (they won two Olympic gold medals and four World Championships), Monsieur Brunet had trained to be an engineer. He brought an engineer's thoroughness to the ice. Nothing slipshod or lazy got by. Figures were a specialty of the French coach, who had been called the greatest figures skater in history when he competed. Scott's figures, the coach recalls, particularly needed attention.

To the work of teaching Scott better circles, loops, and turns, Monsieur Brunet brought his own scientific and philosophical systems of skating thought. Probably no coach in history brought as much deep, long thought to his work as did the Frenchman at Rockton. Scott was probably unaware of the logical and scientific depth of his coach. They simply worked together, slowly and thoroughly. Practice was a painstaking business. Sometimes Scott and his coach gave an hour's attention to a figure, keeping after each desired result until it was theirs. The focus of figures lessons was Scott's body, not the forms his skates traced on the ice. Monsieur Brunet's minute rearrangements of Scott's body position brought Scott's figures into shape. After he began training under Monsieur Brunet, Scott was never again stalled by figures tests.

The fertile skating relationship was deepened by a great mutual fondness. Scott's quick wit and sense of fun delighted Monsieur Brunet. Looking back, he calls Scott at that age a *"petit coquin"* (little scamp). Scott, away from home for the first time since the years of illness, confided in his coach, as if in a father. Scott became, as he has so many times, a son to someone not his parent. The bonding of Monsieur Brunet and Scott may, indeed, have been deepened by the coach's loss of his son, Jean-Pierre, in a highway accident in 1948.

Scott's real parents back in Ohio sent a proxy to watch over Scott in his first extended training away from home. In July 1972, Sue married her high school sweetheart, James Michael Sanders, known to family and friends as Mike. Dorothy gave the couple a honeymoon at the Wagon Wheel. Scott did his best not to burden the newlyweds with too much of his company during the few days they had before naval duty took Mike from his bride. Sue went back to Ohio, and Dorothy talked her into taking a job at the Wagon Wheel until Mike came ashore. So Scott's big sister lived and worked at the Wagon Wheel from mid-August to late November, keeping an eye on him, but trying not to interfere too much.

Besides Scott's move to Rockton, 1972 had brought another change to the Hamiltons. They moved from the big house on Brownwood to a new house in the country west of Bowling Green. The house on Liberty-Hi Road, where Ernie still lives, features a pond in its large yard and is, by any standard, a fine house. But it was a less valuable property than the house on Brownwood. Money realized in the real estate transaction went, for the most part, to Scott's skating.

Competition brought Scott back to Ohio in mid-December 1972, for Regionals in Columbus. The soundness of Monsieur Brunet's figures training was ringingly demonstrated in that competition. Scott was a runaway first in figures, with firsts from all five judges. He went on to win overall. Scott then won Midwesterns, held that year in Denver at the Colorado Ice Arena, a rink that would twice be his skating home in the future. By winning Midwesterns, Scott earned his first trip to the National Championships, which were held in Minneapolis, the site of his letdown the year before in Sectionals. Once again the Twin Cities were unlucky for Scott. He finished last, ninth in a field of nine. For Scott this debut at Nationals was an unforgettable humiliation.

While Scott was swallowing his embarrassment, another student of Monsieur Brunet's triumphed in Minneapolis. Gordie McKellen won Nationals for the first time. Through Gordie's experiences in the next three years, Scott was to learn a great deal about the pitfalls and pressures of a National Championship.

Scott had two teachers in Rockton. Monsieur Brunet ruled his skating. Off the ice, Scott was guided by Gordie, who acted as role model and big brother to Scott. Five years separated Gordie and Scott but, in spite of the age difference, they were close friends. "He took me under his wing and showed me things. He developed the fight. I never was much of a fighter until Gordie. . . ." Nor was Scott much of a girl-hound or a beer drinker or carouser, until the unsupervised contact with older skaters at the Wagon Wheel let Scott explore such big-kid delights, with Gordie watching out for him.

In stories of athletes on their way to greatness, much is always made of the constant, grinding work that goes into a championship. Scott, indeed, worked hard through his career, at least six hours a day of intensive practice and training, day in and day out. But six hours on the ice leaves a lot of waking hours off the ice. And the off-hours at Rockton were like teenage heaven, a pack of high-charged kids free to entertain themselves in the Wagon Wheel's facilities and each other's rooms, far from the classroom and parents and all other obstacles to fun.

Precocious experiments in romance and general hilarity were rampant in Scott's dorm. Scott himself was a terror with practical jokes: Vaseline on toilet seats, Ben-Gay in other kids' bathing trunks. A favorite prank was to fill an album jacket with shaving cream and put the opening of the jacket under somebody's door. Stomp on this arrangement and the room was decorated with shaving cream. Rockton, Scott recalls, was like a year-long summer camp.

Rockton had other peculiarities unforgettable to anyone who

worked on its ice. The buildings that housed the rinks were ill-suited to their purpose, and the result was a perverse indoor climate. In warm weather heavy fog would settle over the ice, fog so thick that freeskating was dangerous. Monsieur Brunet would send Scott and Gordie around the rink with a sheet held between them, trying to clear the air of the wet haze. Fog was thickest at the day's beginning. Bodies moving out on the ice seemed to dissipate it. Summer ice is bad everywhere, but summer ice at Rockton could be atrocious. The combination of inadequate building insulation and failing refrigeration equipment sometimes softened the Wagon Wheel ice to the point that it was no longer ice. The skaters held swimsuit parties on the rink. The enduring memories of any Rockton veteran include those fogbound mornings, and skating through puddles.

Gordie's contributions to Scott's maturation went far beyond frivolity, much as the two of them loved frivolity. Gordie, Scott recalls, made him feel like a skater, not a runt. Part of the strong bond between them was their height—Gordie is barely taller than Scott. Their approaches to skating, too, were strikingly similar— athletic, with emphasis on jumps and personality and occasional humor in performance. Many of their discussions were long and serious, with Scott asking Gordie detailed questions about what Nationals were like, and how the problems of championship were best handled. Scott wanted to know so he'd know what to do when he was champion. The older skater talked freely. Gordie had few doubts that Scott would, someday, hold the National Championship. When Scott's time arrived, Gordie knew, Scott would be the best.

Scott had another year of being less than the best. This was the 1974 season, when he was fifteen, his third year as a Novice. The win at Midwesterns in 1973 gave him an automatic berth at Nationals, which were in Providence, Rhode Island. Scott's showing there was a slight improvement over 1973. He was next-to-last, ninth out of ten.

In summer of 1974 Scott suffered his first debilitating injury, something experienced sooner or later by almost all skaters. He jumped out of his upper bunk in the dorm at Rockton, caught his right foot on the lower bunk, and shattered an anklebone. A lengthy recuperation with a cast and, of course, no skating, ensued. Virtually as soon as Scott's cast was off he competed in a summer competition in Columbus and won. The injury still looked terrible and hurt fiercely, but Scott simply forgot about the pain and skated, an act of mental control that skating has demanded of him many times since.

Meanwhile, events in Bowling Green had taken a disturbing turn. A mark appeared on the breast of Dorothy Hamilton. The spot was diagnosed as melanoma, and removed. So began a surgical hide-and-seek with cancer that would end only when cancer killed Dorothy. At the outset, though, there seemed to be a great deal of hope that the cancer could be defeated. Once again, as it had been when Scott was little, the home life of the Hamiltons was disrupted by hospitals and doctors.

Dorothy still taught at the university, in spite of her increasingly bothersome illness. She pioneered a curriculum in personal and family relationships, teaching a course in intimate interpersonal life that word of mouth among students had made into a campus hit. Her course had a waiting list every time she gave it. Students who came into contact with Dorothy were devoted to her. She brought a great deal of herself to the lectern. When death closed in on her, she asked one of her classes to write essays on facing death.

It was some time, though, before Dorothy yielded to death. While Scott was in Rockton, she maintained good cheer, ever optimistic that the battle against cancer could be won. Surgery took Dorothy's breasts and female organs. Chemotherapy brought on raging sickness. For long months Ernie and Dorothy rose every Wednesday morning at 5:30 to make a two-and-a-half-hour drive to Columbus, where she was inoculated with a virus that was supposed to induce an immunological reaction to her cancer.

Ernie was appalled by his wife's suffering. With every reason to break down, Dorothy's spirit remained intact. Self-pity and bitterness did not disfigure her consciousness as she fought for her life.

Scott girded himself for another competitive season, his first as a Junior. His figures were strong in this period. Sixth Test, part of Scott's entry to Junior level, went well. Scott was third at Midwesterns, and seventh at Nationals in Oakland, California. A good deal of progress was manifest in Scott's skating, but he had yet to soar in competitions. For the first time, freeskating was the problem. Scott was strong in figures, but competition nerves played havoc with his final events. He was, in the words of a blunt observer of those times, "Blowing it."

During this period when Scott's skating stood on its launchpad, unable to take off, Dorothy took a sudden interest in her son's living conditions at Rockton. She had gotten wind of the spectacularly carefree life-style of the dorm kids. Miss Kohout had run a tight ship at the Wagon Wheel, but she had left Rockton to marry skating's media star Dick Button. Thereafter, life for the Rockton ice kids became like a beach blanket movie. But Dorothy soon imposed an adjustment in her son's arrangements. She moved him out of the dorm and placed him in the home of an attorney, Milton Fischer, who lived less than a mile from the rink.

The Fischers had a daughter who skated, a son Scott's age, a swimming pool, a trampoline, and a basketball court. As all his host families have, the Fischers adored Scott. He adjusted immediately to parental supervision, always agreeable and willing to get along. Mrs. Fischer, Scott recalls, was a spectacular cook. A particular favorite were snickerdoodles, a species of sugar cookie rolled in cinnamon.

Home life may have contributed to the successes of the 1976 competitive year, although the return of the Fischers' oldest son forced Scott to move back into the dorm for the fall training prior to the competition season. Mid-1975 also brought important changes in Scott's coaching. Pierre Brunet retired, leaving Scott in the charge of Mary Ludington, who had been a style coach and choreographer for Gordie. At the time of Monsieur Brunet's departure, Scott's training was already a team effort, with Mary concentrating on freeskating and competitive program preparation, and the venerable Frenchman on figures, with some attention to freeskating technique. With Monsieur Brunet's retirement, Evy Scotvold, another coach of national stature, began to work at Rockton. Evy and Mary, who prepared Scott for the 1976 competitions, later became a husband-and-wife team and coached at Janesville, Wisconsin, not far north of Rockton. The Scotvolds trained David Santee, who would fight Scott very hard for his first National and World Championships in 1981.

Scott had lost not only his most important coach to date in 1975, but also his off-ice mentor. Gordie McKellen left amateur competition after the 1975 season. He was National Champion for the third consecutive time, seemingly a strong prospect for a medal in the 1976 Winter Olympics. But Gordie, always an original, decided that life at the top of the skating heap was not the sort of life he wanted to lead just then. He didn't like the pressure, so he ended it. Today Gordie coaches in Rockford. He is married to Kath Malmberg, another veteran of Rockton's glory days.

For Scott Hamilton, 1976 promised to be a season unlike any other season. He learned from his parents that it would be his last. Skating could go no further. The family's finances had dried up. Dorothy and Ernie had to re-mortgage their house to finish the 1976 season. This was to be his last chance to really triumph, to do something in National-level competition. Scott won Regionals. He won Sectionals. His first events at Nationals were strong. He found himself, on the eve of his final event, in a very strong position.

Scott was all set to win, a stunning triumph for a skater who had been seventh the year before. But his spirits were very low. The hours before his final event found Dorothy in a hotel room in Colorado Springs, soothing her son, who was despondent because his skating career was about to end.

Dorothy, who wore a sling because her arm had just been operated on, knew something that Scott didn't know, something she wasn't supposed to tell him. On their way west to Colorado Springs, the Hamiltons had stopped in Chicago. There they met the O'Laurels (this book's only pseudonym, for reasons which will be explained later). The O'Laurels were a wealthy North Shore couple who had invested in the rink at which Carlo Fassi taught in Denver. Carlo wanted to coach Scott. The O'Laurels, Frank and Helene, had agreed to pay Scott's way, training and all expenses.

This stunning good fortune was owed, in part, to the judge from Cincinnati who had helped settle Scott at Rockton. Nancy Meiss had told Carlo, a one-man world power in skating, about the gifted boy from Ohio and his family's money problems. The coach in turn spoke to the O'Laurels. Carlo had told the Hamiltons not to tell Scott the good news before he skated at Nationals. He was afraid the tidings would unnerve the seventeen-year-old.

Dorothy thought otherwise. "I think I know my son better than Carlo does," she declared, and told all. Dorothy had indeed known better. Scott brightened and won the 1976 Junior National Championship.

The win brought Dorothy a moment of happiness that must have paid in great measure for her years of sacrifice on Scott's behalf. In those ultimate moments of competition, Dorothy was as nervous and reluctant to watch Scott as she had once been when she sent her poor sick boy to the skating rink for the first time. She couldn't watch Scott freeskate. To this day Ernie has a hard time watching Scott compete, a reluctance conditioned in the years with Dorothy. Scott's mother paced behind the stands when Scott was about to skate the long program at the Broadmor in Colorado Springs. She heard the audience booming above, and one of skating's important people took hold of her and pulled her toward a place where she could see the ice. Ernie can't remember who it was, judge or official, who hauled Dorothy up to see Scott. But he can remember what was said. "Come here, Dorothy, I want you to see something. I want you to see the future World Champion." The world was beginning to see Scott as Dorothy had always seen him.

After the Junior National Championship, Scott looked ready for a brilliant career. It seemed even more promising in the light of his new alliance with Carlo Fassi. In 1976 Carlo coached both singles skaters who won gold medals at the Winter Olympics in Innsbruck. The success of Dorothy Hamill and John Curry crowned him as a kingmaker in his sport. With powerful European connections and skaters from all over the world, Carlo and his German-born wife Christa seemed more than mere coaches. They were a formidable skating syndicate. The word in the skating world was that they accepted already accomplished skaters and groomed them for international championship, using their standing in the skating world to promote their skaters' success.

Scott's association with Carlo would turn out to be disappointing. But in spite of the unhappy outcome, Carlo gave a gift to Scott's skating future without which there might have been no future. By introducing the O'Laurels to the Hamiltons, Carlo had seen to the solution, once and for all, of Scott's money problems, which are the worst problems facing most figure skaters. Once the O'Laurels started paying, Scott never needed to give a thought to the cost of anything connected to his sport.

The Hamilton family had two new members, Frank and Helene. Almost instantly family friendship and shared affection for Scott loomed larger than money. Scott stopped at the O'Laurel house in Winnetka after Nationals for his first encounter with his benefactors, who had already met his parents. Scott was absolutely beside himself to meet the people who had saved his skating. He was particularly delighted with Mr. O'Laurel, whom he called "Big Frank." Frank was far less interested in skating than his wife, but he was crazy about Scott.

For her part, Helene remembers a boy who was rather more open and animated than most seventeen-year-olds. He seemed younger than his years. Helene's indelible memories of her skater include the image of Scott hanging out of the window of the car that was taking him to the airport. He waved and shouted and carried on until the car was out of sight.

Scott moved in with a family near the Colorado Ice Arena. He endured a few months of home life more strict and regimented than he liked, skated, and carried a full load of classes at the nearby public high school. The school in Rockton that Scott attended in the fall of 1975 had dropped Scott in his second term, because of poor attendance. This seemed to jeopardize his chances for graduation in the spring. But between John F. Kennedy High School in Denver and Scott's school back in Bowling Green, which gave him a load of lightning coursework after Nationals, Scott assembled enough credits to graduate. He wore cap and gown at the June commencement ceremonies at Bowling Green.

In the summer of 1976, Scott took an apartment in a new complex adjacent to his skating rink. There he led a colorful bachelor's existence for the next year, living with the speed and freedom of a college boy away from home for the first time. He drove a Volkswagen Beetle.

Scott's relationship with the Fassis was initially cordial and productive. He passed the final figures test that qualified him for Senior competition. In his new Senior status Scott crossed the Atlantic for the first time. He placed second and third, respectively, in tandem summer competitions held in the Alpine cities of Oberstdorf, West Germany, and St. Gervais, France. This was an auspicious beginning in international competition.

Dorothy missed her son's first trip to Europe. She said she'd go overseas with him the following year. Carlo was very encouraging to the Hamiltons, telling them that Scott might be an Olympic

Champion by 1984. For the first time Scott was hankering after skating's greatest glory. Previously the Olympics had seemed ridiculously out of reach. But his National Junior Championship made all things seem possible.

An injury kept Scott out of the 1977 Regionals. The Midwesterns were a near-disaster, but Scott squeaked by in third place, thereby qualifying to compete at Nationals as a Senior for the first time. There, both short program and long were debacles, and Scott dropped to a ninth-place finish. That showing in the 1977 Nationals, held in Hartford, was made even more agonizing for Scott because it was the last competition that Dorothy saw.

Dorothy saw Scott skate for the last time in an exhibition at Fort Wayne, later that winter. The exhibition fell on a Friday night. The following Monday, Ernie drove Dorothy to Columbus, where she checked into a hospital and remained about ten days. Dorothy had known for some months that she was dying, telling certain friends and acquaintances that her situation was hopeless. Her sons knew the gravity of her condition but seemed to avoid acknowledging the inevitability of its conclusion. They continued to deny that their mother was dying until death made further denial impossible.

Before it came for Dorothy, death had visited a house once very familiar to her. The beginning of 1977 had brought the news, completely unexpected, that Andy Klepner was terminally ill. The family doctor who had been such an important character in Scott's early life was dying of cancer. Dorothy sat with her old crony as much as she could, knowing that her turn was coming fast. Dr. Klepner's illness was mercifully brief. He was dead within a few weeks.

Dorothy came home from Columbus and stayed at home for about a week and then went into the hospital in Bowling Green. Going into the local hospital was part of her plan. Dorothy wanted to die near home. Toward the end, further treatments were suggested, but she turned them down. Painkillers had been offered to her earlier, but she refused them until it was impossible to refuse.

Skating took Scott away briefly, and brought him home again. He skated in the annual show at his home arena, but Dorothy was too sick to attend. The O'Laurels had come, at Dorothy's insistence, to see Scott skate at Bowling Green. Plans had been laid in happier times for Scott's sponsors to share his triumphal annual homecoming with the Hamiltons. Ernie took a videotape of the show to Dorothy's hospital room, but she couldn't watch the whole performance. She was too tired.

A week after the Bowling Green show, Dorothy lost consciousness for the last time. Ernie, who kept a constant vigil at her bedside, sleeping in a chair in her room, began to go home to sleep. He had reached a point where he could no longer stay in that room day and night. About a week after Dorothy lost wakefulness for the last time, Ernie came home at about 11:00 P.M. Scott and Steve, sensing something momentous, went to the hospital and stood watch in Dorothy's room for an hour or two. She died in the early hours of May 19, 1977.

The O'Laurels did not come to Bowling Green for the funeral. They didn't want to further burden the Hamiltons in the hectic days of funeral and burial arrangements. When Sue called to tell the O'Laurels of her mother's death, Helene asked about Scott. Scott, she learned, was sitting on the bank of the pond in the Hamiltons' backyard. He wouldn't talk to anybody.

Dorothy's death left Scott with a feeling that he had let her down by his weak performance at Hartford. He owed her better than that. After her death he made a resolution that carried him through the next few years—which were difficult ones—to his years of championship and finally to Sarajevo. The connection between Scott's mother and his skating still drives Scott. The memory of Dorothy rings in all of his triumphs.

Still in Ohio, Scott phoned Carlo Fassi. Have everything ready for me, the skater told the coach. Have my long program ready.

Have my short program ready. I'm not messing around anymore. This is it. That's all there is to it.

So began Scott's final climb. He rose steadily from then, with only one reversal. But seen from 1984, Scott's bad final year with Carlo Fassi seems to fit into the rise. A last taste of defeat in 1979 may have been necessary to push him to what followed.

In the competition seasons after 1977 and before the 1980 Winter Olympics, four Senior men fought for the top three positions at Nationals, vying for membership on the U.S. World Team, which in 1980 would also be the U.S. Olympic Team. Charlie Tickner ascended to the National Championship in 1977 and held on to the championship, which put him out of the others' reach. David Santee was a World Team veteran, who did well at the 1976 Olympics, so he, too, enjoyed a certain ascendancy. The fight for the top three positions became a fight between two relative newcomers, Scott Hamilton and Scott Cramer.

Scott Hamilton won his Regionals in 1978. He was third in both short and long program. He finished third overall, a stunning break into the U.S. World Team for a man in his second year of Senior competition. Scott finished eleventh at Worlds in Ottawa, Canada, a respectable showing for a man new to Worlds.

But 1978 brought news that destroyed his relationship with Carlo Fassi. The coach was going to train Scott Cramer, the particular enemy of Scott's ambitions. Scott's trust in his coach was shattered. His training for 1979 had already been disrupted when he heard the news about Cramer. Scott had badly hurt his right ankle, tearing and straining it to the point that he was in and out of casts all summer. "I loved skating and I wanted to keep going, but I couldn't train the way I did before," recalls Scott. "And I didn't think anybody cared."

Scott rallied for Nationals. Everything told him that he was in danger of getting pushed out of the top three, but he went to Cincinnati to fight for his place. He thought he skated very well, but the judging went against him.

Scott was furious . . . and at a loss. He wouldn't rise any further in partnership with Fassi, because the spirit of partnership was destroyed. But he was afraid to leave Carlo. Scott watched the World Championships, in Vienna in 1979, on television in Ohio. He swore he'd never watch Worlds on television again.

In March, Scott went east with his personal effects and his dog. He settled into a big house in suburban Philadelphia, becoming once again a surrogate son and brother to a host family. He started training at the Philadelphia Skating Club and Humane Society Rink in Ardmore under Don Laws, a coach of medium standing who had taught at Philadelphia for over twenty years. Scott had left the supercoach for a man he had grown to know and trust in recent years. Something about Don Laws spoke to Scott, something that seemed more important to him than a record of skaters with gold medals.

So Scott was Don's special skater, and the two of them conspired to take over figure skating. Don told Scott to kill whatever remained of the old Rockton good-time boy. It was time to get serious. Don gave Scott stature on the ice. He wasn't short anymore when he skated.

Don and Scott showed the power of their partnership on the eve of the Olympic year. In autumn 1979, Scott won the Flaming Leaves competition in Lake Placid, which that year was an Olympic preview. He beat the current U.S. and World Champions at Flaming Leaves, an annual competition now called Skate America. Scott began his big win with a fourth place in figures. He got angry and won short program. Short program put him in a position to win, but the idea of beating all the men he had ached to beat for years so unnerved Scott that he talked with a sports psychologist. He told the psychologist how terrifying it was to think of beating those guys.

"I can give you some solid professional advice," the psychologist said. "Screw 'em."

Scott couldn't believe what the man had said. "Screw 'em?"

"Screw 'em."

Scott skated a triumphant long program, a ringing beginning-to-end triumph that excited the whole skating world.

Of course skaters don't just take over the sport after something like that; they pay their dues. Scott was third at the 1980 Nationals. He went to the Olympics wanting to finish in the top ten. But after he was there, he said he wanted to finish fifth.

He did exactly that, skating what may have been the night's best long program. But what the world remembers about Scott at Lake Placid are the pictures of him in a ridiculously large cowboy hat, carrying the American flag at the opening ceremonies. It was a special honor conferred on him by his fellow team members.

The 1980 Worlds brought another fifth-place finish. In the spring of that year, Don Laws took over coaching at the Colorado Ice Arena, filling a position created by the departure of Carlo Fassi.

In the following season, the way for Scott Hamilton was cleared by post-Olympic retirements from amateur status. Scott could take over. He did, winning the Nationals at San Diego and the Worlds at Hartford.

# Denver

*December 8–31, 1981*

# 4

# Sweetheartland,
# or Scott Has a Bad Day

Denver is a place utterly unlike the oozing, potting-soil flat-lands of Wood County, Ohio. You can look west, out beyond Denver, and see the planet itself breaking through the brown leather ocean of the Great Plains. The bedrock in this giddy part of the continent comes up and does tricks.

You can never quite get into Denver, and you can't quite get out of it. It is a vast agglomeration of tract suburbs, where the ground never heals, the houses don't look finished. The ambient dinge of Denver's southwest side was accentuated, on December 8, 1981, by gray-brown waterlessness, with no snow to cover up the dead lawns and dust, and overhead, a dome of orange pekoe smog. Thank God, to say the least, for the mountains. The ground-level schlock is not so bad when you can look up over the Mister Donut sign into His eyeballs.

So went my thoughts on the way south across Denver's out-skirts to the Colorado Ice Arena to meet my fellow mudlander, Scott Scovell Hamilton, who in the exactly two years since I had met him had become World Champion, an amateur sports television celebrity, and—almost—a household word.

The Colorado Ice Arena shares the area's fast-buck tackiness. Coming at it down Evans Avenue from the east, CIA—so habi-tuées call it—presents a blank bluish metal-panel wall that could be the back end of a factory outlet. But the sign out front said that this was the rink. More signs in the entranceway said that CIA was the skating home of World Champion Scott Hamilton, and the former skating home of Olympic champions John Curry and Dorothy Hamill. You'd think a rink that had known these skating demi-gods would show a little class, but CIA's lobby brought to mind the locker section of a bowling alley, an alley put up not too long ago but already wearing out.

Of course, bowling alleys are not alive with teenaged girls in tiny skirts and flesh-colored tights, as the CIA lobby was at that moment. Figure skating rinks and competitions and exhibitions crawl with particularly sleek and pampered-looking schoolgirls. And nothing in the world has the heartbending perfection of one of skating's princesses in full regalia.

I had left the earth as I had always known it and was standing for the first time in Sweetheartland, a place peopled largely by perfect girls in tights and skates. I cannot think of Scott Hamilton without thinking of such Sweethearts, for it was their land in which he lived when he was an amateur figure skater. Wherever I followed Scott, these stunning women, the pride of their home towns and home ice rinks, abounded. We skateless adults were an awkward minority.

But then I was in CIA's big rink, a chilly warehouse with a floor of concrete-colored ice and gray air. The rink was ringed by battered hockey boards and lined along one side by bleachers. Two teams of pairs skaters and two singles skaters and Scott Hamilton, Champion of the World, were whipping long oblongs around the rink, breaking out of their orbits now and again to jump, spin, or joggle out a line of footwork. They zoomed in counterclockwise orbit, at the speed, more or less, of in-town traffic just before rush hour, with eyes backward and to the sides and anywhere but where they were going. A crash, you would have thought, was imminent, but no one ran into anyone else or the boards. The refrigerator chill poked through goose down and wool, but the skaters worked in shirt sleeves. The upper half of

Scott Hamilton was covered with only a purple Malibu, California, T-shirt that day, yet he was flushed, like a jogger on a warm afternoon.

The sound of fourteen blades free skating was exactly the sound of a room full of meat-cutters working like maniacs. Close the eyes next to the rink, and the illusion was complete of people in long white coats knocking hindquarters into steaks and roasts as fast and as loudly as they could because the boss had just yelled at them. The freon-clammy air echoed with all the sounds that cutting tools make: long saw strokes. Whizzing fast gashes through flesh. Bone scraping. Axes whacking. And steel on stone, honing edges.

You could tell, right there in the CIA, without knowing a thing about figure skating. You could probably tell without having seen skates before, or ice, that Scott Hamilton was the best. Seeing him on the ice was a physical, palpable encounter with sublime high quality. Dozens of reasons can be given for why Scott looks so good skating, even as he was, at that moment, gliding over to get Kleenex from his coach. But some of this difference is inexpressible.

Scott was smaller than most of the others, even the women, but his smallness was transmuted to largeness on the ice. In any crowd, even among the megaskaters at the World Championships, he was the one that drew looks. The small man was made very big by the perfect match of himself with what he was doing. When Scott skated, there was no part of him that was not skating. Don Laws, looking back to when he first saw Scott, recalled, "There was no error in Scott's skating." Don meant that nothing was there that should not have been there, not a molecule. Scott back then had not been the best in the world, but Don had seen with great clarity that nothing in Scott would prevent him from becoming the best, and then still better. He was made for skating; skating was made for Scott. The marriage of the man and his work was breathtaking, even when he coasted to the boards to blow his nose and have a word with his coach and the newly arrived writer.

The meat-cutting sounds of blades on ice were drowned out in a wave of iron noise and human screeching. Skaters like raw, lowbrow rock and roll, the kind that sounds like a human sacrifice in a steel mill, and somebody had started a tape screaming out of the rink's speaker system. Scott gave his used Kleenex to Don and went back into orbit, picking up speed.

He went swooping backward into a far corner of the rink, holding a pose that suggested a T'ai Chi master doing an airplane for charades. He was poised on a flexed leg, with his free leg—skaters ride one skate at a time—reaching out behind him. His arms stretched winglike out to the sides, the left a little forward, the right arm back. The apparent wind from this rearward swoop pulled his hair toward his face, which was set in expectant, pouting concentration. For the instant it endured, the pose was statue-still but full of future movement, a rocket on the pad at T-minus three seconds, vapor and flame already boiling around.

Then he was off the ice into a whiff of smoke-colored black like his stretch pants, purple like the T-shirt, and pale bloody orange like Scott himself. He had escaped this dimension into what should have been, for him, an easy everyday triple Lutz jump.

No unaided nonskating eye could pick out what happened. We owe the following to Scott, who some time later took an afternoon to explain a number of his maneuvers on the ice. What happened just then was that he dropped his free leg iceward until the toe touched down and he went up over the leg like a vaulter going up over his pole. The flexed leg he was riding snapped straight, also pushing him upward. Scott started the jump backward, but at takeoff he threw his left arm around and twisted forward into a closed-up mummy clutch of hands across chest and feet together. In this tightly bound vertical position he was supposed to rotate three times around, counterclockwise, before gravity hauled him back into contact with the ice. In a good jump these blur-speed rotations in the air had to start stopping at the precise instant that would give Scott time to unfold himself into airplane position and come to the ice in a quiet glide, again backward. The unfolding from mummy into airplane checked the rotations.

Cause and effect blend together in the accelerated dimension of triple jumps. What was required for a jump to come off was that Scott had to start the jump when it was starting and stop it when it stopped. His skating goes beyond the limits of language and three-dimensional brain pictures. Scott himself found talk about skating mechanics very taxing and tried to avoid it. Asked what made a triple jump go, he said he had no idea. Among skaters, triple jumps are a religious question. Each has his own ideas about how they are created.

Scott had a hard time with the causal theoretics of his jumps, but he knew a good jump from a bad one, and excellent from very good. A large part of his proficiency in skating is his minute feel for the quality of his own performance. Another aspect is that anything less than the finest performance angers him.

The jump that started just after Scott blew his nose was bad; indeed, so bad that it failed all together in mid-blur, leaving Scott hovering skewed and embarrassed before he came down into a messy scrape of ice shavings. "Aaaaargh," he gargled in a voice purple with rage that carried over the rock and roll. He went back to the takeoff point, fussing at the ice for clues as to what had gone wrong. The ice, apparently, revealed nothing, and Scott high-throttled away for another go at the jump.

The next attempt failed, and the one after that. Scott's rage turned more purple and then deepened further into a frightening black.

A triple jump going bad offers the skater two options. One is to make a split-second, semi-voluntary decision to stop rotating early and land after only one or two turns. The other is to commit oneself to a triple and hang on to the jump and try to finish it in spite of the problems, which can mean a nasty ankle-wrenching landing or a crash. The semi-voluntary abort is called "popping." *Semi-voluntary* is the operative word because things that go on during triple jumps are not all deliberate. In blur dimension Scott was piloted by little men in his brain who operated half independently. This had to be so because in blur dimension things happen faster than the whole brain can think about them.

An artful pop in competition can look like a double- or single-revolution jump that was always meant to be just that. Everything in competition has to be prettied up and sold to audience and judges. In practice, though, Scott's jump failures were obvious. The memory picture of these pops is of Scott hanging over the ice like a parachutist caught in a tree, arms and legs out, eyes pointed down between his feet, looking silly and waiting for somebody to rescue him. In memory Scott stayed off the ice, hanging and looking silly, for some time. But of course it all happened in a flash.

Scott thought popping was a loathsome failure of nerves, the way out for yellowbellies. He liked the hero's option, bringing down a crippled jump like Clark Gable at the stick of a bomber with two engines on fire and the crew bleeding from Nazi shrapnel. To hell with hitting the silk, we're going back to England! Failing, Scott always said, showed you at least had guts.

But the little men who piloted Scott were sometimes tired or underconfident or scared, and so they popped without orders. The result was friction between command and the boys at the controls. You could tell, on December 8, that the top half of Scott's brain wanted the bottom half shot for cowardice.

Now and then Scott came to the boards at mid-rink where Don Laws was standing, and they talked about what was going wrong. "I wasn't ready," Scott said on one of these passes. "I went up and my upper body went so far ahead of my lower body."

"Start with the knees," Don counseled.

Starting with the knees didn't help. Nothing helped. The badness of this bad day, which Scott later said was the worst in his five thousand days of training, went up a notch, and I was soon witnessing full-scale demonic possession. The Champ barked in a phlegmy baritone that was nothing like his real voice. The growling and noise was dreadful, with the evil one chasing Scott around and sinking in claws so Scott couldn't finish his jumps.

The Champ's rage literally knocked over the other skaters, one of whom fell down every forty-five seconds or so. Skaters, coaches, and bystanders looked and felt profoundly uncomfortable, but there was a general effort to carry on normally, as if we could ignore and make go away the fact that Scott Hamilton, Champion of the World, was acting like a dangerous maniac. But the Champ's wrath was bigger than the rest of us, much bigger. On a good day Scott can tickle seventeen thousand people into giddy happiness, bouncing them out of their seats for ovation after standing ovation. A delayed broadcast of a good performance and a fast-shot interview afterward with Dick Button can bring sunshine into America's living rooms on the darkest Saturday afternoon. On December 8, though, Scott's power was turned backward and he sucked all the light and oxygen out of the Colorado Ice Arena. We were helpless victims of the evil side of the force that emanates when Scott skates.

But then the overwhelming black rage vanished into boyish sorrow. Scott bent double at the boards next to Don. His hand held the top of the boards, and his face smashed into the back of his hand.

"I don't see any sense in prolonging this," Don said to Scott, who stayed bent double. Don meant that the disastrous practice session ought to be cut short, and we could all go to lunch.

Scott, in his bottomless sadness, misunderstood. "I know, I know. This will be the last year. I don't think I can take this anymore."

Skater and coach moved away from the center line along the boards to a place where no one could hear what they were saying. Don put on a face-splitting smile and went to work trying to haul his champion out of despondency. He went at it with great energy and conviction, but you could tell, from fifteen yards, that all this effort came to nothing.

Scott's most-of-the-time girlfriend Kitty Carruthers called Don the "Silver Fox," which was not a bad name for him. It expressed the coach's feral middle-aged good looks. You could tell that Don had been a smoothly good-looking young man. You could also tell that going silver had upgraded his handsomeness.

"I'd like to look like Don just once in my life," Scott said about his coach. "And see what I could get away with."

"Silver Fox" was not, at any rate, a bad name for the coach, but "Silver Wolf" would have been better. Don was a major predator, too substantial to be a fox. His pale brown eyes were positively lupine and the association was furthered by Don's behavior during full moons. At the full moon, clear or cloudy, Don Laws couldn't sleep, and his days were so hypertense that those around him got the jitters. You could sense behind the pale eyes this creature trotting in deep snow, ravenous for blood, closing in on the caribou herd over the next ridge.

The wolfman in Ivy League clothing is not the only picture of Don. You could also see, quite clearly, a career path not taken. Don very nearly went into the U.S. Central Intelligence Agency after the Korean War. He had served in Korea in an army security unit and the federal government let him know that he could spy for life if he wanted to. Don chose instead to get back into figure skating. But almost thirty years later you could see the federal agent that Don might have been, a dapper man of action, six feet and an inch and a half, 190 pounds, equally ready to kick in a door or go for drinks in Georgetown. All graying federal agents in movies and television resemble Don Laws. He was born and raised in Washington, D.C., and he always looked like a man working under secret orders from the Capitol.

Wolf or G-Man, Don Laws did not look like a man who ought to be capering at the edge of an ice rink, with a silly wide grin, putting on a get-happy show for a person ten and a half inches shorter and eighty pounds lighter than himself. At the close of the worst practice in Scott's fourteen years of figure skating, we were treated to the ludicrous sight of Don carrying on like Miss Frances on the old "Romper Room" television show. He beamed, flapped his arms, patted and poked, and put friendly hands on Scott's shoulder. But the target of all this cheering up was beyond reach. Moodwise, Scott Hamilton had become an object so heavy and dark that all matter and light around it was pulled downward and lost. The gleam off the coach's teeth went spinning into Scott's black hole.

"Meet us out in the lobby," Don said. He and Scott left the rink.

Forty minutes thereafter this tall silvery man and a very small young man came up out of the hall that ran out of CIA's lobby past the video games and men's and women's bathrooms and lockers to Don Law's office. These were the happiest guys you ever saw. The effect just then was that Scott Hamilton was an identical twin whose brother was a criminal psychopath. The normal brother, who was walking up to me with Don Laws, was by all appearances an incredibly centered, happy-go-lucky guy, as unlike the poor, cracked ice maniac as he could possibly be.

"Hello, ugly," Scott said. "How you been? Let's go eat. You like Chinese?"

# 5

# Fortune Cookies and Tea

After a few days on the Hamilton Trail, this sort of mood leap would seem natural. But on that opening Tuesday, Scott's instantaneous change of state brought on inner-ear disturbances. You would have been ready for anything after that bad practice—anything but what ensued, which was a delightful lunch in a Chinese restaurant a couple of minutes by Don's BMW away from the rink. Like all things in southwest Denver, the place looked like a coin-op laundry from the outside. But the food was good.

"Oh that." Scott and Don were chuckling over the savage events at CIA. "That wasn't as bad as it looked."

How bad was it? Well, they were saying, it was bad, but a sort of badness that wouldn't last. It was, in fact, a good sort of badness, because it was good to be bad like that at CIA, in relative privacy, a month before competition. It was good to get it out of the way. It would be bad, indeed, if it cropped up later.

So what brought it on?

The amazing badness, according to Scott and Don, was the result of Scott having to be perfectly good for four days running down in Colorado Springs, at a show at the Broadmor. Being World Champion, which Scott had been since Thursday, March 5, 1981, had required Scott to be good almost continuously for ten months. For show audiences, for the press, for everybody.

Scott's capacity for goodness had been absolutely exhausted down at the Springs, so what was left was the residual badness of a very, very good year. It had to come out some time.

Scott and Don began talking about the psychology of World Championship badness with pleasant clinical detachment, as if it had all happened some time ago, to somebody else. You could see that they were keenly interested in what was going on, but you wouldn't have thought that they had a great deal at stake, which was *everything:* the long run to the 1984 Winter Olympics, three more National Championships before the Olympics, two more Worlds. A global sports reputation was at stake. Not to mention the chance for a brilliant professional career.

The whole situation, to the newly arrived outsider, seemed critical. I, of course, had been absolutely unprepared to see the happy-go-lucky male skating sweetheart of network television going berserk on the ice. The spectacle initially brought on the notion that this was going to be one of those psychological sports tragedies in which a gifted jock's psyche is destroyed by fame and the monstrous pressures of competition. Possibly the greatest natural-born skater of all time, the narrator of the tragic scenario was intoning, poor Scott Hamilton fell victim to permanent, overwhelming badness. The whole world was saddened by the loss. Final video: Scott, gray at twenty-four, a woolen lap robe, tokens of past glory in his trembling hands, his mind a thing of shards. . . .

But coach and skater were ready, as the waiter brought us shrimp with lobster sauce and chicken almond ding, to dismiss the incident or, at least, to put the incident in its place. So they ate and talked in one of their characteristic modes. This was their happy-duet mode, Scott and Don together when things were fine. The effect was that of a French horn and a clarinet, with the horn playing a mellifluous, serious melody while the clarinet broke in now and again with comic flourishes. Don Laws generally spoke earnestly, in a strident falsettoed baritone. While he spoke he wore a fixed wolf grin. He spoke with the overemphasis that belongs to schoolteachers and all those who have to spend their days explaining things to children. The overemphasis was sweetened by the saccharine lilt common to men who spend a great deal of time talking to women. The men in the skating world talk this way, like third-grade teachers who do interior design work on the side, because they do, indeed, spend a great deal of time explaining things to children, and almost as much time humoring the children's moms. Smooth talking was de rigueur for an adult male in figure skating. Don was about as smooth as you could get, but there was nothing timid in his smoothness. Deprived of the normal sports-world outlets for male aggression—growly vituperation, spitting tobbaco gobs, punching people—Don Laws had developed smiley verbal nastiness to a science. He was intensely proud of his deftness with what he liked to call verbal stilettos. He'd mime sticking the stilettos in and turning them, grinning with wolfish glee.

No stilettos were going in at the Chinese restaurant, though. Don was laying out the big strategic picture. This was the only time in many hours of talking with Scott and Don that the big picture, which encompassed everything between then and the 1984 Winter Olympics Games in Sarajevo, Yugoslavia, was discussed. After that, the overview was lost in the short-term tactical situations of the 1982 competitive season. When a competition lay in the near future, nothing but that competition existed for Don and Scott.

While Don carried the melody, Scott broke in with raucous counterpoint. His habit, in company, was to quip rather than talk, throwing in sentence fragments, most of them meant to be funny. In this conversational mode, Don was the straight man and Scott the comic, undercutting and overcutting what the coach was saying. Now and again, this business would stop, and the coach would roll his eyes, make an exaggerated sigh of exasperation, or gently reprimand his skater. But Don's impatience was an affectionate fraud, a way of showing that they enjoyed each other's company. The essence of the relationship between Scott and Don was a very elastic familiarity. Sometimes they were father and son, with flare-ups of filial resentment and rebelliousness, and fatherly imperiousness and grief. In the chummy mode in the Chinese restaurant, they were big brother and little brother, siblings with a considerable age difference, so they weren't jealous of each other. There were many modes in the Scott-Don relationship, and they all were elemental and deep. These two men, you could tell, were mutually entangled to the point that they worked for much of the time as one person. Most marriages don't have anything like the deep mutuality shared by Scott Hamilton and Don Laws.

But the glue that bound Scott and Don together was not mutual affection—although they did, clearly, like each other. The glue was not so much the love of one human for another as it was the love of two men for something else. In March 1979, they had formed a two-man combination for the purpose of doing everything that could possibly be done with Scott Hamilton's brilliant talent for figure skating. The commitment was reaffirmed and deepened after the 1980 Olympic year, when they saw that they could take over the skating world and rule it until 1984.

In that world, the skating world, all their shared purpose and devotion was wagered on ridiculously short, risky performances. About thirty minutes—ten minutes in three competitions—on the ice in front of judges lay between Scott and Don in the Chinese restaurant and the 1982 World Championship. The sum of Scott's competitive performance time between December 1981 and the Sarajevo Winter Games would not equal two hours. This was a nervous, high-risk world. And the tension and hazards tied Scott and Don together more firmly than those of us who live in less chancy worlds can be tied together. They were combat buddies, welded into manly intimate interdependence because they needed each other to survive.

The quest for gold in Sarajevo was this pair's sole *raison d'être*, but they rarely considered the quest in the long view. They rarely talked about it, that is. You got the idea that each of them made some sort of silent, private obeisance to the ultimate purpose every day. But it didn't come under discussion. What did come under discussion was the micro-view, the day's triumphs and failures in practice. And when talk about skating ran out, which it generally did in a few minutes, Scott and Don would wander into ritual, light conversation that was pursued for fun and release more than it was supposed to be an exchange of information. They usually spent a lot of time, as Scott put it, just jokin' around.

It later became very clear that the jokin' around was part of their winning formula. At the competitions that season, when things were serious, indeed, and Scott and Don labored under an amazing tonnage of seriousness, it was nearly impossible to get them to be serious. When the two were off the ice together, seriousness couldn't last for more than a minute or two. You could get them to talk about skating and reflect and answer carefully individually, but in tandem they were always jokin' around.

But those nervous times at competition were still comfortably in the future on December 8, and for the first and last time Scott and Don got serious and talked about everything, from their teaming-up in Philadelphia to Sarajevo.

Just about then, Scott Hamilton said something that he said at least once a day for the ensuing three months. "It's hard," he said. "It's harder than I ever thought it was going to be."

Scott generally sang out the "It's hard," in a clear descending alto that rang for some seconds on the word "hard." What he meant was that it was damnably difficult to be World Champion. The skating that had rested so lightly on him two years earlier weighed on him now, and it gained weight every day. "It used to be fun," Scott said. "Now it's a job."

Scott's brilliant skating talent floated him rather easily into world preeminence in 1981, Scott and Don were saying. The competitions had been hard fought, but winning the first time had been simply a matter of laying down the best possible performance and letting victory take care of itself. "Now," Scott was saying, "I've got to earn it."

To earn the World Championship for the second time meant making an even more emphatic, solid demonstration to the world that Scott Scovell Hamilton was the best male figure skater. But being World Champion made it difficult in all ways to be the best skater. "It's hard. It's really hard," Scott reiterated. "It's never been this bad before."

Scott, the two of them were telling me, was at the center of a web of internal psychological difficulties and external pressures that made it impossible for him to train with the clear-headed, easy devotion that he knew back in Philadelphia. World Championship had brought him into manic-depressive mood swings. The high days, Scott said, were higher than before. But the low days were lower than ever. We had just seen the worst possible practice session. Such badness, Scott said, was absolutely unknown before his World Championship. "I was really hungry for it before. Now that I've got it, it's really hard to stay hungry."

Winning the championship in 1981, skater and coach explained over fortune cookies and tea, absolutely transformed the psychology of the 1982 season. It was easy to be ravenous for something Scott didn't have, and to bring all the Champ's energies to one voraciously competitive moment to take what he didn't have. The incentives, then, had been outside Scott. Now everything had moved inside. Somehow, Scott had to fabricate for himself the mental conditions that would make him a winner again. But the goal was less substantial now. Formerly there had been somebody else to beat. Now Scott had to beat himself.

World Championship had brought Scott exposure that dissipated the energies he needed to form his new, internal victory synthesis. The eye—the public eye—was always on him. Formerly he had two- or three-month stretches of unbroken practice time at his home rink. But the championship had brought with it new pressures to perform in United States Figure Skating Association–sanctioned exhibitions, like the showdown at the Springs. Scott, as World Champion, was worth a great deal more money to his sanctioning body than he was before. So, there was new pressure to do shows and bring money and glory to local skating clubs and the USFSA. Everybody wanted Scott to *do* something.

Public pressure was coming to bear on Scott outside the skating world, too. The World title had made him a minor celebrity outside of his sport. So there were more reporters around than ever before. This new celebrity was making it hard for Scott to travel, or eat in restaurants, without being recognized. "Ooooo," people were beginning to say, "you're Scott Hamilton, aren't you?" So Scott was signing napkins and menus where he had once known the same privacy as the rest of us.

If Scott held together, these new pressures would lose their dreadful, overwhelming novelty. But in 1981, it was all too damned hard. "This," Scott said, "has been the worst year of my life. I hope it gets better." The statement, like the "It's hard" song, would be heard almost daily until the ultimate moment in Copenhagen.

The 1982 season, as Scott and Don mapped it out in the Chinese restaurant, was a psychological obstacle course. With less time to practice, less peace of mind with which to concentrate and focus, without the same easily perceived object of desire that he had going into the 1981 season, with less of all the stuff that made him the world-beater in 1981, he had to beat the world again. Scott and Don treated the season as a psychological problem. No one in the Hamilton camp harbored any doubts that Scott had the technical skating stuff.

Actually, the psychology wasn't a question. Scott and Don never, then or later in the season, indicated doubt that he'd deliver the stuff when he had to. The point of the conversation was that training, winning—living in general—was more difficult than it had ever been before. "It's hard. It's so hard."

The difficulties mapped out here are only the crudest schematic of the psyche-management difficulties that faced Scott and Don. The triumphant 1982 season had to be followed by a more triumphant 1983 season, which would lead into the greatest triumph pressure of all, the 1984 Olympic season. Scott had to be hungry. And the world had to be kept hungry for Scott. Each season had to bring improvements and change so the Champ's brilliance wouldn't pall, so the world wouldn't lose its fascination for him. Scott had to keep beating himself, even if the men against whom he competed didn't improve. If Scott didn't grow, he would, sooner or later, lose. For twenty-six months, Scott had to make everything he did brand-new. Just when the world was doing everything to make Scott old, he had to keep pulling out newness.

The approach to Sarajevo amounted to something like the old "Lunar Lander" computer game. Here were Scott and Don, riding a thing that had to land just so in February 1984. All the while they approached the landing they burned the Champ's emotional fuel, firing the retro-rockets that kept Spaceship Hamilton from crashing fatally onto the ice. To win they had to land at the precise moment when they ran out of fuel. Points would be deducted if they still had fuel at game's end. Every day brought the problem of what to do with Scott's fuel. Should he skate at a club show, to increase his public exposure, and maybe rub a judge and the USFSA the right way? Or should he stay at CIA and train? Should he take time out for a studio television interview and get some good press, a necessary part of a happy landing in Yugoslavia, or should he forgo publicity and skate? Too much fuel spent outside of training could bring on a dreadful crash like the one we had that day. And using up Scott's emotional fuel before Sarajevo could mean the worst crash of all. But, on the other hand, to get the most out of the landing on the ice in Yugoslavia, Scott and Don had to burn as much fuel as possible on exhibitions and press and awards banquets and all the other things that didn't contribute directly to preparing for competition. To really, really win, they had to play this lander game carefully, indeed. And Scott was already loaded with all the fuel he'd ever have.

# 6

# Scott Speaks in Quotes

On the Wednesday after the hideous Tuesday, Scott Hamilton started telling his life story to a little tape recorder in the basement of a four-bedroom brick ranch house four blocks east of CIA, on the south side of Evans Avenue. "My life story?" the Champ said. "That ought to be a sure cure for insomnia." Then he made snoring sounds.

Scott started talking at 2:00 P.M., which was the time he submitted himself to interviewing in Denver. His habit was to eat a light lunch and watch his favorite soap operas from one o'clock, when the noon freeskating session ended, to two. At two he would shut off the television and go downstairs to talk.

The hour of lunch and soap operas was the beginning of a midday lull in Scott's training day that lasted until 6:15 P.M., when he went back to the rink for forty-five minutes of compulsory figures and then an hour of freestyle practice, during which he practiced his two-minute short competitive program. Scott's training day began at nine o'clock in the morning. He had two "patches"—skating talk for sessions of compulsory figures practice about an hour in duration—then a brief late-morning break followed by the noon freeskating session, in which he practiced the long competitive program. Saturday was Scott's day off the ice.

The place where Scott did this eating and TV watching was the home of Dr. and Mrs. Henry Landis, the parents of Scott's best friend, Brent Landis. Scott had lived there since he and Don moved to Denver in September 1980. Scott had an upstairs bedroom, but he liked to talk downstairs, in a rec room adjacent to Brent's bedroom, because the basement afforded privacy and kept us out of the Landises' way.

The best way to begin an afternoon session with Scott was to show up early and watch him taking in his soap operas. The Champ was a highly involved witness to the prurient and tangled events on the screen of the little color television in the Landises' kitchen. It all delighted him, and he'd cackle and give a running commentary. "See that guy there? He's a really, really good guy, and everybody's been screwin' him over. . . ." Scott had the ability to memorize scenes that he particularly liked and play them back, verbatim, for a few days after seeing them. One scene that got to Scott that week was when somebody asked a big hunk of a male secretary what he liked to do in off-hours. "I play with girls," the secretary said, absolutely deadpan. That, Scott thought, was hilarious, and he reran it for us repeatedly.

The best times for watching Scott watch soap operas was when Brent was around. The two were almost equally well informed on the programs, with Scott seeming to hold the edge in up-to-the-minuteness, probably because he was home in the early afternoon more regularly that December. (Brent was studying at Metropolitan State College in Denver.)

Almost no overtly intimate or affectionate remarks passed between Scott and Brent in these early afternoons in Denver. This absence of showy friendliness gave away what really went on between these two, which was friendship so deep that they barely needed to speak to each other. They were in sync; they simply understood. The few things they did say to each other while the soaps played were brief locutions that meant almost nothing to the newly arrived listener, but which brought on satisfied smiles of mutual understanding. As only the closest friends can do, Scott and Brent communicated in code.

The bond between Scott and Brent was symbolized by a bracelet worn on the Champ's left wrist, which dated to the time of his mother's death, when he lived in Denver and trained under Carlo Fassi. Brent had an identical bracelet, worn and lightly grimy like Scott's. The meaning attached to the matching bracelets, which looked like nylon rope, was somewhat obscure. For Scott, the bracelet seemed to be a rather powerful linkage to his mother and the commitment to skating he had made to her memory after her death, as well as a link to fellow bracelet wearer Brent. It was, among other things, a good-luck talisman, which Scott said he would cut off during his last amateur competition, in the 1984 Winter Olympics season. Then, and no sooner, would he remove the heretofore sacred wristband. Brent was characteristically taciturn about why he wore his own bracelet. No, he indicated, the bracelets didn't carry any profound messages. They had stayed on, he said, because they had to be cut off once they shrunk onto the wrist, and he simply hadn't felt like cutting his off. Brent had an opinion about whether Scott would cut his off after the Olympics, as he had vowed to: "Betcha ten to one he doesn't."

Dr. Landis was a family practitioner, "Ace" to Scott, who called the World Champion "the King." The doctor, obviously, was taken with Scott, as was his wife. The Landises were both from North Dakota, and had brought from the northern plains a folksiness that humanized what could have been an inhumanly upper-middle-class house. Mrs. Landis, a cheery, intelligent American dream of a wife and mother, called her house "homey." It was a somewhat expensive version of hominess, with appointments beyond the means of most families: the dock and the two-hundred-acre lake in the backyard, for instance. But it was, in fact, homey, because of the hominess of the Landises themselves.

The relationship of the Landis household to the big blue skating meat locker down the street was peculiar. They weren't a skating family, but they had housed some of the world's premier skaters. It had all started when they put up Billy Schneider, from Los Angeles. Then a Landis girl brought home a new friend, Dorothy Hamill, who was training under Carlo Fassi at CIA and who eventually won the 1976 Olympic gold medal. Dorothy, Mrs. Landis thought, was going to stay overnight. But she moved in. One of France's best skaters has lived with the Landises. The Landis house, in effect, has been a loving orphanage for the teenagers training at CIA. The family has been enriched by the arrangement, they say. And, of course, the poor homeless skaters have gotten much-needed hominess from their hosts.

It goes without saying that a profound linkage was formed when the household that loves skating orphans was connected with the greatest skating orphan of all time, Scott Scovell Hamilton. Scott became, as he can become anywhere, a member of the family. He got his clothes washed, his pants shortened, his favorite dishes prepared, such as steak and Black Forest cake. The Champ, incidentally, was reported to be a good eater. He didn't have a special training diet, just lots of good food. The Landises also gave Scott an ear, listening to his troubles after a bad practice day and his joy when things went well. They tried to protect him, screening the ever-growing number of phone calls. "We see how tired he is," Mrs. Landis said. "He's always so tired when he comes back from trips."

The most precious contribution from the Landises was not the time and attention they gave him, but, rather, a negative contribution, something they didn't give him: trouble. They didn't try to come into the skating world and take something from him. Scott repeatedly said how deeply he appreciated that the Landises did not follow him to competitions, or claim time—his time—at the few shows and events they did attend. They simply loved Scott, and left his skating and his world glory alone. In three months on the Hamilton Skating Trail, these were the only people encountered who seemed to accept Scott without the whole nervous business of World Championship creeping into the relationship. Deep in the competitive season, Scott would sometimes have fits of pained vituperation against his family and loved ones, everyone with whom he was close, except the Landises.

The choice of living with the Landises was not dictated by economics or other circumstances. Scott had a virtual *carte blanche* to draw money for living expenses, so he could have lived alone if he wanted to. He had, in fact, rented an apartment next to CIA during his first stay in Denver, training under Carlo Fassi, when he was eighteen. But independent living did not suit the Champ. Since that apartment experiment, he had elected to live with families. The enormous effort he gave to skating created in Scott a boyish dependency on other people when he was off the ice. You just couldn't picture Scott doing his own laundry or cooking or—especially—going home to an empty apartment.

So at two o'clock on the day after that bad, bad Tuesday, Scott started speaking into the tape recorder in the basement of the Landis house. His mode of dress was teenage casual: blue jeans, a colored T-shirt, and nylon running shoes, which is what Scott wore nine out of ten days in 1982. His color phase that afternoon was bluish and pale, which meant he was still tired from the Broadmor ice shows. Most people's mental image of winter athletes includes rosy high color, but figure skaters, except those just back from vacation, have a prison pallor. Scott's complexion was pale even by comparison to the other skaters. His skin was transparent and it could show an enormous range of color, from the red-orange flush when he skated all-out, to a cadaverous blue-gray when he was wound-down and tired. His normal complexion was a porcelain-pale flesh tone that brought to mind a baby's skin, or the skin of someone long confined in a hospital. Scott could look fragile, even deathly ill, when he wasn't skating.

The message of fragility was carried only by Scott's face, however. The Champ's physique, even when he lounged in the Landises' basement, betrayed enormous, unkillable strength. His strength didn't show in muscle bulges as much as it showed in detail. Scott Hamilton was illustrated anatomy, without a teaspoon of excess flesh, every muscle-strand and tendon standing out. Healthy veins rode down the crown of his biceps from the shoulders. On the days when he sat for his interviews in a bathrobe, bare-legged, his legs showed the ropy veins of a laboring man's arms. The gorgeous complexity of tendons, muscles, and veins fanned out into the Champ's feet, a man's size six. Scott's feet were tiny compared to most men's, but they weren't tiny relative to the body they supported; they were perfect, as were all his limbs and bodily detail. Scott lacked the outsized parts that would have told you he was small. His gnomish face was, perhaps, a little large, but still nothing like the big heads of other little men.

The issue of Scott's size, incidentally, which no writer or television announcer has failed to mention and, in many cases, belabor, disappears when you get to know him. Once you are acquainted with Scott Hamilton, he ceases forever to be small. He also ceases to be boyish, which, like smallness, has been made an integral part of his national image. Scott's physiological rightness in proportion to himself, and his amazing rightness for his work on the ice, can, indeed, give the idea that he is a man's proper size, and the rest of us are wrong.

His first words, as were many of the words from the tapes made during the ensuing three months, had to do with a woman. But he quickly dropped the subject and started talking about the bad practice, which led him into a ninety-minute interview that he would give in more or less the same form for the next two years. The interview—a bad word, it was really a monologue, with short pauses for the reporter to ask questions—was a very satisfying, frank-sounding hash that included the big commitment to skating made by Scott and Don, biographical details, plans for how he wanted to change the image of figure skating into something with more manly *brio* than Sweetheartland, and on and on. The year had been hard. He suffered for want of a social life, but it was worth it because skating had given him so much. Already he had met the most marvelous and fascinating national celebrities as a result of his World Championship.

He then discussed his personal ideology for competing. The idea, he said, was simply to do one's best, without trying to beat anyone else, and hope that the best would prevail.

Most of what Scott said during the first few interviews in Colorado was true. It jibed, at any rate, with what he said in subsequent conversations. But this was a pre-cooked version of the truth, which he could regurgitate for anybody with notebook or tape recorder. He was speaking in quotes, with the self-conscious unselfconsciousness of celebrities telling us about themselves. Soon the boy from Bowling Green had mastered the art of "being himself," without being himself at all. Scott is, indeed, a master of pseudospontaneous opening up. Always there is the illusion that Scott Hamilton has chosen you, and you alone, for some special confidence. In the skating world, which I was about to enter, I met dozens of people convinced that each had seen something in the Champ that no one else had seen, that each held a unique piece of the Champ.

This isn't to say that Scott was insincere. This facility of un-confidential confidentiallity was, probably, a protective reflex. What came out of his mouth had to be somewhat prepackaged. The skating world, more gossipy and petty than any country town, was no place for unburdening oneself. You could never be sure what your listener was going to do with what you said. Scott had by then acquired a celebrity outside of skating. A too-loose tongue for a reporter or the camera could sink his ship. On the other hand, there were risks in being closemouthed. The skating world, the confidence-hungry press, the TV public, had to hear *something* from the Champ. And it had to sound like the real thing.

In three days, though, Scott exhausted his supply of words with quotes around them. The pre-taped stuff started to run out in a session that closed with a discussion about competitiveness and winning. Scott was saying that he didn't like some of the emotional changes wrought by his success. The commitment to skating, the growing pressures and emotional trouble, was making it hard to be a person, Scott said.

"I don't want to pay the price of not being a person," Scott said. "I want to be a person that someone can turn to when they need help. Not when somebody comes up and says, 'My daughter doesn't want to skate anymore. Would you talk to her, please?' That's dumb! If the daughter doesn't want to skate anymore, don't make her skate. But if someone's in a room crying, I'd like to be there for them."

There was, it seemed, a war in progress between the parts of Scott that wanted to comfort the crying and the offensive-defensive components that concerned themselves with winning and being World Champion. Those parts couldn't care less if somebody was crying. Scott was distressed by the barrier going up between him and the rest of the world. "I've seen too many people put out this wall that's impenetrable. And I just didn't like them. I thought they were just too cold." Nevertheless Scott, at the end of 1981, had a wall under construction, and the cold was creeping in. It was hard, damned hard, he said, to hang onto personhood.

Other issues came up alongside this business of how hard it was to help somebody alone in a room crying if you were World Champion. In Scott's mind, they all went together. What you had was a right way and a wrong way. The right way included putting oneself at the disposal of others, knocking down the wall, training with a pure heart, and winning with an angelic devotion to the sport that was absolutely unconnected to any desire to beat other skaters. It was wrong, Scott said, to want to beat the others.

Anybody who knows Scott's competitive history knows also that all of his big advances have come when he was pitting himself against somebody else, no holds barred, doing everything in the world to win. Well, Scott said, that's true, but he hated that sort of competitiveness.

To the first-time listener, Scott's moral dilemma seemed terribly poignant. There was trouble here, not as terrifying as the trouble out on the ice on the terrible Tuesday, but sad trouble. A sincere young man, a nice guy, being robbed of his niceness.

Eventually, I'd learn . . . and begin to doubt whether these mood vagaries of the Champ were anything more than extremely exciting and changeable emotional weather. Because Scott had a fit of idealism and guilt at two-forty-five on an afternoon in Denver, and because he was able to carry the listener with the depth of his idealism and guilt—this, I would discover, did not necessarily mean that idealism and guilt were the major themes in his life. To assume that you knew something permanent and true about Scott on the basis of a highly convincing display of emotion was like making a visit to a place when it was snowing and then assuming, on that basis, that it always snowed. The only assumption that you could make on the basis of an afternoon with Scott was the assumption Mark Twain made about New England weather: If you don't like what it's doing now, stick around because it will change.

So, we'll leave to the ages the unanswerable question of what meaning was contained in Scott's utterances about rightness and wrongness. The point is that at this juncture the audible quotation marks that made his words into something just like you hear on television disappeared once and for all.

They disappeared at the precise moment that side B of that tape cassette ran out and the machine clicked itself off. Scott paused momentarily, thinking, and then made an observation in a reflective, measured tone of voice, as if he'd been thinking in isolation for a long time and not talking in quotes. Once he said this, he never talked in quotes again. "You know," said Scott Hamilton, "I really have to hate somebody to win."

# 7

# Nailing the Long Program

The music in Scott's 1982 long program added up, very roughly speaking, to a sonatina, a little three-movement creation that hit hard and loudly initially, then softened and slowed, and then built into a noisy finale. The only wrinkle in the simple sandwich design was a brief comic dance at the end of the andante middle movement. In a not-too-close hearing, the four-minute-and-thirty-six-second pastiche seemed to hang together. But close listening told the truth. What you had was an act of musical abduction, five passages spanning 150 years of composition: three ballets, by three composers; movie music; and a synthesizer piece, all kidnapped from their home works by Don Laws and forced to perform together for Scott. It is a tribute to the coach's skill in tape editing that the opening blast of the music for *Mutiny on the Bounty* seemed to lead into a section of Prokofiev's *Cinderella*, followed by a piece of Rick Wakeman's "Seahorses," a snippet of the pizzicato from Delibes' *Sylvia,* and a brassy finale belonging to Tchaikovsky's *Swan Lake.*

The 1982 long program soundtrack lacked the musical interconnectedness that would bind its pieces into a whole. Without Scott the five kidnapped musical moments were strangers, sitting together in a cassette without a common purpose or voice or subject matter. But with Scott skating, marvelous things happened. The strangers got into a happy clutch and sang a wordless anthem to Scott.

Competitive programs represent a musical/choreographic/athletic junk sculpture. The final product is a collection of opportunistic borrowings, sometimes from outlandish sources. The genre is full of surprises. The most unlikely pairings of sound and movement can explode into high art. Skating has a magical ability to pull stunning beauty out of music that was never beautiful, not even close to beautiful, on its own. Out of "Seahorses," a pretentious but trivial synthesizer ditty, Scott extracted a performance that was stunning the first time and every time. Scott went through that andante section in every long-program practice in the 1982 season. Every time he did it, the thing that he made out of "Seahorses" skewered his beholders and held them out over the aesthetic abyss.

Such moments were the big reward for watching figure skating. A kid swooped and jumped to a piece of musical trash and whammo—you were sick with bliss, full of sad wonderment that was sad because such moments are so brief. More susceptible Scott watchers were apt to cry when the Champ was having his moments. They couldn't help it.

Compared to other skating programs, Scott's 1982 music was rather old-school. In 1982, there were World-level programs that were all rock and roll. Scott, of course, loved hard rock, and pumped himself up for competition by listening to raunchy heavy metal. But on the ice he embodied something that couldn't be expressed with electric banshee wails. His skating was a pure product, plain and simple, an unembellished presentation of the beautiful things that can be done by a man on skates. The taste implicit in Scott's skating was much too fine to be paired with the music that the Champ himself loved. So Scott wasn't rock and roll.

Neither was he balletic. Skating's great balletomane, John Curry, won the 1976 Olympics with a program based on *Scheherazade*. Curry, as much as a skater can be, was a *danseur*. His program was as close to a dance performance as a gold-medal skating program could be. And behind this evocation of dance on ice was an idea absolutely not present in Scott's performances. Curry seemed to be reaching off the ice, frustrated with the expressive limitations of his sport, trying to fuse skating with ballet. Scott Hamilton's skating never implied dissatisfaction with skating. He stayed in his medium, always trying to skate as superbly as possible, without trying to do anything but skate.

The music in Scott's 1982 long program formed a transparent vessel into which all of Scott's abilities could be poured. In this vessel, man, movement, and sound could fuse into a protracted supreme skating moment. Four and a half minutes of raw skating power, and blinding skating beauty, beginning to end. The long program didn't always work that well, though. In Colorado, the mix of technique, choreography, and music was not sufficiently fine and evenly blended for beginning-to-end chemistry. Parts of the program caught fire every time—the "Seahorses" section always worked—but the program run-throughs were, for Scott watchers, a series of buildups and letdowns. Just when things were heated up and about to burst into glorious flame, some technical glitch would snuff out the fire.

To the beginning skating spectator, technical troubles in the long program were perceived as aesthetic failures. Unless the technical problem was grossly obvious (and Scott's problems were not generally grossly obvious), unless what went wrong really stuck out, what you saw was a section of the program that didn't quite happen. Without knowing a thing about skating, you could measure the success of a run-through by how much joy it gave you. If a run-through blotted out everything in the world but Scott, and Scott gave you everything you wanted in the world, then you could be sure that you were seeing good skating.

Of course Scott's perceptions of success and failure were not aesthetic. He was at the very heart of the machine, at the controls. Success and failure to him were matters of technical accomplishment. Between skater and nonskater there was an unbridgeable gap in understanding. Only Scott knew what it took to create his skating effects, what it felt like when all went correctly. The Scott watcher could only react. Conversations across the skating gap went something like this:

"God, Scott, that was really beautiful."

"Yeah. Well, it went pretty good that time. Everything was pretty solid, except the triple toe loop in the slow part was terrible. And I need to work on the spins."

"But it was so beautiful."

"Uh, thanks."

So when the Champ soared, the earthbound Scott watchers would gabble and cluck their appreciation, telling him when he got back to earth how great, how fantastic, how beautiful it had been. Scott had his own expressions for success. One was "nailin' it." Triumph was nailin' it to the wall.

On Tuesday, December 29, Scott nailed the long program. Maybe not to the wall, but closer to the wall than he had yet gotten. It was a moment, you could tell, that everybody had been waiting for. Nobody would have said such a thing, but coach and skater were listening to a nasty angst whisper. "How come," the whisper was saying, "he hasn't nailed it yet? Isn't it getting kind of late?" Maybe, the thing was whispering, he wasn't going to get it together this year. Maybe he wasn't going to nail it, ever again. This sort of apocalyptic doubt was always around in the hypertense 1982 competitive season.

The burden of fighting back fear rested mostly on the coach. Poor Don spent a great deal of time with a smile pasted on his face. The forced good cheer brought to mind the plucky British army officers in old movies. "Right-oh," they say. "Little difficulty, eh? We'll do our best, sir, not to worry." Then ten thousand throat cutters come screaming out of the jungle, and that's that.

You'd say to Don, "Everything going all right, coach?"

And the grin would answer you, "Suuure, sure. He's not quite in focus yet, but he'll come around. Everything's pretty much on schedule."

The truth was that by December 29 of the two previous competitive seasons, Scott had nailed his long program a half dozen times, maybe more. But of course Don wasn't going to say out loud, "I'm getting a little worried. He should have had eight perfect run-throughs by this time. He doesn't have any." Opening the door to defeat by saying such things was out of the question. In the phenomenally nervous world of global-level figure skating, it wasn't a good idea to say that something might be amiss, not to anybody else, not even to yourself. Even if something went wrong, it couldn't be acknowledged, and the unacknowledged wrongness had to be willed into rightness. Since Scott had to win, everything that led up to the big competitions had to be part of a victory. The immense will-work, like the work of staying cheery, fell mostly on Don. For the next two and a half months, until the night of the men's long program in Copenhagen, Don's grin did most of the talking for him. When the subject was Scott's skating, no matter what was happening, the grin would tell you, "Yes, yes, everything's fine. Nothing to worry about." The level of concern, or lack of concern, had to be divined from signs other than what the coach was telling you.

The level of concern on December 29 was, by all outward signs, not terribly high, certainly nothing compared to the dreadful typhoons of anxiety that lay ahead at Indianapolis and Copenhagen. The mood was watchful. Scott and Don had been waiting for something, and they were starting to worry about what was taking that something so long. The mood communicated itself dimly to CIA's other skaters, and whoever watched the practice sessions. As 1981 closed, Scott became the focus of all of the CIA skaters' attention, and there was a general atmosphere of expectancy in the rink.

Back in early December no particular deference had been

shown to Scott in the noon freeskating sessions. When he ran through his long program with music, the other skaters stayed out of his path in the unlooking manner that skaters have of giving one another the right-of-way. He wasn't, in any obvious way, a big deal to the others. But by December 29, Scott had ascended to a highly visible leadership at CIA. His long-program run-through had become an important event. When it started, most of the other skaters went to the boards and watched. A few would finish what they were doing before stopping and watching, but nobody skated all the way through Scott's long program in the last days of December.

On the twenty-ninth, when Scott gave Don the nod that meant that he was ready for the long-program tape, all activity halted and all eyes went to the man in T-shirt and black stretch pants with the run on the behind. The white hiss from the tape cassette started. Time to watch Scott. Time to see if he was going to nail it.

# 8

# Warship, Octopus, Jester, and Young Apollo

So there was Scott, hauled up into a pose somewhat taller than it was possible for a man of five feet, three inches to be, up on his toes, with his right arm stuck skyward, the right hand flattened and rigid. Scott sighted along the back of his raised right arm. While his right arm and his eyes went upward, his left arm stuck adamantly down, like a steel tether, an anchor cable, holding him momentarily still while he strained to move. This opening pose was charged with energy, every bodily detail showing strain. His fingers were bent backward with muscle tension. The tendons on the left side of his neck snapped tight like ship's rigging. The blood boiled in a red-orange fog over his face and neck and exposed arms.

He waited momentarily for the music in his opening pose, and held the pose briefly after the first sounds, an ominous orchestral growling. Then a brass fanfare, tum ta-dah ta-dah, the notes low and dark. These notes were the herald of something powerful, threatening. Danger was coming up over the horizon. The music here was lifted from the opening moments of *Mutiny on the Bounty*, and the image from the sound was of a Royal Navy man-of-war, sails jamming skyward, one hundred guns, four hundred men flogged into a killing unit by sadistic officers. This gorgeous fighting machine smashed through white-capped swells, a vision of terror to those who would oppose it. The image materialized in the music and Scott embodied the image. This was skating's ultimate weapon, an instrument of world empire. The opening section was an exhibition of the weapon's firepower.

As the brass was beginning the fanfare, the anchoring left arm was lifted, and both hands went up into what could have been a charades depiction of a ship under sail. The arms were forty-five degrees above the horizontal, Scott's hands flat with the horizon at the ends of the uplifted arms. Then hands and arms came downward as Scott corkscrewed out of the opening stance into a fast backward swoop into a corner of the rink.

Thirteen seconds into the music the orchestra was convulsed in a percussive climax. Just as cymbals crashed, Scott exploded off the ice into a triple Lutz jump. This jump had absolutely failed to detonate, time after time, three weeks earlier on Scott's worst practice day. But on December 29 he nailed the Lutz, firing himself with his toe pick into a clean column of human smoke. The smoke cleared with Scott pumping into the other corner at the same end of the rink. Almost immediately the orchestra convulsed and crashed again, and Scott shot off a triple toe loop —like the Lutz, a toe jump—an ice-pick explosion with Scott rifling into the air. Then he was down and out of the corner, rushing toward the rink's center. As he skated, the orchestra's fit of martial violence went on. It crashed again, but this time he didn't jump. He chopped an arm out to the side. His face in this opening cannonade was a stern military mask, defiant, but composed and still. This was Admiral Hamilton on the attack, a man whose element was the smoke and the roar of battle.

Scott went plowing out into the middle of the rink. At the next orchestral crash he sailed up into a double axel. The jump was high and arching, a trajectory more like a flare floating upward than the boom-flash concussion of the opening toe jumps. And unlike the toe jumps, Scott flew into the axel going forward. This was about twenty-five seconds into the program. The orchestra's mood changed somewhat, leaving the violent fanfare and going into an insanely fast march, with the brass making double-time oompah-oompahs and the violins chittering in upper registers. The sound was still martial, but the suggestion of wild speed was being added to the image of dangerous firepower. Scott charged, maneuvering and aiming himself around the rink, and then he squirted up into a triple Salchow. The blur-speed image of the toe jump was explosion and flight, a gunshot, but the Salchow gave a microsecond picture of the two feet coming together and Scott being smoothly squeezed upward, rocketed rather than shot into the air. There was no toe explosion because he went off an edge into the jump. In the closing twenty seconds of the long program's first minute Scott banged off a couple of minor jumps and another triple toe loop. At the end of the first minute he fell from the air into a crouched spin, flying-change sit, and he turreted around near mid-rink.

The mock battle began to wind down after the first minute. The music brightened and we were seeing flourishes that were not as savagely ballistic as the opening bombardment. A Russian split, and then another, with Scott sitting bent at the waist with his legs in the horizontal, the legs obliquely wide open, and Scott's fingers reaching for his toes. The illusion of the Russian splits was that Scott sat impossibly high in the air, an altitude effect caused by Scott's pulling his legs up off the ice into the splits. His jumps, probably, were higher. But the illusion showed Scott at least ten feet off the ice. After the splits he rocketed into a quick double Salchow, and then threw himself into an Arabian, a move in which his upper body went horizontal while his splayed legs snapped through the air behind him. By this time the orchestra had relaxed, abandoning the martial violence entirely and swooping into stringy climaxes. These last few moves were coordinated with the final crescendos.

Then there was a Wagnerian horn call. Scott's skating, too, had relaxed by this time, and he moved through a series of what looked like semaphore signals. The signals said that the battle was over. Scott had won. The horn was a final victory song. A minute and forty seconds into his long program, he stopped, with hands held high, a reproduction of the opening pose that was expectant but not as tense as the original. When the music started in the program's second movement, there was no battle. Where there had been noise and Scott explosions, and Scott smoke, there was hush and clarity.

"Seahorses" was playing now. Scott floated down out of the movement-opening stretch to the first notes of a sweet, short melody played on what sounded like a celesta, but with a suggestion of wetness: underwater music. Scott, too, was transformed. His movements still showed power, but this was power implicit in profound bodily stillness.

The music's title, "Seahorses," almost evokes the picture of Scott moving through his program's slow part. Almost, but not exactly. What came to mind was, indeed, a sea creature, but Scott had become something stronger and more supple than a seahorse. The thing that appeared was an octopus—not the absurd bag of meat and tentacles out of water, but an octopus in its own element, the king of the shallows, intelligent and powerful, capable of transforming itself into any shape.

The slowness in the program's underwater section was an illusion. Scott maintained a speed across the ice far beyond most recreational skaters, and performed three double jumps, a triple, and a combination spin. This was a concentration of energy into a quiet body line. Scott changed his body format in the slow part. No longer in the violently active vertical position of the opening, he moved into fluid horizontals. He gave the illusion of a body swimming horizontally. Of course he was standing up—gravity and anatomy compelled him to—just as he was standing in the opening section, but somehow he managed to destroy the perception of erectness with horizontal leg and arm extensions. For the next minute and thirty-five seconds, Scott swam and changed shape for us.

He tentatively explored this new body of his, making long extensions upward with his arms. Then he changed shape for the first time, lying flat in the horizontal and rotating in a camel spin, a move that turned the perceptual world on its ear. Scott's rigidity and control in the camel position momentarily gave the onlooker the idea that he had mastered gravity. Of course he was held off the ice by his skating leg, but the rest of his body somehow lent credibility to the notion that he had levitated, floating free, and by sheer mental magic was rotating a leg's length off the ice. This illusion collapsed as Scott shrank into a sphere, low on the ice. This was a sit spin, which then flowered upward into a standing spin, as Scott assumed a chalice shape, a wineglass formed by the man spinning on one foot with the free leg held out and his arms up in a V over his head.

The magic creature of one thousand shapes swam again, but something startled it, and Scott squirted off the ice into a triple toe loop. This jump had seemed like artillery in the opening, but in "Seahorses" it went up fluidly, a swelling synthesizer chord trailing behind it like bubbles. The triple toe loop closed the first minute of the program's middle section. The "Seahorses" melody had played through twice, increasingly elaborate and supported by electronic chords. It started again, building to an intensity that jetted Scott into a pair of double axels.

The pair of axels, performed in quick succession near the rink's center line, each shooting toward opposite sides of the rink, was one of the program's most sublime moments. The jumps went up so quickly that Scott seemed to start the second before the first came down to ice. So here was a twin arching fountain of Scott Hamilton, a truly bravura display of body shape. The twin axels came at the musical climax of the "Seahorses" sequence. In the section's last fifteen seconds, the music simplified itself into the sweet opening bell melody. Scott affected one last shape transformation. He wound himself into a standing cylinder, created by a slow spin on a bent leg, with the free foot cocked in front of him and his arms held still, palms out, as if he were shut in a narrow cylinder, pushing outward. With the turning, Scott's body line spiraled, so what we saw wound downward, like a turning drill bit. Here, in the slow-drilling cylinder, the "Seahorses" section ended. Not a ripple disturbed the rink's surface at this wonderfully calm moment.

The calm, however, did not survive; music began again. Scott was pulled out of the sea, to flounce through a choreographic joke that brought surprise laughter out of his fellow skaters. This thirty-second interlude was such an outrageous twist in the program that it always came unexpectedly, even to those who knew the program by heart, as most of the Scott watchers on December 29 did. So the other skaters started and laughed, tickled by the Champ's bogus ballet. The musical accompaniment to this burlesque was the pizzicato from Delibes's *Sylvia*, a universally familiar trifle that has been used to make fun of classical music and dance as much as it has been used in its real setting, a mythological ballet. Spike Jones once wrecked this pizzicato, and old cartoons abused it repeatedly. Now Scott Hamilton was having a go at it, tiptoeing through an intricate destruction of serious ballet on ice.

The bogus ballet—Scott called it the futzy section, because he futzed around in it—was a clean break with long-program tradition, which dictated that performances be serious. That the Champ injected humor into his big competitive presentation was a testament to an overweening confidence in his technical abilities. Nobody but the world's best skater would dare to clown in front of judges and expect to win. Breaking up a world-beating display of technical prowess with a joke put an element of risk into the performance that made it even more overawing than an all-serious *tour de force* would have been.

The sense of humor smiling out of a great skating program also made the Champ more lovable. The effect was the same as seeing a sense of humor in a public figure. What could have been inhuman was suddenly human, accessible. So the futzy element raised the stakes in this program's competitive game, at the same time dissipating the arrogance implicit in Scott's skating power. We could *like* Scott now.

At this point the watchers relaxed. And for the first time, the Champ turned to us. His attention had gone inward during the opening battle and the undersea stillness, but during the thirty-second joke he faced the people watching him and presented himself, making a self-deprecating shrug first to one side of the rink, then the other. As the orchestra plunked and he capered to the plunking, he stopped twice and shrugged to us. His face wore the distant sadness of Emmett Kelly and other melancholy clowns. The futziness didn't grab for laughs; it simply unwound itself, with Scott closing each musical phrase in a quiet "So what?"

Besides bringing a comic break in the heretofore serious material, this section brought an entirely new body picture of Scott into the program. Only here did his movements show a human upright on the solid earth. A flowery meadow, you would have guessed, and Scott was tiptoeing through the tulips. The flow and flash of freeskating was halted momentarily while he clowned.

But almost as soon as the image of Scott the jester was given, it was taken away. The self-deprecating tulip-tripper was sucked up into a thundering triple Salchow. The thunder boomed out of the pizzicato's last note, and a messenger from heaven flew down out of a cloud as the rink's speakers started blaring the program's finale, a brassy gallop from *Swan Lake*—uptempo, circus-style music.

The choreographic picture Scott made in the last fifty-five seconds was erect and manlike, but something more than human. He became, for the frantic final minute, Zeus' gorgeous son, Apollo, ripping up the clouds on the way down from Olympus, dazzling us, his people, with godly largesse. This was especially evident in the first part of the finale, as he flashed through a curving footwork sequence, casting hands outward as if throwing something to the mortals far below. Up went a double Lutz, and then a lightning line of footwork and a double axel. The tricks were coming more and more quickly, building like the end of a fireworks display, when everything goes up at once. The high-speed barrage of movement brought to mind the program's beginning, but the opening and closing sequences were really quite different. The first was percussive, a series of sharp explosions. The finale was building into a seamless smear of motion.

The last discreet jump was a delayed axel about thirty seconds before the program's end. This was a modified single axel, a long stag leap forward off the ice. Scott hovered momentarily in this leaping-stag pose and then closed into a quick one-flash rotation. The jump was the signal for the big skating potlatch, with Scott throwing to his audience absolutely every maneuver that could be given away in half a minute, a cosmic casting of pearls that seemed inhumanly high-speed but accelerated still more. Scott went into a fury of giving-away. You saw a man-blur hurtling around the rink through a Russian split, half loop, half loop, double Salchow, and a Hamilton trademark, quick turns, with Scott hurling himself around and around, his skates skipping him stonelike across the ice. Then the blaring final notes as Scott went into a scratch spin that vaporized him momentarily.

That's it, you would have thought. The gorgeous young Olympian had disappeared, gone forever to the clouds. But, miraculously, he came back to us, in the form of a little man, flushed and shaken by the deep breaths that wracked him as he moved slowly toward the boards, where Don Laws stood.

The other skaters clapped and shouted. The burden that had weighed everybody in the great gray icy meat locker was gone for the moment. And the man who had been most heavily burdened was now the most unburdened. "Verrry nice, verry nice," Don was cooing, his face split into a gleaming silver grin that was not even a distant relative of the offensive-defensive grin that had occupied his face exactly four minutes and fifty seconds earlier. This was the real thing.

Scott, however, the man who had taken the weight off the Colorado Ice Arena, was not grinning. It might have been that a grin would have taken up more energy than he had to give at that moment. "So there," he said to the weight that had just been lifted. "Bastard program!"

Scott Hamilton, first row left, at age seven and appearing quite ill. *(photo courtesy Richard Hall)*

After only a short while on the ice, Scott, at age nine and seated on the floor at right, is a new person. *(photo courtesy Richard Hall)*

*(Left):* March 1968. In his first Ice Horizons show, Scott starred as a jack-in-the-box. *(photo courtesy Clifton Boutelle)*

*(Below):* Scott, first row right, played on this Youth Hockey team in 1968. *(photo courtesy Clifton Boutelle)*

*(Right):* Scott prepares for Ice Horizons 1971. *(photo courtesy Clifton Boutelle)*

*(Below):* November 1971. Scott Hamilton (center) and Scott Tyson practice figures under the eye of Herb Plata, a skating professional and coach at the Bowling Green State University Ice Arena. *(photo courtesy Clifton Boutelle)*

*(Above):* In March 1975, at a Bowling Green hockey game, Scott Hamilton and his parents were given a small amount of locally raised money to support his skating. Scott, wearing an Afro that season, showed his happiness, while Marian Mason, wife of the Bowling Green hockey coach, gave his parents a check. *(photo courtesy Bowling Green State University Office of Public Relations)*

*(left);* Lake Placid, February 13, 1980. A proud Scott Hamilton carries the American flag at the opening ceremonies of the XIII Olympic Winter Games. Scott placed fifth in the overall men's competition. *(photo courtesy Wide World Photos)*

# Morristown, New Jersey

*January 6–12, 1982*

1982 Eastern United States Figure
Skating Championships

# 9

# Morristown

The quickest way from the industrial/agricultural mud plains of the lower Great Lakes to Morristown, New Jersey, is a predawn DC-10 to Newark and a rented car. The cheapest car available on the morning of January 6, 1982, was a brown Datsun with a heater that didn't work, which made the trip west from Newark damnably cold. But there was no time to turn around and fight with the car rental people back at the airport. Scott Hamilton at that moment was beginning the initial phase of his premier qualifying competition in the 1982 competitive season. By the time the big red-eye businessmen's special hit the runway in Newark, Scott and thirteen other Senior men were warming up for the first of three compulsory figures that together would make up thirty percent of the competitors' final standings in the 1982 Eastern Sectional Championships.

By the time I reached the seven-year-old William G. Mennen Arena, which belonged to the Morris County Park Commission and stood in a light-industry outskirt of Morristown, warmups and first figures were over and many of the entrants were in the lobby awaiting the next competition phase.

The lobby of the Mennen Arena, like the lobbies of most municipal skating rinks, resembled the foyer of a recently built junior high school, spartan and solid, the floor an icy sheen of waxed tile. Seen from that foyer on January 6, the 1982 Eastern United States Figure Skating Championships could have been a flower sale, student science fair, or any other locally run event overseen from big folding tables by mothers volunteering their time. Ten skaters who were going to make it to the 1982 U.S. World Team would compete at Easterns, but the atmosphere that day was hypo-energetic. It didn't at all *feel* like a big-league sports event.

The doors straight ahead went to the ice, and down a hall to the right was a snack shop serving the sort of limp fast food you get in skating rinks. The refectory also featured video games. In front of one of these games stood a little man wearing a voluminous tan coat blown up with goose down. The man was destroying squads of bugs and mushrooms. A silver-plated taller man was kibitzing with the mushroom killer. So stood Scott and Don. The video games would turn out to be a likely place for finding Scott at Easterns. If he wasn't at the hotel or on the ice at Mennen Arena or the South Mountain Arena, where some of the practice sessions were skated, and if he wasn't in a car somewhere between the hotel and the rinks, if you looked all over and he wasn't there, you could find him shooting laser bolts at things that lived on a screen.

"Heyyyy, ugly," the Champ was saying. He said it was almost time to go back to the ice, for his second figure. Just killin' time between figures.

A field of nervousness enclosed Scott. He talked reflexively, without necessarily listening to the things coming out of his own mouth. He paid almost no attention to the words coming out of other people's mouths. If you spoke, he'd say "Oh yeah?" or something equally disinterested. Clearly the brain had gone elsewhere.

When it was time to go back to the ice, Scott shouldered his lumpy red skate bag and he and his coach went to the doors that led into an airier and somewhat larger, in seating capacity, version of the rink back in Colorado, but still with meat-locker air and the harsh wavelengths of overhead lights. Perhaps a score of people were perched in the stands. Figures at a sectional competition, even when the champion of the world was about to skate, do not draw crowds.

Very funny things were happening. Seven people without skates, all of them with little boxes hung from neck straps to solar plexus level, stood at center ice. They faced our direction and pulled numbers out of the boxes and a voice read off the numbers, which were integers and decimals, four-point-one, three-point-nine, and so on. When they were done showing their numbers, the box people put them back in their boxes.

Behind the group a skater snaked himself through a figure. Then he skated to the front of the box people, and stood. He made a mysterious gesture across the ice with his arm. At a signal from the box people he pushed off and wound himself through a big figure eight. He repeated the figure eight several times, lost in concentration, alternating feet, forwards and backwards. The box people watched everything he did, equally lost in contemplation of the guy doing his figure. Then he skated away from the box people, and they shuffled on cold-weather boots to the patch of ice where he'd skated. The group began a minute perusal of the ice, bent over and shuffling in an oblong, so everybody got to look over every part of the section where the skater had made his figure eight. Sometimes they'd stand and take long views of their piece of ice, sighting down their arms. One man had a paint brush, which he used to sweep away ice shavings.

Meanwhile, another skater was running through his identical foot-switching, forward-and-about-facing figure eight, behind the judges. They showed us numbers again, and the voice read the numbers. The skater behind them skated around to the front of the box people, and the chain of events began again.

The game, you might have concluded, was that the skater dropped something, and the box people had to find it. Of course the ice examiners with boxes around their necks were judges inspecting and rating tracings put on the ice by the skaters.

Obviously. There was, however, something about this event that suggested arcane happenings. The hush and mad absorption of the small group of spectators, judges, and skaters, all given over to something so obscure, plus the measured, ritual pace of skating and judging—suggested otherworldly goings-on. This could have been a cult practice—a sacrifice, you might have thought, a spell-casting, a way to look into the future.

The event, actually, was all these things. The skaters were sacrificing to skating's great god, Edge, showing how many hours and how much attention they had given to him through ritual edge control. They were trying to cast spells on their competitors and the judges with the power and beauty of their offerings. They were, moreover, really and truly looking into their futures. A skater's final standing in competition has a great deal to do with his performance in figures. Standing in a ranking competition is a strong omen of what will happen in the next competition. For Scott, success at Easterns was not simply a matter of beating everybody else there. He had to have a win with heavy magic on it that would emanate for three weeks all the way to Indianapolis and enchant the Nationals judges and Scott's opponents. His effort here would figure for the rest of the season, and, in a dim, oracular fashion, all the way to 1984.

It was almost time for Scott to do his paragraph double three, the second of the three compulsory figures required of Senior-level skaters in 1982. In the U.S. and all over the skating world, the International Skating Union–stipulated figures that year were inside rocker, paragraph double three, and back change loop. At each competition they came up in that order, with all the Senior men skating each figure before moving on to the next. Scott, of course, had won the inside rocker at Easterns. He appeared down at the far end of the rink, wearing a blue nylon outfit that looked like a high-priced jogger's suit, but with refinements in fit and cut beyond off-the-rack running clothes. The outfit's top was really a body suit, a long-sleeved jacket with a bottom like a dancer's

102

leotard so it couldn't come untucked or be pulled crooked. A stripe ran down the sides of the outfit, from the armpits down to the waist, the same stripes running down the trouser's outside seams. The stripe was supposed to be a bold highlight, emphasizing Scott's ramrod bodylines, but the effect didn't quite come off. The stripe was too thick for Scott, and the result was somewhat awkward-looking. With that stripe the figures outfit looked drapey and large, like a pair of pajamas.

We'll now try to learn, by means of a standing mental exercise, about the basics of school figures, and the figure Scott was about to perform at Morristown. Rise, reader, and put make-believe skates on your feet.

Consider carefully the shape of the blades on your skates. Since they are figure skates, they curve, rocking upward at the toes. The blades do not come to single knife edges—each comes to two edges, slightly more than an eighth of an inch apart, with a round hollow between edges. Each blade, in miniature, is something like an old-time double-runner sled.

If such a sled could move along balanced on one runner, it would turn with the curve of that runner. Balanced on the left runner, moving forward, the hypothetical sled goes to the left. Balanced on the right runner, it goes to the right. If the sled stayed in motion, and stayed on one runner, it would go in circles.

Of course sleds are made to ride flat on both runners. But figure skates—particularly when the skates are doing compulsory figures—are made to run on one edge at a time. Only one edge. Only the correct edge.

Edge is the practical and theoretical basis of figure skating. It might be an exaggeration to say that edge is everything in skating, but not a great exaggeration.

So you and everyone else standing on figure skates have four edges. The edges have names. Left and right. Inside and outside. The left foot's left edge is Left Outside, LO in schematic skating shorthand. The left foot's right edge is Left Inside, LI. In edge

103

language, inside/outside is relative to one's own legs and feet. Completing the quartet are Right Inside, the right foot's left edge, and Right Outside, the right edge of the right foot's blade.

Pick up your left foot, poise yourself on your hypothetical Right Outside edge, and make believe you're moving forward. This is RFO in shorthand initials, Right Forward Outside. This imaginary exercise should make it clear that RFO takes you in a clockwise circle, curving continuously to your right. Complete the imaginary circle, and, at the starting point, shift to your Right Inside edge, the right foot's left edge. Pretending to continue the forward motion, you'll make a counterclockwise circle, curving continuously to your left. Finish this second rotation, and you have a figure eight. You have, in fact, made one tracing of a fifth test figure called the one foot eight. The one foot eight is the basis of the paragraph double three. We'll think through the one foot eight before cracking the latter, more complicated figure.

The diameter of each of your pretend circles ought to be about three times your height, perhaps a few feet larger, but not smaller. Scott's circles were about eighteen feet across.

A figure is not complete after one passage around it. At the return to your starting point, which is now the meeting of two circles (this juncture is called the center in skating language) you transfer to your left foot and repeat the entire one foot eight. Moving around the figure on the left foot means using different edges. RFO made the first circle, clockwise, curving continuously to the right. LFI, Left Forward Inside, goes over the same circle in the same direction. The second circle, which was RFI, is now LFO.

In competitive figure skating in 1982, a two-lobed figure, such as the one foot eight, was traced six times, three times on each foot. In competition, a skater had to be prepared to start each figure on either foot. The starting foot was chosen by officials just before competition in each of the three figures.

The first time around a figure is done blind, without guiding marks on the ice. It is, in fact, illegal to orient a figure along hockey lines or somebody else's figure. You start on clean ice, making as best you can a perfect design. The circles have to be absolutely equal in size and squarely lined-up.

In skating parlance, the first trip around a figure is called laying out the figure. Subsequent trips are tracings. Figures are judged by both overall layout, and neatness in tracing. The first trip around a figure has to be true to an invisible ideal. The next five circuits have to follow the first as closely as possible. The mind skates first—the skater's brain down-loading everything it knows about a figure, willing it to appear beneath the feet. Then the eye skates, following the line the mind made. Finally the skater abandons the figure to the scrutiny of judges, who compare it to their own mental images of perfection.

To skate a good figure, you have to use correct edges, and use them in control. Speed becomes a factor in the execution of figures. You've got to push off from the center with enough speed to carry around two eighteen-foot circles—a distance of about 120 feet—enough speed to flow and keep control, but not enough to go wild.

Behind these accomplishments is a science of balance and body control that involves head position, shoulders, the arms and hands, waist, knees, and—especially—the free foot, the foot held off the ice. Every joint and appendage and organ takes part in the creation of a compulsory figure.

For the reader, who has been left standing, there's one more thing to do, and that is to walk around in a circle. If you don't have room for an eighteen-foot circle, walk in a circle that fits the situation. Walk around once, clockwise, going forward. Then, on the second circuit, walk forward one-third of the way around the circle, 120 degress of arc, and then turn around and walk backward, continuing in the original clockwise direction. At two-thirds of the way around, 240 degrees, switch direction again, and finish your circle walking forward.

In the paragraph double three, the skater has to turn around twice in each circle. He begins each going forward, then turns and glides backward through a third of each circle. Two-thirds of the way through each circle, the skater must turn around again, and return to the figure's center going forward.

Even a primitive walking simulation shows the complications added by the turns, which, technically speaking, were three turns, hence the name paragraph double three. (Paragraph, in this case, means the same thing as "one foot" in one foot eight.) The constant direction switching, with its momentary disorientation and losing sight of the circle, makes it possible to walk out of a circle. It goes without saying that on skates it would be far easier to lose the circle.

The floor exercise has ended. You can sit down now.

A few words about turns. Turning in figure skating means turning around, a near-instantaneous reversal, back to forward, forward to back, on one foot, without the other foot touching down. As in all aspects of compulsory figures, the seemingly simple business of about-facing is highly formal and complex. The three turns in the paragraph double three—four of them, two on each circle—make concavely rounded peaks jutting into the circles. They are called "three turns" because they're supposed to look like the middle part of the Arabic numeral three. The skater rotates his foot into the turn, makes the edge switch at the turn's peak, and then skates out of it on the other edge. It all takes place in two blade lengths, one going in, one coming out. At no point can both edges of the blade touch down. Edge errors, like a flatted three turn, will not go unnoticed, or unpenalized. Edge writes a very clear record of itself on the ice, and judges are trained to read what it has written.

There is no end to the minutiae and technicalities of executing, and judging, a world-class double three, which, relative to some of the other figures in the Senior repertoire, is simple and straightforward. The points of the two three turns in each circle should be directed at the center of their circle (not to be confused with the figure's center). The change of edge at the figure's center must be no longer than a blade length. The USFSA rulebook gives nine rules for correct carriage, telling, among other things, what to do with the toe of the free foot (it should point downward and outward) and how the hands should be held (no higher than the waist, the palms held easily, naturally, and parallel to the ice).

Beyond these technicalities and the mere geometric perfection and neatness of a good figure, there is an overall quality that can be seen and felt by those who know skating well: command, power. Virtuosity that can shine in scratches left on the ice. Brilliant free skaters are not always brilliant figure skaters. In 1982 Scott was brilliant both ways. Judging would show him to be the best compulsory figures skater in the U.S., and second-best in the world. To those who understood what they were seeing, the dimpled circles he scratched in the ice at Morristown were as dazzling as the high-speed impossibilities that drive Scott's free-skating audiences wild.

# 10

# Insane, Insane Again

Scott's preferred frame of mind for doing figures in competition was an alert but vacant state that was like the less profound trances achieved in transcendental meditation. The idea was that a part of Scott's mind concentrated absolutely on the figure taking shape beneath his feet while the larger portion of his consciousness floated in unconcerned emptiness. The percentage of the Hamilton brain doing the figure was exactly the amount needed for the figure, and no more. The rest of the frontal lobe was allowed to think about whatever it wanted. What it couldn't do was worry or get tense about the figure, because that could bring on bodily bind-up, which would do violence to Scott's circles and turns.

Don liked to make a last-minute contribution to Scott's thinking. In warm-up, just before Scott did his figure for the judges, Don would give his skater a few things on which to concentrate. Of course Scott had been taught everything there was to know about doing his figures. But Don liked to remind him of two or three technicalities. Don really liked to see a few glitzes—a little bit of trouble, but not too much—in warm-up. Two or three minor problems would give Scott something to think about when he competed, which would prevent him from trying to hold the whole figure in his mind while he did it. Don said that was no good. So the problems limited and gave shape to Scott's thinking. What Don really didn't like to see was a problem-free warm-up.

Then there was nothing to think about, and the Champ's brain could drift away.

So here was Scott, part of whose consciousness was completely devoted to a compulsory figure, moving among the features pointed out by Don, while the rest of his mind floated along balloonlike, doing whatever it wanted. Sometimes this balloon played music while Scott skated, like a radio. Scott couldn't have endured music playing on the rink's speakers while he did figures, but music in his brain didn't bother him. Brain music, indeed, had been playing when he did his best figure to date as of January 1982. That figure was a left inside rocker at the Norton Skate competition in fall, 1979, in Lake Placid, Scott's first big win in international competition. The song was a bubblegum disco tune called 'Makin' It," by David Naughton, who had made a name for himself in Dr. Pepper commercials.

"So I," Scott recalled, "was singin' that song, and thinkin' about girls and stuff like that while I was skatin' the figure. And it turned out great."

During the paragraph double three at Easterns, Scott's mind balloon was echoing with music much darker than "Makin' It." "Insane, Insane Again," a cut off the J. Geils Band's "Freeze Frame" album, was new then and very big with Scott. A visual representation of this music would be a violent jumble of lines and angles, a psycho-killer's doodlings. Having heard "Insane, Insane Again," it's nearly impossible to believe that the same skull could accommodate this electronics-age noise and the elegance and perfection of Scott's paragraph double three.

But the strange texture of mental music and compulsory figure competition gave Scott no trouble. He pressed himself into the flat bodily knife-edge that cuts perfect circles in the ice. His face drooped in a gray-blue bloodless mask of concentration. He pushed off and rode through the figure once, fast through the first circle and then more slowly through the second as friction ate his initial speed. His skate made a throaty metallic rolling noise on the ice, like a steel rollerskate on concrete that started quickly and then slowed until it almost halted. The near-halt came as he returned to his figure's center after completing the second circle. Then he pushed off again, and the wheel sound rolled fast again, interrupted by the surgical "swi-switch" sound of the three turns, two in each circle.

What put Scott through these instantaneous about-faces, front to backward, back to frontward, was, to the spectators off the ice, very mysterious. Without flailing out, or putting down his free foot to push himself around, or doing much of anything, he switched direction. The effect was that Scott was turned around by an invisible linkage that drove him through the figure like a machine tool. But of course Scott was doing it all himself, storing up the energy to switch around and then releasing it by scissoring his legs and swinging his shoulders.

The rink had a library hush. Even a cough flew high over the ice and echoed. The judges were as lost as Scott himself in the figure he was creating. Don stood off the ice, leaning on the boards, lost, too, in some sort of telepathic link with his skater. The spectators kept respectful silence. And all the while voices none of the rest of us could hear were singing to Scott, chanting a string of disjoint phrases over a background of frenetic double-time electronic noise.

When Scott came back to the center of his paragraph double three and skated out of the figure, the thin applause rattled again, and the judges started hunting over Scott's ice. Scott's numbers were in the low-to-mid fours, a slight dip from the scores in his first figure; but he remained ahead of everybody else and left the ice looking quite satisfied.

Don later explained that the paragraph double three was the hardest of the 1982 season's trio of compulsory figures for Scott. The scores dipped because this particular paragraph double three wasn't quite up to par. It was, however, world-class. Certainly it was much finer than anybody else's paragraph double three at Easterns. Don, too, was satisfied.

The Champ was affable but somewhat distant and tense as he took off his skates. He put on his running shoes and quickly marched with Don out of the arena and turned left down the hallway to the snack bar. He bought a cup of coffee and played some video games.

Within an hour Scott was back on the ice in front of the judges, doing the final of the three compulsory figures, a back change loop that earned the highest scoring of his three figures, with a top mark of 4.7. Scott seemed quietly happy about his loop, and Don pronounced it exceptional. On this high note, skater and coach went back to the Madison Hotel for lunch. The hotel restaurant, they said, had surprisingly good sandwiches.

It would later become apparent that this enthusiasm about the food was as much a part of a skating competition as the just-completed compulsory figures. For the first day or two the hotel food tasted great. Then, inevitably, it turned to clay.

# 11

# Cleopatra of the Ice

Music here, sphinx music, with an oboe, and drums going *bim pumpum,* and all the other movie-score trappings of the Pharaohs. Caitlin Carruthers, Kitty, Sweetheartland's own Cleopatra and Scott Hamilton's *femme fatale*—his *femme* near-*fatale* really—is about to be carried into view. On Wednesday night she floated across the rink at Morristown, lolling eight feet over the ice, stretched out like a carnal queen on a dais of leopard skins, shining an alabaster smile of self-satisfaction and regarding both banks of her frozen Nile with bland possessiveness.

The skating of Kitty and her brother Peter, the reigning U.S. Champion Pairs team—who, like Scott, moved to National Championship for the first time in 1981—was a royal procession with Peter serving variously as Kitty's divan, barge, litter, chariot, and throne. The impression of the Carrutherses' performances was that everything—the tricks, the music, the screaming audience—was solely for the pleasure of this sensual and self-indulgent dark queen. It was Peter's job to satisfy the queen's endless appetite for airborne thrills. So he carried her above his head while she lay prone, balanced on his hands. They did this, too, with Kitty supine. At times she rode him upright in the air with her hands thrust downward and holding his, which were raised high above him.

These poses up over her brother's head were ridiculously dangerous. A rut in the ice or something out of balance could have put either Carruthers, or both, into the hospital. One of the indelible memories of the 1982 season is the collapse of a lesser-known pairs team's lift. The crash occurred at Indianapolis, in competition. The man fell backward and the woman, who had been balanced above him, came down, driving his head against the ice. The man's hands went to the back of his head in a moment of poiseless agony, but then he and his partner recovered and smiled and waved. Blood from a split somewhere under the man's hair was running down the back of his neck as they left the ice, still smiling. As pairs accidents go, this was not terribly serious. Kitty seemed entirely oblivious to the fact that she might be micro-seconds from the emergency room. Whenever she was in the air her look was one of selfish and abandoned delight.

A few days after Easterns Scott would record a voiceover commentary for a television production of the Superskates exhibition. Watching a TV monitor, which was showing a videotape of Kitty sailing along over Peter's head, Scott called her, in a pensive, awed way, "the girl who loves to fly."

The over-the-head lifts were the least of Kitty's flying tricks. Peter threw her up into jumps resembling Scott's jumps—axels, Salchows, and Lutzes—with the queenly distinction from singles jumping that Kitty was spared the effort of vaulting off the ice. Peter propelled her, and she rotated and landed on her own. In the Carrutherses' most hair-raising maneuvers, Peter threw Kitty up and she twisted and spun and then he caught her before she could smash her brains out on the ice. Her facial expression was lost in the aerial blur, but as soon as you could see it you'd see the wide smile.

And of course there was the bread-and-butter trick of pairs skating, the death spiral, where Kitty defied skull fracture by getting as close as possible to the ice while Peter crouched and pivoted and whirled his sister around him. In the death spiral Kitty lay back in queenly recumbency, holding Peter's hand and riding one edge of one skate while she whipped centrifugally. The

113

moment of high drama in this maneuver came when Kitty dropped her head back and her short-cropped hair brushed the ice, which was rushing by dangerous fractions of an inch from her scalp. Ice shavings in Kitty's hair indicated that a particularly good death spiral had been performed. Even though every pairs team did these death spirals, the effect was always thrilling.

Pairs skating was the most circuslike of the four figure skating events. The elements in pairs programs didn't bind themselves into unified performances as did singles or dance performances. What you had instead were series of acrobatic stunts, each performed with can-you-top-this? circus bravura. The choreography tacked onto all the pairs lifting, throwing, and jumping was somehow unconvincing. But pairs skating didn't suffer for this lack of a binding aesthetic. The thrilling stunts made it worth watching.

The Carrutherses' skating, and that of all pairs, involved side-by-side synchronous movement, with the man and woman performing single jumps and spins simultaneously. The lifts and throws were separated by relatively long interludes when both skaters were down on the ice. But the vital moments, the seconds that really counted for the audiences, judges, TV commentators, and Kitty Carruthers, were those moments when Peter launched her, and Kitty flew. In memory she will always fly, always with that mad smile.

Many of the 1982 women skaters had been taught to smile during their competitive performances, but even high in an arena's cheap seats it was impossible to mistake those enamel grimaces for looks of happiness. Kitty's ice smile was the most sincere, and infectious, of any. Her brother, by contrast, looked preoccupied, even worried. He smiled as if making an effort to be pleasant. What he looked like, really, was a court functionary trying to anticipate the caprices of a difficult little queen.

The Cleopatra identity for Kitty—my invention, not hers—is a consequence of her dark beauty. Kitty was a novelty among U.S. women skaters in that she looked Mediterranean. Like Scott,

Kitty had been adopted. Her ancestry was Lebanese, and her looks were an absolute mismatch to the Scottish surname Carruthers. She was, too, an ethnic mismatch to her brother, a sturdy Dutch and English mix, who, like Kitty, was adopted in infancy from the New England Home for Little Wanderers.

Peter was two years older than his sister, who was twenty in the 1982 season. She was five-one, he five-eleven. She weighed just less than one hundred pounds, and Peter one hundred and fifty-five. You might have thought that Charles and Maureen Carruthers, a physics teacher and an art teacher, had intentionally selected a big baby boy and a tiny baby girl and brought them home to Burlington, Massachusetts, just to raise a championship pairs team. But the Carrutherses, like the Hamiltons, adopted their little wanderers with no idea that their kids were going to drag them into Sweetheartland.

So here, in Morristown, we first encounter Kitty, who was, in spite of her pint-size and rather childish manner of expression, powerfully magnetic. Kitty's consummate physical toughness became clear one evening when she sat in a hotel room where a skating-world reception and cocktail party was about to get underway. My gaze went to one of Kitty's hands, which lay splayed and weary, like a bricklayer's hand at day's end, against her thigh. The hand was squarish and meaty, large for the woman to which it belonged. It wasn't at all a cute hand, as Kitty could be cute, and the presence of such an obvious working-class entity deep in Sweetheartland was startling. Somebody, you would have thought, was going to ask it to leave. But the hand was a valuable discovery. In itself the hand told a story about Kitty's flying that was entirely different from that told by her smile. While her teeth showed ecstacy, the hand coupled and uncoupled from her partner like a machine, keeping Kitty from danger. The hand, like Peter, worried and worked while the incisors celebrated.

A turning of the hand showed a trio of purple-red scratches strung between elbow and wrist on the inside of Kitty's forearm.

These were deep scratches, as if Kitty had pulled her arm from a crocodile's jaws. She explained that a death spiral grip had slipped and she and Peter had had to claw to keep hold of each other. She laughed with friendly disdain at the wincing her scratches brought on.

"Oh, that's nothing," she said. "You should see the bruises I've got on my ribs." One side of her upper torso was a mass of painful black and blue, she said, and chuckled again, this time flirtatiously. "But I can't show you that."

At Easterns word was that Scott and Kitty had broken up, and there were rumors, which you could sometimes hear from either, or both, of them, that they were getting back together.

We're going out onto thin ice now, thin ice over unfathomable waters: the romantic life of Scott Hamilton, specifically the heart entanglement of Scott and Kitty, which was the big show during the 1982 competitive season. There were smaller shows, for both of them, since they had ostensibly parted, but nothing as compelling as the big one.

What, exactly, was going on between Scott and Kitty in 1982 was unfathomable, in spite of both participants' willingness to talk, very freely, about their involvement. The situation seemed equally unfathomable to Scott and Kitty themselves. No matter what they said they were doing in the 1982 competitive season, they appeared to be doing something else. At the same time that both would privately admit that they couldn't get along, they would also aver that it was impossible to imagine life without each other. So they simultaneously acted on both impulses, and glossed over the impossibility with the most ridiculous fiction in the annals of love: "No matter what happens," they said, "we'll always be best friends."

Scott and Kitty were, indeed, a textbook case of young love in the 1980s, in which the difficult business of sustaining a romantic entanglement with another person is made nearly impossible by the introduction of the modern rhetoric of mutual regard and

116

psychological awareness, endless self- and mutual examination, and, in general, too much egotism and too much talking. In the 1982 season they would meet for long confrontational "working it out" discussions, at least one per competition, which lasted into the wee hours. From Scott's reports, these seemed to be strategic mutual withdrawal negotiations, with the subject being how to safely disengage the affections.

They had met in 1976, in Boston, at the Jimmy Fund benefit exhibition. Scott was Junior National Champion, and Kitty and Peter appeared because they were locally well known skaters. They started dating at the 1978 National Championships, in Portland, where Scott made his surprisingly early break into third place and onto the U.S. World Team. But Scott lived in Denver then, and Kitty was on the East Coast, so the romance was rather casual, on and off. When Scott moved to Philadelphia and Don Laws in the spring of 1979, he was close enough to Kitty, an hour down the road at Wilmington, for bigger things to happen. Things happened until the summer of 1981, about six months before the 1982 Easterns. Then they decided to go steady no longer. But they somewhat inadvertently kept going together, unsteadily. The attraction between skating's pale king and dark queen was so compelling that you could imagine them staying half in and half out of love indefinitely. You could imagine that, at any rate, in 1982.

The conditions of life in Sweetheartland were responsible in large part for Scott and Kitty's emotional dilemma. Those circumstances that made romance between the two inevitable at first went on to make the romance impossible to continue and at the same time impossible to break off. Scott and Kitty, when they met, were dreaming the same dream, the championship dream, and strove together unjealously to become champions.

The greatest dream moment of all was the 1980 Winter Olympics, when the Carrutherses and Scott belonged to a U.S. Figure Skating Team so close-knit and simpatico that it called itself the

Dream Team. (The teams sometimes, but not always, name themselves. The following year the Americans dubbed themselves Wazoo World Team, because of their highly consistent performances on the exhibition tour after the 1981 Worlds in Hartford. Scott had a Wazoo World Team T-shirt that he still wore in 1982, and the skaters were still making and drinking an unctuously sweet ice cream drink called Dream Team Punch, which was invented in the Olympic year. Apparently no name caught on for the 1982 World Team.) At the 1980 Winter Games Scott and Kitty had been going steady for about six months. There, in the Olympic village at Lake Placid, among the Dream Team that consisted of their favorite fellow skaters, Scott and Kitty enjoyed the dream of perfect romance. Nothing was missing. Both had everything they could have hoped for in skating that year, which is to say inclusion on the 1980 Olympic and World Teams. But neither was considered a medal hopeful at the Olympics, so they existed without the dreadful championship pressure that would come the following year. In both skating and romance Scott and Kitty enjoyed risk-free freshness, and they floated young and in love through the picturesque mountain town that was electrified with the attention given to it by the whole world. It was, they both recalled, fabulous. A dream.

Scott and Kitty had, by January 1982, taken hard emotional body blows from each other. But nothing could tarnish the golden dream of the 1980 Winter Olympics. When either brought up that time at Lake Placid, which included an Olympic Valentine's Day, he or she would stare into middle distance, as if scenes of that interlude were being projected on a screen. The memory always silenced them momentarily and provoked sighs. "It was just," either one of them would say, "so neat."

Things stayed neat for about a year after the Olympics. Scott and Don moved to Denver in September 1980, but the romance survived long-distance. In February 1981, Scott and Kitty's competitive dreams started coming true. Both became National

Champions at San Diego. A few weeks later Scott, at Hartford, Connecticut, woke up to find that the ultimate skating dream had been realized. He was World Champion. But while their skating kept getting more and more "neat," Scott and Kitty found their romance becoming increasingly un-neat, and finally it became a burden that they agreed to lay down. But then they kept picking it up again. Momentarily things would be as neat as ever, then the neatness would vanish, and they'd be fighting or engaged in the hours of verbose negotiations that are the acceptable 1980s substitute for fighting.

Domestic squabbling is not part of our mythic picture of athletes. A movie about Scott would show him in some sort of clear-eyed meditation, or prayer, or patriotic self-dedication before victory in an international competition. But before one of his non-ranking wins that preceded the 1982 Easterns in Morristown, Scott stayed awake until two in the morning arguing with his girlfriend. He then skated a stunning long program. Fussing about a girlfriend—mainly Kitty in the 1982 season—occupied a great deal of Scott's off-ice private conversation. This strife was an inevitable part of competition, as routine as the practice schedules and hotel lobbies and room service. "I always have girl problems at competitions," Scott said in advance of Easterns, as part of a briefing on what I should look for in my first trip to a competition. He then answered, no, the problems didn't really hurt his concentration. It was in fact somewhat beneficial to have a low-key soap opera happening off the ice, something intense enough to be distracting, but not overwhelming. "Then I can say, 'Women! To hell with women!'" Scott explained. "It gives me something to take my mind off skating."

So there was probably a therapeutic value to Scott's sporadic difficulties and confusion about Kitty and what the two of them were going to do. It would be wrong, though, to say that this was all there was to it. Scott was genuinely saddened by the breakup, as was Kitty. It seemed they had done all they could do to be each other's one and only but were beaten by forces inimical to love.

"It hurt," Scott said in memoriam. "We had shared a lot. We shared Olympics. How many times do you get to go to Olympics with your girlfriend? We shared everything. She saw more sides to me than anybody has ever seen. She's seen me totally ecstatic. She's seen me really competitive. She's seen me mellow. She's seen me upset. She's seen me at the point of self-destruction. In every way possible. She didn't understand all the time, but she was always there."

What ended it? "You always need a bouncing board. You need somebody to stabilize things. If you're both trying to do the same thing—then you don't know how to help each other."

Kitty concurred that skating success had much to do with romantic failure. "It was a lot easier," she said, "when neither of us were National Champions, because we didn't have the pressure. And now, when we're at a show or competition or something, we're thinking about our skating more and more, and defending the titles. It kind of ruined our relationship. . . . Everyone always says once you've made it to the top, everything gets smooth. But it's a lot worse. It's just harder."

On the other hand, it was hard in the heat of competition mind battles not to lean on your oldest and best combat buddy. The egocentric demands of competition that made lasting and smooth-running love between Scott and Kitty impossible also threw them back together and pushed them toward lover-like intimacy. Championship skating, which they chiefly credited with breaking them up, made them particularly *need* each other. So, in and out they went, driven by their infernal emotional machine. In Sweetheartland, in 1982, there was no escape.

Love in Sweetheartland seems to be different from love on the rest of the planet. These world-class skaters were mainly in their late teens and early twenties, the age range when heart murmurs are loudest and most compelling. But the skaters didn't listen to their hearts with the same credulity shown by other young people. They didn't abandon themselves. They seemed to hang back, and they listened to skating's cold commands a great deal more closely than they listened to love's hot whispers. The result was a certain emotional incompleteness in the skaters' personal affairs. There wasn't a realistic level of drama. Passion was always brought up short, and things never quite resolved themselves.

This was all rather difficult for the outside observer. Scott and Kitty in the 1982 season would act a great deal like any other willful and passionate pair who were breaking up. They did things to destroy each other's minds. But they didn't react like normal young men and women. They didn't have the satisfying option of a screaming breakup scene. Any sort of low-class public nastiness was out of the question. They particularly did not have the healing option of not having to see each other again. Skating demanded that Scott and Kitty were never away from each other for long. Skating dictated, moreover, that even if Scott and Kitty wanted to shoot each other and strangle whomever was the object of the other's flirtations, no matter how deep their momentary pain and murderous anger, they had to rein it all in. The rules of Sweetheartland said that you always had to keep smiling the civilized, aren't-they-such-nice-kids, Sweetheart smile. Scott and Kitty were laboring under the very heavy curse of perpetually being good.

Skating threw Scott and Kitty together, and skating broke them up. At Easterns skating was again throwing them together, putting them in the same hotel and pitting them simultaneously against the hideous mind monsters of competition. Fighting the ice demons made our poor skaters long to warm themselves at someone else's heart. Competitive moments could be cold and desperately lonely. What they needed, really, was a best friend or more, all the human heat they could get. Kitty and Scott needed each other much more than they needed to be true to their earlier resolve *not* to need each other. And there wasn't sufficient time or psychic energy, as battle with the ice monsters closed, to reflect on their need, or fight it.

I had by that time recorded dozens of feet of audio tape of

Scott telling about how he and Kitty had once and for all broken up, how their ship of love had been rammed and sunk by jealousy and overcompetitiveness and the stress of championship, and on and on. It was too bad, Scott said, but that was that. With that in mind, it was surprising to see Scott hanging on to Ron Ludington's left arm when Caitlin and Peter Carruthers, 1981 U.S. National Pairs Champions, skated their first event in a ranking competition in the 1982 season. "Yea, Kitty and Peter!" the hundreds of spectators at the William G. Mennen Arena were screaming. Music started, and Kitty went up into the air and began another year of her opulent reign.

Ron Ludington was Kitty and Peter's coach, a past National Champion pairs skater himself and head coach at the Skating Club of Wilmington, a globally important center for training pairs and dance teams. Luddy—his name in Sweetheartland— was balding. Since his athletic preeminence in 1960 he had expanded into what was once called "a fine figure of a man." Luddy looked like a prosperous Old World master brewer, well-nourished but muscular. You wouldn't want to take one of his punches. He dwarfed Scott, and seemed completely oblivious to the fact that this small boyfriend of his best pairs woman was at his side. He seemed oblivious to everything, in fact, but his best pair, whom he watched somewhat haughtily, arms folded and face lifted so he was sighting down along his nose.

Scott explained later that he was standing with Luddy because standing there when the Carrutherses were competing brought them good luck. He always stood with Luddy like that. The coach didn't mind at all, Scott said, because anything that helped Kitty's frame of mind on the ice was okay with Luddy.

Good luck or not, the spectacle of Luddy and Scott in tandem throwing all their psychic power at the Carrutherses was ludicrous. They looked like a bear and a spider monkey deep in concentration, trying to keep Kitty airborne through psychokinesis.

# 12

# A Man Cannot Serve Two Mothers

"You've got to help me," Scott said, as he often said such things, on the run, in a busy swoop through the lobby of the Madison Hotel. At these competitions, Scott bustled through crowded places, as if he were late for something terribly important. The idea was to discourage those who wanted to say something, ask a question, engage in any number of ways the attention and time of the Champion of the World. Such an engagement, multiplied hundreds and thousands of times, could bring poor Scott to screaming nervous exhaustion. So he made himself somewhat engagement-proof by going fast. You had to rush to keep up with him.

Trotting along, Scott would say things to friends and acquaintances that normally would call for some minutes of reflection and follow-up conversation. But since this was Scott Hamilton in a hurry, what you got was the initial message, and maybe fifteen seconds to reply, and then a perplexing vacuum. There was always plenty of time to wonder what on earth Scott had meant by what he said to you as he trotted by. Every day someone in Scott's entourage was mulling over one of these bulletins. You always had the idea he really *meant* something, and that it was vitally important to divine the meaning.

"You've got to help me work this out," he was saying Thursday morning. "It's a balancing act. I've got to figure out how to balance two women."

It should be pointed out that the rhythms of a skating competition are markedly different from what appears on television. Television shows you one climactic moment, the long program, with at the most five minutes of contributing interviews and background material. The skating video comes with Benzedrine-fast-and-loud voiceover by sportscasters who are paid fortunes for their ability to pump frenzied excitement into absolutely any event. "A wonderful, wonderful performance by a great champion!" they shout over the airwaves, and we in the home viewing audience—since we see nothing more of skating than this video—get the idea that skating really resolves itself into wildly dramatic climaxes, and that everything leads up to these climaxes.

Seen in person, figure skating was absolutely nothing like these high-adrenaline distillations. It was all rather diffuse to those around Scott and, by all appearances, to Scott himself. After all, at any skating competition the Champ spent at least an hour in hotel restaurants and snack bars for every thirty seconds of his long program. Time spent in practice was greater than the time spent in competition. Time off the ice, time spent neither practicing nor competing, stretched vastly longer than time on the ice. So, it was possible to forget that the purpose of a competition was competitive skating. The firsthand impression was sometimes that skating competitions were social/professional gatherings with trips to ice rinks provided only as a relief from the real business at hand. The real business was milling around, organizing breakfasts, lunches, and dinners with different people, gossiping, and being social. So the week in Morristown exists in recollection as a combination sales meeting, sorority reunion, and jamboree of the world's sleekest teenagers.

Anybody who has spent a week or so at an event based in a hostelry knows a great deal about the atmosphere of figure skating competitions. As time passes the business that the gathering was supposed to serve diminishes in importance, replaced by interpersonal intrigues and other delicious trivia. At Easterns and subsequent competitions in 1982, the big video sports drama of victory and defeat was lost in the hotel-bound soap opera.

Every day, for Scott, had a story, some absorbing chain of events real or imagined that most of the time had nothing to do with his sport. He'd wake up talking about whatever it was and unload the story on you in pieces through the day, at meals, on the long drives to practice rinks, and in his hotel room. Usually the story was a personal drama: Kitty or another intrigue or problems with Don or maybe with members of his personal entourage.

After figures Scott introduced an off-ice drama that was going to play for the rest of Easterns and at Indianapolis and Copenhagen. This was the story of two women. The first of these women was Helene O'Laurel. Helene and her husband had been Scott's source of skating money since he began training under Carlo Fassi in 1976. By virtue of being a rich widow living alone (her husband, Big Frank, died in 1979), Helene earned herself, in this book, a name not her own. Helene—Mrs. O to just about everybody—had come east to Morristown to do genealogical research as well as to see her investment skate. Mrs. O's great-great-great-grandfather was supposed to have been born in Sussex County in 1755. Sussex County had once been part of Morris County, so she had come to Morristown, in part, to look up family records. When Mrs. O was absent from the rinks or the hotel during the first few days of Easterns, she was hunting through local archives for some trace of her ancestor. The search turned up absolutely nothing, and on the day of short-program competition, the day after figures, she went out to give it one more try, but then gave up the effort and took a drive in the country and settled into watching Scott skate at all his practices and last two events.

Mrs. O had given $80,500 to the USFSA Memorial Fund on behalf of Scott Hamilton by the end of the 1982 season. She gave little or no thought to what it cost to book a last-minute flight to New York, rent a car, and live and eat in a relatively high-priced hotel for a week—Mrs. O, along with the rest of the skating crowd spillover, was staying at the Governor Morris Motor Inn.

Her trip to Easterns cost more than many Americans' family vacations. This is not to mention her weeks that year in Indianapolis, then Denmark, and subsequently wherever Scott went in the U.S. or abroad. "I'm lucky," she observed in the stands at Morristown. "I can pretty much afford to do what I want to do." What she wanted to do, apparently, was watch Scott. Virtually all of Mrs. O's recreational trips since her husband's death had been to Scott Hamilton's ice. "I suppose you'd call it a hobby," she said. "He doesn't owe me anything. But I derive a great deal of pleasure from watching him skate and perform."

A woman who could afford pleasures as rare as sponsoring an athlete and following him around the world to watch him compete, a minor oil magnate, who lived in one of those towns north of Chicago where folks are socioeconomic peers of Morristownians, such a woman, you might have thought, would money up her appearance with emeralds or a chinchilla or something to signify that she could afford the things she could afford. After all, everyone else at Easterns was trying to look well-to-do. But, said Mrs. O, "I don't go in for jewelry or things like that." Her dress was plain and anonymous. You might have guessed that this was Scott's great-aunt, a country widow who had saved for some time to take a trip to see her grandnephew skate.

This camouflage worked even in conversation, her words coming out in deliberate, consonant-heavy cadence. She gave the same slow attention to listening that she gave to speaking. Mrs. O, except for a dozen early years in Indiana, was a lifelong Chicagoan, a graduate of the University of Chicago, member of university boards, in many respects a leading citizen. This background, with or without money, could have called for the assumption of a nasal overeducated superciliousness. But Mrs. O's mannerisms, like her dress, smacked of the corn country from which her immediate forebears had emigrated to Chicago.

Mrs. O's habitual expression was a friendly smile, her laugh a deep chuckle, which we heard frequently. She was too reserved to be called jolly, but she was close to jolly. There was, however, much more present than a slow-talking friendly old country aunt. The eyes gave it away. They weren't unfriendly—most of the time they were very friendly, actually twinkling. But underneath the twinkle was cool alertness that watched very carefully. Like grocer's scales, Mrs. O's eyes were constantly weighing things, calculating the value of what they saw. Not value in dollars, but value in Mrs. O's moral-ethical scheme: hard work, duty, devotion, all ennobled by faithfulness and kindness and courtesy. These were the things that Mrs. O prized and watched for. Her late husband Frank and she had made successes of themselves while hewing to these virtues. So she believed in them, and dreamed the American dream. Scott Hamilton was, among other things, an American Dream horticultural project for Mrs. O. She watered him with money, for the satisfaction of watching him grow. "I think," she said in the stands at Morristown, "an investment in people is the best investment you can make."

Mrs. O, like absolutely everyone else older than the Champ in his inner circle of acquaintances, professed to feel some parenthood. She didn't have a son, or a daughter, but if she had had a son, she'd want him to be like Scott. And like the other members of the Champ's court, she put herself at his disposal. "I'm here if he needs me."

Sitting next to Mrs. O at the morning practice Thursday, January 7—short program day at Easterns—in the bum-polished old wooden folding seats in the South Mountain Arena was a woman roughly fifteen years Mrs. O's junior who was also there if Scott needed her. This was Barbara Camp, Mrs. Robert Camp, woman of the Haverford, Pennsylvania, house in which Scott had lived while he trained under Don at the Philadelphia Skating Club and Humane Society's rink in Ardmore. Compared to some of the beminked and diamond-soaked ice mothers at Easterns, Mrs. Camp was simply attired. But hers was not Mrs. O's fashionless simplicity. Mrs. Camp dressed in the subdued, sporty, classical-conservative style usually called preppy. There was quiet quality to Barb Camp.

Mrs. Camp didn't want to talk about herself and her skater, because she didn't know me at Easterns, because she didn't trust anybody to treat the details of Scott's personal life responsibly in print, because she thought that the very idea of a book about Scott was objectionable, that such a thing wouldn't be good for him, and finally because the bond between Barb Camp and Scott Hamilton could not be talked about. Not that there was anything to hide—it was inexpressible.

Asked how many children she had, Barb would say she had five —not counting Scott. The room on the second floor of the Camp family's house was now and forever Scott's Room, even though another skater was living in it by January 1982. When Scott took over that room in March 1979, it had become his, and he became the son of the mother of the house. Forever. Barb was perfectly aware of Dorothy Hamilton and her preeminence in Scott's life. No, she said, she couldn't hope to take Dorothy's place, she wouldn't want to. But in Dorothy's absence, Barb had put on the mantle of Hamilton motherhood.

"I like to mother," Barb observed. "I think I mother pretty well. When my children started to leave the house and go off to college, I had empty rooms, and I don't like empty rooms." She had, before and after Scott's tenancy, sheltered tennis players, students, and other skaters, but by far the strongest maternal bond formed was with Scott. "He really is my sixth child. I really feel that way."

Barb was rooming at the Madison Hotel with Kitty Carruthers. Kitty, like many high-strung national skating stars, didn't like to stay alone at competitions. She needed somebody to lean on, and Barb was volunteering. Kitty was Barb's number-two skating surrogate child in the 1982 season. There were others, among them Kitty's brother Peter, who belonged to Barb's brood of "chickens."

"They're all my chickens," said this most expansive of mothers. And knowing her you might wish that you, too, were one of her chickens. Life would be more bearable and sweet if Barb Camp were there to drive you to the shopping mall for a haircut, badger you to go to the dentist, mend your clothes, and stay close at hand all day long, working on a needlepoint belt with the insignia of your favorite cars on it, all of which Barb was doing for Scott at Easterns. Barb Camp embodied a dream of womanhood as compellingly television-American as the American Sweethearthood that the skating princesses embodied. Our National Mom.

The differences in Mrs. O and Mrs. Camp's bonds between themselves and Scott—the one moral/philanthropical and the other biopsychological—crystallized into disagreement over an issue that neither acknowledged, but one that surfaced as acquaintance with the Hamilton entourage deepened.

"I wish to God he would come back to Philadelphia," said Barb Camp. The idea held by Barb was that Mrs. O had engineered Scott and Don's removal from Pennsylvania to Denver, and that the two of them were in great moral danger because Denver was impossibly far from the people who truly loved Scott, who were qualified to protect him from the hideous psychological and spiritual monsters that World Championship had loosed on him and his coach. Only the Philadelphia variety of love could slay the dragons of international celebrity.

Mrs. O was equally anxious about the Champ and his inner well-being, but her solution to his purported problems was entirely contrary. Gooey mother-love, to Mrs. O, was mental poison for a twenty-three-year-old man. What Scott needed was to learn to stand on his own two feet and do for himself and make his own decisions, all of which he would never do if he had a surrogate mother to lean on.

At the core of both women's thinking was an absolutely identical impression that Scott was being carried by powerful currents toward a cataract in which his soul was going to be drowned and that he had to be saved because it didn't look as though he was going to save himself. What, exactly, was imperiling Scott Hamilton was hard to pin down. The danger defied definition, but always it was with us, this vivid impression that Scott was going over an invisible edge, and that we absolutely had to rescue him.

Scott was aware of all the theorizing and side-taking. "Nobody else knows what I'm thinking or doing," he told the cassette recorder, "but everybody has his own theory. And everybody's telling me not to listen to everybody else."

In many of Scott's forty-odd taped interviews, he fretted about being under emotional siege and got angry about being surrounded by people trying to storm his inner being, but it is equally true that he would have been distraught if Mrs. O and Mrs. Camp and the rest of the Scott people quit spending most of their waking hours worrying about him. That, you could tell, might have been unbearable.

The well-intentioned fuss and worry would exasperate and occasionally enrage him. But it would have been difficult for him to cut free from the tangle of apron strings or umbilical cords of his multiple mother-son, auntie-nephew, sister-brother, woman-man connections. So Scott had learned to live with the tensions disguised as a difference of opinion between Philadelphia and Denver and mother-love versus the hard lessons of young adulthood.

Mrs. O and Mrs. Camp sat down next to each other. The South Mountain Zamboni woke up and roared a mournful song while it made long oblongs on the ice, eating the top inch-fractions of frozen water and excreting a sheen of unfrozen water. The machine erased entirely the ice writing left by the Junior ladies and men, who had practiced from 8:30 to 9:30 that morning, the session before the Senior men. The shining smear of liquid behind the Zamboni froze and dulled to opalescent gray, like jelly-jar wax. Then the Zamboni made its final pass down the arena's middle and off the ice toward its stall.

While the Zamboni bellowed in the arena's dim morning, Scott Hamilton took off his running shoes and pulled on free-skating boots and sutured together the parallel rows of hooks that made the boots snug on his feet and ankles. Thirteen other Senior men put on their skates, some bantering and some silent and self-absorbed. Coffee in cardboard cups smoked in the coaches' hands. It was like dawn in a caddyshack down next to the ice, boys and men rousing themselves with jokes and caffeine, the quiet ones doing mental stretching exercises, everybody getting ready to go to work. The Seniors going onto the ice mingled briefly with the Juniors coming off, who were out of their skates by the time new ice was being made.

Halfway up the arena's steep slope of seats was a roost of skating mothers. They sat in a loose flock, close enough for a word or two and bland smiles of recognition when new mothers chose seats and nested. The skating mothers of Senior men had been watching their sons practice like this for a decade or more, and everybody knew everybody else. But in spite of this acquaintance they weren't talkative. Communication consisted mainly of ritual greetings followed by mute sharing of the mysteries of skating motherhood. By the looks of these women, being the mother of a skater held bottomless maternal joy. The force of feeling in the mother's gallery at the South Mountain Arena miraculously hurtled the Senior men back through the years to infancy, and sucked them off the ice to their mothers' laps, where they all fell asleep. That, at any rate, was what the beatific expressions of satisfied motherhood said.

But then the skaters went onto the ice and swooped counter-clockwise like so many birds let out of a cage. All hostilities between Mrs. O and Mrs. Camp ceased, and all eyes went to Scott.

# 13

# In and Out of the Swamp

It was happening again. The seats tipped forward when Scott Hamilton swooped in his counterclockwise warmup strokes. The seats tipped, and the Scott watchers fell out of this dimension into Hamilton's own dimension, where nothing but Scott existed. His skates shot charged particles into our solar plexuses. Scott on the ice became such a perfect projectile that you could feel the projectile going through you, ghostlike.

The sensation of seeing Scott freeskate was what it had been in Colorado, an aesthetic overload. It was possible, looking down at him from the mother's seats in New Jersey, to feel like a tourist looking up at some scenic wonder, gaping and struck dumb. The spectacle of Scott warming up with his competitors was like a barracuda swimming into South Mountain Arena. You were afraid for these other poor boys.

Seeing him skate made all sensations possible. The sublime moments of watching Scott were as apt to arrive at these pre-competition practice sessions as in competition, or exhibition programs.

I came to like practices best of all, because they gave such extravagant amounts of time for watching Scott skate, compared to, say, the four and a half minutes on the ice in a competition long program. In the practice sessions Scott's programs were broken into their component jumps and spins and lines of foot-work, and each warmed up before a complete run-through with music, which came in the middle of the practice. After that the shaky parts of the program were worked over until the session—most of them lasted about forty-five minutes—was over. This made for a highly satisfying study of Scott skating, with leisure to really examine his tricks and memorize how they went in the program. Besides, practices had a very appealing intimacy. They were like a virtuoso's master classes, or going to dress rehearsals, which to a culture vulture are more delicious than performances.

I was, by that time, a Hamilton vulture. I wanted all of his skating that I could get. The aesthetic bliss that came from his skating started happening the instant he hit the ice. The sensations caused by his warm-up circuits of the rink were as strong as when he shot off his technical best. It wasn't what he did, but the wonder of him doing anything on skates. Scott Hamilton had that self-contained perfection that makes Japanese connoisseurs pay fortunes for certain rocks or prize goldfish. He had all the power that truly beautiful things have.

I wasn't the only one rhapsodizing over the Champ on skates. You could see the Scott people going over the edge when he went onto the ice. They'd sink into gorgeous sadness, close to crying, or they'd chew a smile and give away secret giddiness.

At Easterns, Scott and his competition were like an Arabian horse and a dozen caribou. You might have thought that this naked preeminence would bother the other men's mothers. But the Champ sent a shiver of smug delight up into the broody moms at center ice. He ennobled the morning practice. It was, apparently, a fine feeling to have one's own son working out with Scott Hamilton. It was fine, that is, unless you thought your kid had a chance of beating him. Later in the season we would encounter mothers of skaters who dreamt of knocking off the Champ. For those ladies, Scott's practices were Purgatory. But no such competitive self-torture was evident at Easterns. The skating mothers at Morristown adored Scott, and showed it.

Besides all that bliss, the practice on Thursday morning in

Morristown brought on a case of the psychic bends. Right there I went through a pressure change, which turned out to be a constant feature of these competitions, but was initially bothersome.

Scott's off-ice melodrama—Morristown was only an introductory episode—was a study in emotional frailty, pettiness, egotism, earthbound and narrow and irritating as only the goings-on of a self-absorbed small group of people can be. The familial miasma was, now and again, made suffocating by the mist of smiley Sweethearthood that settled on the world of figure skating. But then just when things were getting to be too much, Scott would put on his skates. And then a cold wind blew away the human swamp gasses and Sweetheart fog. While he skated everything was wonderful.

You could see that for Scott people, going to those practices was like going to church. We sat for an hour in the presence of IT, the ultimate answer, the reason why everybody was spending so much time and money to be there. While Scott skated, the load was lightened, and everything was unquestionably worth the trouble. So different were the swamp and the house of Scott worship that while in one you forgot what the other was like. While deep in one, you could even stop believing the other existed.

The great sea changes that morning brought me to a mystery that I started chewing over at Easterns. The mystery was this: How could a man as obviously agitated and beset as Scott Hamilton was that morning put on skates and become, for forty-five exalted minutes, a demigod? It seemed impossible that a man's existence could include states of being so different as Scott skating, and Scott not skating.

This, it developed, was all wrong. There was no such mystery. This false mystery was based on the assumption that, because Scott's skating could bring such bliss to Scott watchers, skating brought Scott to a similarly exalted frame of mind. It turned out that the Champ didn't get carried away with his own powers the way he carried us away. He was, rather, fairly immune to his own stuff. The bogus mystery was also based on the idea that things like the silent jealousy between Mrs. O and Mrs. Camp really bothered Scott, that his appeal for help was genuine. That, too, was all wrong.

The real mystery, which became clear only much later, was as follows: How did Scott Hamilton convert all of his off-ice petty annoyances into that marvelous skating? A season with Scott showed that he didn't skate in spite of besetting interpersonal problems—in some baffling way he skated *because* of them. Difficulties like balancing Mrs. O and Mrs. Camp, love with Kitty, and anger directed at Don—which was about to become an issue—were part of Scott's winning synthesis. He needed Mrs. O and Mrs. Camp to be jealous, and if they hadn't been jealous he would have sought some other minor crisis that morning.

So when Scott went from the human swamp to the skating dimension and then back to the swamp, he wasn't going anywhere. He was making a conversion of state that was like water turning into ice and then becoming water again. You wouldn't get one without starting with the other. In retrospect it is obvious that when Scott rushed through the lobby of the Madison Hotel on the way to practice and looked disturbed and asked for help, he was not asking for help at all. He was performing a function very like that of the picadors in bullfighting. But he was also the bull, so he stuck lances in his own neck to bring himself to just the right state of madness for the ring. He was deliberately tormenting himself for the sake of his practice that morning, getting worked up over something rather randomly chosen to get worked up for. Something else would have done just as well.

After the practice something else did, in fact, do just as well. Scott lay on his bed in his curtain-darkened room in the hotel. He had just eaten lunch downstairs, and he intended to rest alone in his room, with a nap if he could go to sleep. In the meanwhile, though, there was time to turn on the tape recorder and tell it about new problems. Initially the problem was Don, who in the 1982 competitive season was going to be the bad guy in some of Scott's nastier inner soap operas. In 1982, it was impossible to compete without raging against Don.

So he started. "Well, he's really concerning me, because he was very short with me. And we didn't go through the regular dialogue where I'd say, 'Gee, I'm nervous. I can't do it.' And Don would be calm and say to me, 'Oh yes, Scott, give it a try, and when you do it, think of this. . . .' No, last night, it was, 'I can't do it.' And Don goes, 'Fine! Think that way. If that's what you want to think, fine!' "

Scott might have been starting a vituperative monologue that would last for fifty yards of cassette tape, but just as he began working up a righteous anger against his coach, a thought came that took away all the spleen. Scott was remembering why Don might have been so snippy. It came to Scott just then that Don had to go to Philadelphia to have a growth removed from his arm. For the next several minutes Scott quit playing on his own emotions. Don was going to miss the Friday-morning practice to drive down to a doctor in Philadelphia with Mrs. O. Something bad was growing on Don. And Scott, with fear and sadness in his voice, was talking about his old nemeses cancer and death.

"I think Don was hurtin', I really do," Scott said. "I get so worried about him. It bothers me, it really bothers me. Because it was a carcinoma they took off his arm before. And it was a melanoma, which is scary. And I'm scared. If that develops any more, I'm gonna go bananas. I've already lost a mother from that, and I don't want to lose any more. It's tough, because it comes and it goes and it goes and it comes back. Just zap! And then it won't go away, and it goes inside. All of a sudden whamp! It's in your lungs and the vital systems, and it's out of control. . . ."

Scott went shooting back to 1977, when cancer and death took away Dorothy Hamilton. After a moment he came back fighting, but this time he wasn't shooting at a paper target constructed in the shape of one of the people around him, whom—in spite of all his unpleasant noisemaking—Scott loved and depended on. What materialized in the room was the enemy that had to be faced that night, the thing that had raised Scott and thrown him down and then took him higher than ever before, as high as skaters can go. The thing in the room could throw Scott for another fall, and if Scott started falling from his high place in the world of figure skating, if he started to fall now, he might never stop falling. The fatal plunge could start if Scott didn't win short program that night. Winning, if he didn't win convincingly, could be a dangerous downward slip. When you fought with this thing, you had to beat the hell out of it, every time, or it beat you. Beating it was harder every time, because this thing learned all your tricks and got trickier itself every time you fought. If you weren't better than you were last year, it would win. If it won, you got dumped. And maybe you never got up again.

So Scott was alone, on a wide battleground, empty except for *it.* And the two of them were just in sight of each other, taking each other's measure. Terror filled the room, but Scott didn't shrink from the buzzing fear. This fear was an old friend of Scott Hamilton's. Battle like that about to begin was Scott's delight, his life, his love; and the fear was the dust and sound of his enemy's advance to attack position and, in another six hours or so, the battle that was the first of the 1982 campaign, which would end in March in Copenhagen, which in turn would lead to more campaigning in 1983 and then glory or defeat at the 1984 Winter Olympic Games in Yugoslavia.

Hostilities, of course, had broken out the day before, but compulsory figures never brought on the battle tension that was setting in Thursday afternoon in Scott's hotel room in New Jersey. Figures were serious, all right, and Scott prepared and performed them in dead earnest, but the atmosphere of skating's opening event was always less burdened than that of the two freeskating

137

events. Figures were more like maneuvering for position than committed fighting. On the opening day you feinted and pulled back and chose the ground on which the short program would be fought. These opening maneuvers in a close contest could be the difference between winning or losing, but the skater didn't win or lose in figures. Victory and defeat, destiny in a competition, began to unfold in short program. There the skater and *it* traded the first deadly blows, wounds were given and wounds received. And short program had a battlelike fatality—here Scott began depending on skating's fortunes of war. Control was no longer all his.

"In figures," he observed, "you can control your own destiny. You pick good ice, and you know how prepared you are. In short program, you can rush one thing, get a little nervous, hit a bad piece of ice. Something can happen. And if you miss one element, you get a point deduction. Somebody who doesn't miss one beats you. But," he concluded, "that's the pressure. We'll see what happens."

Scott, who was in a new place, the battle plain, was talking a new way. He spoke in battle language, in a voice that became flat and matter-of-fact. But in spite of the superficial calm, you could feel fierce nervousness behind the voice, and you could sense apprehension and anticipation, equally powerful, canceling each other out so that Scott neither ran nor attacked but stayed there on the bed and went to amazing energy levels. The effect of being close to Scott was exactly that of four cups of coffee, strong and black. It was exhilarating.

Scott spoke more about the short program. "You don't feel anything as far as emotions going into short program. Maybe upset a little, sometimes a little nervous. Once in a while you're so nervous it throws you physically. And the ice feels funny, when you first get on. It doesn't feel like real ice. It feels strange, like you've never skated on it before. That's what it usually feels like in competition.

"I'm not really as ready for this as I'd like to be," Scott said, unemotional and detached from what he was saying. "I'd like to really feel good. But I feel slow. I feel tired most of the time. That's when you're out of shape, coming into competition."

The first wave of nervousness had passed, and the tension subsided. Scott didn't want to talk anymore. He was too polite to say that he wanted to be left alone, but without mentioning it he made it perfectly clear that it was time for solitude. Later, he said, it would be okay to talk, just before five, when he had to go to the Mennen Arena.

# The Combination,
# Floor Exercise Number Two

Scott's fight Thursday night against the nameless, faceless beast of figure skating, which was going to try, as it always did, to make the Champ's mind snap and sabotage his jump landings and cause him to catch a rut and fall flat in his footwork, was going to hinge on one of the seven required elements in the two-minute short program. That element was the two-jump combination, which the 1982 USFSA rulebook said must be double flip in combination with any other double or triple jump. For technical reasons, which we'll touch on shortly, virtually the only jump that could be done in combination with double flip was a toe loop. So Scott and all of the skating world's heavies that year were doing double flip, triple toe loop.

In a jump combination, the second jump had to go up off the first jump's landing foot, with no intervening steps. Every year short program had a combination, most of which were puff pastry to Scott Hamilton. But double flip, triple toe loop, called simply the combination, had always been a particular disaster for Scott. He had never landed double flip, triple toe loop in competition as of Thursday, January 7, 1982. He had landed it in front of audiences only a few times, at USFSA-sponsored exhibitions where he did his short program as a show number. He probably could have won Easterns popping into double-double, which had been good enough to win that year at the National Sports Festival in Syracuse and Skate America at Lake Placid, his two non-ranking international competitions. But Scott's game plan was to beat once and for all the unlucky combination at Easterns. He would have to do double-triple to win at Nationals and Worlds, where there would be skaters solidly in command of it. And the point at Easterns was not to beat the other men at Morristown, none of whom could have gotten ahead of Scott without an act of God. The point at Easterns was to do figures, short, and long that would win at any of the upcoming competitions. In the worried world of figure skating, the Champ was always up against men who weren't there, at competitions that wouldn't be held for weeks and months. To beat the invisible men in time-warp competitions—which were more important than the real-time, corporeal happenings in Morristown—Scott absolutely had to do the combination that night.

Since Colorado, success or failure in the short-program practice hour had been the combination. Whether Scott could land it or not was, indeed, a prime indicator of a whole day's worth. Evenings were dark and horrible when Scott couldn't get it right at least once.

This might seem a disproportionate amount of concern for a maneuver that was just one of seven required in an event that counted for only twenty percent of a competitor's final standings. But the short program loomed large in Scott's competitive strategy, and the combination was its key.

In short program, more than in either of the other two phases of competition, winning was defined negatively, which is to say that winning was a matter of not missing more than it was a matter of outshining other competitors. The rules specified point deductions for omitted or missed elements, and point deductions for extra elements, so there was no way to compensate for missed elements. What you had to do to win was absolutely nail the required seven elements, which were not weighted equally in the rulebook. Missing the combination cost more than any of the others. If somebody else landed the combination and had an otherwise successful performance, Scott was virtually guaranteed to lose. So, in the 1982 competitive season, the short program could have been called—without greatly oversimplifying the case —a combination competition. For the top skaters, this was the whole nut.

With all this in mind, it's not surprising that Scott was worrying. His anxiety was worsened because the double flip combination had been so awfully cruel to him. It had figured highly in the 1979 season, Scott's year of agony, when he came in fourth at Nationals and watched Worlds, held in Vienna that year, on television in Ohio. Not only had he muffed every combination in competition that year, he had lost weeks of training time when it wrecked his ankle in practice.

Scott, incidentally, was not the only skater to have trouble with double flip, triple toe loop. In the 1979 World Championships, it had made a mess of the world's best skaters, cutting down every one of them save one, Vladimir Kovalev, of the Soviet Union, who nailed the combination and went on to win the championship.

Time to stand up. This won't take long, not nearly as long as the standing compulsory figures lesson a few chapters back.

The rulebook specified only that the skaters perform any other double or triple jump in combination with a double flip jump. But technicalities of the double flip made a toe loop the only feasible partner to a double flip, and it was only feasible to do the toe loop after the double flip. A double toe loop would have met the rulebook requirements, but those who wanted to win were doing triples. All other things being equal, a triple would beat a double in competition because it was harder. So Scott's combination was double, triple.

Nonskaters can be misled by the name of the first jump in the combination, double flip, which suggests some sort of gymnastic whole-body flip. Nothing like that here. Whatever flips in a flip jump is highly obscure to the witness.

So, you're on your left foot, hurtling forward at a pretend speed that you couldn't possibly reach unless you're a very good skater. Unless you're a terrific skater, you couldn't do anything but skate at this speed. Any attempted jumps or tricks would be black-and-blue disaster. But, for purposes of this floor exercise, you're Scott Hamilton, so you can do whatever you want. What you want going in this combination is high forward speed. You make a push with your right foot and, skating on the left foot, execute a three turn, just like the three turns in figures but done at breakneck velocity. Now you're going backward on your left foot.

In this pretend double flip, you should flex your left leg into a one-legged half knee bend and at the same time reach to the rear with a straightened right leg. Arms are stretched chest-high, with the left forward and the right rearward. Keeping the pretend backward velocity in mind, drop the right leg until your toe touches the floor. At the toe's touchdown, snap the left leg upright. At this point the floor exercise becomes more mental than physical, because it's impossible to reproduce what happens on the ice. The idea is that you vault over the stiff right leg into the air, the escape from gravity assisted by the upward-snapping left leg.

At the pretend moment you vault and jump off the ice, whip everything leftward and close the arms and legs into a tight package, bolt upright, with the hands clutched across the chest. The momentum of the closed-in body parts speeds the rotations, so you turn around twice before coming down on your right foot. At the end of the jump you're opened into a backward-speeding flexed arabesque, this time on the right foot. Flex the skating leg again, reach back with the free leg, the left, put the toe down for another stiff-legged toe-pick touchdown and upward vault. Throw yourself through three counterclockwise rotations and land on the right foot again, coming down cleanly and swooping in a neat curve on the outside edge away from the landing spot. You've done it. You've nailed the combination.

In Scott Hamilton's personal jump theoretics, the big problem in the execution of this combination was speed. Speed across the ice translated itself into vital jumping energy. "You see," he said, "speed is more or less an insurance policy. You've got to pick up speed to do any jump. And the more speed you have going into something, as long as you've got it under control, the better the odds are that you'll do it. The more speed you go in with, and the more you come out with, the better the judges think the combination is and the better the mark is."

To preserve this speed, Scott liked to skim the double flip jump low over the ice, like skipping a stone over water. Launching himself into a high double flip would have eaten up velocity and energy needed for the triple toe loop. And he'd had to learn to squeeze a little extra rotation speed out of his triple toe loop by crossing his feet during the jump. The more closely a turning body is brought into a single vertical line, the more quickly that body turns. The foot-crossing position made Scott's double flip, triple toe loop possible in 1982, whereas it had been impossible in 1979. Back in June Don had suggested to Scott that he try crossing his feet in the toe loop, to see if it worked better that way. It did, so much so that Scott landed the combination in the first practice session in which he experimented with crossed feet. But the change of technique in a jump he had known for years meant painful retraining that bothered him still in January.

That the combination was the big question—the only question —of Thursday is clear only in retrospect. The things that counted were so tangled up and hidden in Scott's amazing thicket of artificial problems, to which he gave so much voluble attention for personal psychological reasons, that the issue of the combination was at that point highly obscure. Scott mentioned it, but he seemed to be mentioning it in passing. I was, in Morristown,

144

dazzled by the displays of interpersonal volcanics and missed the combination altogether. Only looking backward does it become apparent that on Thursday afternoon the upcoming double flip, triple toe loop was absolutely *everything*. We wouldn't know a thing about the 1982 competitive season until the question of the combination had been answered.

And we wouldn't have to wait long for that answer. The combination went up about twenty seconds after Scott started his short program. He told me about the placement of this short program element in an interview in Germany: "I do a little thing, and I turn around and start picking up speed for it. I like to get the combination over the very first thing. That way I know if I commit suicide or not after the program. Some people like to get their feet under them a little bit and warm up before. I like getting it out of the way. I've always done combination first."

# 15

# The Maelstrom

"I sit here and listen to my raunchy rock and roll. It's confidence inspiring. AC/DC is the best thing to listen to. It's the best! This is my song before competition. It's the best thing in the world!"

The music blasting out of Scott's massive Japanese silver stereo boom box stopped, so he didn't have to shout anymore. "Anyway," he said, "music is very important because it's confidence inspiring and you really get a lot out of it."

The tape recorder was rewinding and looking for "Back in Black," which Scott said was the best music in the world for bringing on just the right frenzy for him to skate like the best skater in the world. The machine found it, and the roaring and wailing came back, louder than before. Talking, even shouting, was out of the question, so Scott communicated with the proprietary beaming of a person sharing a musical delight hitherto unknown to another person. "Isn't it fantastic?" Scott's face was asking while it also answered its own question and said that "Back in Black" was, indeed, fantastic. There was no choice in that situation but to make a face saying that this was an amazingly great song, better than fantastic.

That was a lie. "Back in Black" was awful. It was awful in the same way that all of Scott's favorite music for cranking himself up for competitions, and depressurizing afterward, was awful. Scott loved the most sinister dead-end blue-collar rock and roll, and he brandished his love for those savage noises the way high school dropouts back in Bowling Green showed off obscene home-made tattoos and threw empty Rolling Rock cans out the windows of hopped-up rusty Camaros and punched their girlfriends' fathers. Musically, Scott liked to go back to Ohio, to the wrong side of the tracks. There were, in 1982, some very sophisticated alternatives to primitive rock and roll, but Scott could not find spiritual sustenance in New Wave. He got the juice he needed only out of that music that howled up and down the absolutely uncurved country roads back home. And he got the juice only because that music was so wonderfully terrible.

And even though the music was less than fantastic, things were happening in the noisy hotel room that were quite fantastic. The sensation of being that close to Scott Hamilton while he got ready to warm up in costume for short program compared well to the best amusement park rides, with gravity pulling in all directions while the hotel room whooshed down the tracks and through the overhead loop and around steep-banked curves. The supreme nervous tension of Scott Hamilton really brought on giddy sensations of motion, the kind that would have made little kids go "Wheeeeeeee!"

This was nervousness of an entirely different character than the quiet but tense moments of three hours earlier, when Scott had stood alone on the wide gray battle plain and watched his enemy's approach. That had been meditative nervousness, with Scott emptying himself of everything but him and *it*. Now he was filling, sucking energy out of the high-tech speakers and everything within miles that had anything he needed for that night's performance. He was even getting blood from somewhere. The new blood clouded catsup-colored under his skin and engorged him so every muscle stood out in a distinct lean bundle. Scott couldn't sit still. He crossed and recrossed the room, pacing and pumping up.

"I just had soup," Scott said. "That's all I'm going to have

147

tonight. If you skate full of food, all the blood rushes to your stomach."

"What's happening in your head, Scott?"

"You're just sort of thinking about what you've got to do. What mistakes you generally make and how to prevent them."

The conversation was getting to be like shortwave radio. Contact with Scott was being lost. Momentarily he would come through loud and clear, then fade. "This is what I do," he said. "I listen to really awful rock and roll and pace and get psyched and go through the program about seven times. Self-hypnosis. Total concentration. Do it standing up. Make sure every one of my muscles is so warm, by the time I get there, they're ready to go, before I get onto the ice."

Loss of contact. The pacing was turning into Scott's short program, with him miming on the carpet all the things he had to do on the ice. Contact came back. "Well, I'll be leaving for the rink at five o'clock. I'm gonna drive over with Mrs. Camp. I think I skate at eight."

"You'll be at the arena for three hours?"

"That's fine. That's all right. Then I'll leave right after that. Then I'll probably want to be alone, from the warm-up on. Just pace, and get my head together."

A confusing reflection on last year's Easterns: "I don't feel like I'm in as good shape as I was last year. Last year I came to this competition and—it wasn't here, it was in Philadelphia, uh Wilmington—and I was pretty ready. Boy, best short of my life! Last year at Easterns. Triple Lutz double loop—Snap! Pop! Best double axel I've done in a long time. And I really nailed it. But, in fact, I was more ready. But I feel about the same going into short as I did last year. The difference is last year I knew I could do the combination, even though it was a harder combination than double flip, triple toe. This one I'm just not sure of. . . . I should have enough confidence in it—I land it more than I miss it in practice. Practice this morning gave me the confidence I might land

148

it. It's *dumb!* This is one head-trip year. . . ."

Scott broke out of his entranced pre-competition war dance and looked around for a copy of a newspaper that had an article in it that he said made him really mad. He started reading the article. The part that Scott hated quoted him saying that he and Don wanted to put the humor section in his long program because "Everybody's so boring we thought we'd give it a try." That passage, Scott was saying, was an egregious misrepresentation of what he had told the reporter. He had plainly said that long programs were the same thing over and over, repetitious, and that it was time to break them up a little bit.

"That really makes you mad, Scott?"

"Yeah, because it makes people think I'm cutting everybody in the sport down, saying I'm better because I'm doing something new. That's not what I said at all! I would never say anything like that about skating in general—'Everybody's so boring . . .' What do people think when they read something like that?"

Then he was up and so far into his short-program trance that further communication was impossible.

Scott put on his short-program costume in the boys' locker room of the William G. Mennen Arena, which was under the stands at mid-ice. The costume was surprisingly heavy in the hand, to the touch a lot like the stretchy polyester doubleknit in suits and sport coats.

This was either a lucky or an unlucky costume, depending on which part of Scott's rambling utterances you believed. "Every time I've competed in it, I've missed. Well, no—I mean I missed the combination. It feels funny in the air because the pants are kinda big, on the bottom. It's maroon with jewels on it, one piece, and you feel naked in it. See, I don't know why I consider this outfit bad luck. It's this year. Last year I never missed anything in it. I like it, I guess. I won Worlds in it last year. I won Nationals in it."

* * * *

Before going over to the rink, Don was much less communicative than Scott had been. The coach left the hotel later than Scott and spent considerable time in the hotel's restaurant with Mrs. O, the two of them bent conspiratorially across a little table in the atmospheric darkness. No, he said, he didn't want to answer any questions about how he got ready for competitions. After he was done talking with Mrs. O, he was going up to his room to rest for a few minutes.

Don's standoffishness was purely clinical, without a hint of rudeness or hostility. He seemed to have made a cold decision that once the conversation with Mrs. O concluded, his attention would go to Scott and Scott's skating and nothing else.

Don, encountered shortly thereafter, was simply not where he was standing. What could be seen was there; the rest was gone. The loss of contact was not like the erratic mental fading-in and fading-out of Scott Hamilton. Don's attention was shut off as if a switch had been thrown.

At the rink, Don came back, rather festive, joking and hurrying along the boards. Then when Scott warmed up, Don was gone again. You could stand next to him during the long silences when Scott tried the different parts of short program and never be tempted to talk to Don, so obvious was the fact that nothing existed for him but Scott skating. Don watched his skater with an expectant half grin. He showed by minute expression changes that he was going through each trick with Scott. The half grin would droop when Scott went into a jump and then widen into a satisfied real grin when Scott landed it. "That's a boy, that's it," he seemed to be saying silently. Don gave exactly this sort of neutral encouragement to Scott when he coasted by the boards where the coach stood. The Champ would then make self-deprecating jokes that said he was afraid. The coach's quick responses said, "There, there, that's all right," or "Don't worry, you've done this before." That, at any rate, was the gist of what

Don told Scott. He spoke to his skater like a trainer talking to his skittish horse. The soothing sound of a familiar voice was more important than what the voice said.

The coach showed emotion only once, when Scott glided by and said that he wished to God he understood the combination, because if he had a better mental grasp of the thing he'd know how he could do it.

Don gave him a five-second scolding. "I don't care if you understand it or not. Just *do* it!"

The first competitive event of the evening was Junior ladies long program. The arena was a little less than half-full for Junior ladies, with more people coming in all through the event. The second competition was Senior men's short program, and the last, and most important, was Pairs long program, Kitty and Peter's final event.

The voice of a skating crowd is entirely different from that of the fans watching a mainstream team sport. No baritone roar and basso murmuring between roars, as in football. In the Mennen Arena you heard the raised voices of hundreds of early-teen girls and boys with unchanged girlish voices. Adult voices did very little to bring down the piercing, ultra-high frequencies of all those kids. At its loudest, the sound was like the squealing of teenaged girls hysterical over their favorite star. When the crowd got really excited, your ears hurt.

Scott took off his costume after warm-up and sat in the stands near the center line, exactly across the rink from the boys' locker room, where he would put his costume on again later. There was a break in the boards where he would get on and off the ice and where Don would stand when he was skating. The Champ wore his usual jeans, running shoes, and warm-up suit over a T-shirt. He was within smiling and helloing distances of Mrs. O, but a few rows below her and to the left. He seemed pleased with himself, but jittery, holding forth at high speed on a rapidly changing array of topics. In this hour before his short program, Scott became a television with somebody switching the channels.

He went down across the rink and by the boards where Don was standing with Jim White, a skater from Seattle who was being coached by Don at Easterns, and the three of them made jokes.

He went back and sat next to Mrs O. "I have to start pacing," he told her, and left. Mrs. O, who had been watching Scott skate since 1976, said that Scott had always paced before his competitive performances. It used to be that he would ask his mother or maybe a group of people to pace with him. These days he wanted to do it alone.

7:50 P.M. Scott was going to be the first skater in men's short program, which was supposed to start at eight o'clock, but was now expected to be fifteen or twenty minutes late, maybe more.

Scott was out of his street clothes and back into his maroon costume. The cuffs of the costume were turned up and his feet wore the nylon running shoes.

Scott was staying at the same side of the rink as the locker room and the gate in the hockey boards where the skaters went onto the ice. He'd go down to the corner of the rink and then come back, having quick words and handshakes with a lot of people, always staying in motion.

7:55 P.M. A pack of Sweethearts ran down the Champ and waved programs in his face. He signed autographs.

7:56 P.M. Scott: I twisted my arm and I couldn't move it, going into my combination.

Don: Well, twist it the other way.

Scott: I really want to land that sucker tonight.

Don: You will land that sucker tonight, Scott.

Don turned and asked if he could hit Scott. Then there was gleeful boxing horseplay, the kind that breaks out between fourteen-year-old best friends carried away with high spirits, loving punches. ·

7:57 P.M. More uncertainty. Scott fussed again about the combination.

Don: Just *do* it.

Scott: (Musing, to no one in particular) I really want to hit that sucker. . . .

7:59 P.M. Some jokes about judging with a skating mother. No, not a mother, a coach, a small dark woman from New York. Scott made a lewd grab at her rear end, and didn't let go. So she grabbed Scott's, and they walked along the boards, hands barnacled onto each other's seats.

Scott went down to the back corner of the arena, beyond the stands, where the floor was covered with rubber matting. Alone on the rubber, he started to dance through his program.

Scott: I feel okay. I'm just trying not to worry about it.

Near the rubber matting was a table with a display of India Earth Cosmetics. Scott looked at a competition program at the table, and then looked at the cosmetics.

Then he wanted a drinking fountain. He was thirsty.

8:02 P.M. Don: Who is that? You've got to find out who that is. . . .

Some guy was hanging around down by the boards, with lots of cameras. Don absolutely had to know who he was and what he was doing. It turned out that he was nobody, just somebody else's friend. He wasn't doing anything.

8:04 P.M. Back at the India Earth display, by itself in the back corner, near where the rubber mat was on the floor. The coach whose butt Scott had squeezed was at the makeup display, and so was Scott. She put on makeup, and he watched. They both thought this was hilarious.

8:05 P.M. Scott back with Don at the boards. He was worried, but he had just thought of a reason not to be worried.

Scott: And to think I only have to land this thing three times. And then I'll never have to land it in my entire life. Ever.

For a saccharine moment Scott became his endearing self with his coach, the sweet, nice, figure skating kid. Awww . . .

Scott's face, when his momentary good cheer went away, was worried. Worried, the mobile features stretched down into seriousness so intense that it was comic. The jaw in these serious moments was the prominent part, and Scott looked like the old-time movie comic Stan Laurel.

Nobody in Sweetheartland looked like Oliver Hardy.

8:10 P.M. Mrs. Camp made a ceremonial visit to rinkside, where Don and Scott and Jim White were standing. She gave each a queenly, motherly, deliberate kiss, as if such kisses were worth a lot, and wished each good luck. Then she went away.

In all that hypertense craziness down by the ice, Mrs. Camp's visit could not have been a great distraction. Nothing was making much of an impression on Scott at that point, anyway. But her actions made Don furious. Skating mothers. There's no room for skating mothers at ice-side in a competition. *That's* where they belong, he indicated, making a theatrical gesture toward the stands.

The incident triggered a building fury about such distractions. Just that morning, Don went on, Mrs. Camp and Kitty had been talking to Scott when Scott should have been skating. Don had to yell at Scott. Next time he was going to yell at Mrs. Camp.

Most of the Senior men were back on the rubber matting, jumping and dancing through their moves. When they weren't making jokes, they looked terrified.

154

Scott and Jim were affable and brotherly under an indulgent Uncle Don. Scott, the older brother, gave advice to Jim, who was worried about his double axel.

Scott: Pretend you're somebody else doing the double axel. Think of somebody who's got a really good axel, and pretend you're him.

Then Scott and Jim started flipping coins. Whether or not the coins came up the way they called them was supposed to say how things would go. They flipped for double axel, then combination, then the whole short program.

Scott went to Don, who was making conversation about certain mixed drinks with somebody's father.

Scott: It's so dumb to be nervous like this! I've been on the ice in front of people one hundred and fifty times this year. I only have to be out there for two minutes. Why should I be nervous? That's dumb!

He walked away as if what he had just said closed the issue of nervousness once and for all.

8:15 P.M. Scott's skates were on. A great squall line of tension passed over us and we were in wind and hail. The lightning in this final nerve storm was a series of jokes cackled out by Scott. Gross jokes, a particularly awful species of joke in which the joke-teller gave different definitions for gross, jokes meant to be funny by virtue of stupid loathesome bad taste. Everybody laughed. There was nothing else to do.

Then a group of Senior men were released onto the ice for a brief warm-up. When the other boys came off the ice, Scott stayed on, circling back and forth near Don. Then Scott's name and his club were announced; the cheering was like sharp pencils poking into our ears. He went out onto the rink and hauled himself into a tall pose with his arms at shoulder level, straight out to the sides. Scott's opening stance suggested a crucifix. He wasn't the man but the cross.

155

The screaming stopped assaulting our ears, and just as the crowd quieted, white noise came over the sound system, which meant music was about to begin. It began and Scott skated.

The opening was a whining soprano chord on an electronic instrument that sounded like a power tool. Drums beat out scratchy sixteenth beats in the background. Scott was stroking the rink for speed to send up his combination. Then he was flat-out flying backwards. Just when the chord went up, Scott went up into the combination, and then landed the double flip and went up again and came down out of the triple toe loop. Mr. Clean. As he came down the crowd squealed as if he had done something delicious to each person.

The big question was answered. Don was smiling, and nodding a delighted "Yes, yes . . ."

There was no time for getting carried away with the gorgeous skating, or anything else. In Scott's short program, you had seven questions to ask, and then you had to see Scott's answers. The asking and answering took exactly one minute and fifty-six seconds. There was only time for asking and answering and these results.

> Combination? Yes.
> Flying camel spin? Yes.
> Double axel? Yes.
> Sit change sit spin? Yes.
> Double Salchow? Yes.
> Combination spin (a sequence of spinning with changing positions and a change of foot, not to be confused with the combination)? Yes!
> Footwork (hundreds of choppy steps eating the length of the rink, with building musical frenzy in a jazzy drum solo)? Yes!

The final wild affirmative, which had Don crazy with happiness and the crowd hitting new decibel highs, was a blurred final spin that turned Scott into something like a tall mushroom. The music stopped, and the kid's relief and happiness broke through the blank self-absorbed mask of him skating. When he wasn't skating anymore, he beamed, and bowed, and glided over to Don.

"Good, good," Don was cooing. "You were a little slow, but that'll pick up."

"Yeah," Scott said. "I felt a little slow. I'm so glad it's over." He had to talk when wracking breaths let him talk. He held the boards and looked down, and then got off the ice, thanking the crush of people who told him that he had been just fabulous.

The truth is that it's impossible to remember seeing a short program in competition. What was seen at Morristown was like a dice toss, or a man being shot out of a cannon. A buildup. Suspense. Then the thing itself, which happened so quickly you were immediately seeing the results of what had happened.

The results at Morristown were very good. The dice came up boxcars. Scott survived the cannon shot.

Then the speakers were saying what the seven judges thought. Technical merit, a 5.7 and 5.8s. Composition and style, 5.8s and 5.9s.

Scott had gotten better numbers, but just the same, these were great numbers, absolutely good enough. None of the Hamilton people were going to worry about Scott getting passed in short program at Morristown.

Scott went to change. While Scott was in the locker room, Don explained that one of Scott's spins had been unbalanced. One part was stronger than the other. The short program had been technically perfect, so there were no point deductions. But the glitchy spin weakened the entire presentation, so the technical merit scores weren't as high as they could have been.

The combination could have been done more quickly, Don said. With more power. What Scott needed was more speed, "Just speed, speed across the ice. All the way down, in and out, the whole program. But it'll come. He'll do it."

Scott returned in street clothes, high color gone, breathing easily. He looked thoughtful, quiet. "I need a Coke," he said, and dogtrotted out of the arena.

# 16

# All the Minks Screaming

By five o'clock Scott was awake and pacing in his room, sucking up the deranged screaming that came out of his boom box. Nervousness more savage, and more inward, than before short program. Scott was not talking.

Scott's long-program costume was light blue, the same sort of stretchy knit synthetic as the short-program costume, with a spray of jewels across the chest. The light blue outfit was a two-piece, shirt and trousers. The shirt was really a body suit that went down between the Champ's legs, like a leotard. The idea was that a body suit would stay straight on Scott's upper torso. A shirt might have pulled crooked or loose in a way that would look messy or disturb Scott's own sense of alignment.

The suit went on just before six o'clock, when Scott and the other Senior men at the 1982 Eastern United States Figure Skating Championships were to have a half hour on the ice at the Mennen Arena. Nobody was laughing his way into practice, as the guys had laughed a day earlier. Terror was showing, even though everybody was trying not to look terrified. The old veteran Scott Hamilton wore a combative pout that said he was damned mad, ready to fight. His jumps flashed down cruel and precise, as if he were drilling to kill enemies with the blades on his feet.

While Scott skated, Don put on the "everything's okay" grin and kept it shining in Scott's direction, nodding "Good, Scott,

good, good . . ." at his skater's jumps. Meanwhile, talking side-
ways, he pointed out that there was a pattern to Scott's nervousness. At short program, Scott was noisily nervous. Before long
program, the nervousness became quiet. No, no, he said, there
was nothing to worry about. "He's like a lion in a cage," Don said.

Then Scott was back with the coach, out of the long-program
costume. The Zamboni made ice for the first of the evening's
three competitive events, Senior dance original set pattern. Then
came Junior ladies' long program and, finally, Senior men's long.
Scott, because he was leading, skated in the last group of men.
He wouldn't be competing for almost four hours.

The crowd was already big and noisy before the ice dancing
started. Everybody was charged up by the world-class skating that
was going to happen that night, and almost everybody had something for Scott to sign, and loving messages. "You're great, you're
just great," they were saying. "Could you sign this one, and this
one, too?"

Scott, very quickly, had more than he could take. "I've got to
get out of here," he growled. And so, walking fast and protecting
himself against more autograph requests with a force field of
nervous preoccupation, Scott got out of there.

Don said he guessed Scott was going back to the hotel. He
didn't have to be back until about nine.


The coats at the Mennen Arena were fabulous. Thousands of
fur-bearing animals had laid down their lives so the gorgeous
grownup Sweethearts packing the bleachers and sucking cola in
the snack bar could be warm on a cold night at the end of the
year's coldest week. The scene would have given a mink or an
ermine or a poor little chinchilla nightmares for the rest of its life.

And the coats—lavish as some of them were—did not approach the dollars in ice time and coaching and probably special
tutoring and room and board and travel expenses spent on just one
of those Junior lady figure skaters who did her long program

Friday night, in the hours before Scott's big four and a half minutes. Ah, Sweetheartland . . .

Sometime during Junior ladies' long program, while Scott was still pacing and listening to more horrible music back at the hotel, the evening got to critical mass. Enough important skating people were reacting with a sufficient number of globally significant skaters and promising young skating meat—in a chemically excited medium combining ice and music and big-dollar suburban socializing—for Easterns to really start cooking. The Big Event–energizing was further driven by the television crews down from New York to tape possible footage for later skating coverage, and the presence with the cameras of Dick Button, the former great skating champion and current media incarnation of figure skating. But a lot of the night's radioactivity was coming from the man listening to AC/DC back at the hotel, Scott Scovell Hamilton, Champion of the World, who, in a couple of hours, was going to give the final measure of glamor to that Friday at Easterns.

So Easterns went from being just another nighttime event out in the suburbs, with moms and dads and kids and not much more throb than a high school musical, to being an absolutely gurreat evening event that acted as an egotistical nerve tonic on everyone in the Mennen Arena. The headiness was exactly the same as a gala opera opening, or a tennis tournament, or telling the cabby to stop at the international terminal instead of the doors where the planes go to Des Moines. In a world where the vast majority of places are wrong places, we were in the right place. Nothing is as good as spending time in the right place.

Don Laws was loving it. "Hey," he'd exude from his place in the long line snailing back to the snack bar, "nice to see you." Don, you could see, was a big deal in Sweetheartland. This was the seaboard where he had coached for twenty-one years, so he was a particularly big deal. We were, indeed, deep in the Silver Wolf's old hunting grounds. His old acquaintances, you would have thought, were going to start throwing their underwear at him. But they limited themselves to high-hormone exchanges that mostly had to do with mutual acquaintances who had just gotten to Easterns, or were going to get there any minute. "Oh he's [or she's] here?" the Wolf would growl insinuatingly. Then it was time to break off, and Don would suggest drinks or something, later. Subsequently Don would give me a quiet aside telling who the woman was, a pro, a judge, somebody's mother or wife, whatever. The Champ's coach also included amazingly intimate bits of gossip.

Don bared his teeth in proprietary delight, as if the parade of ice women were a special surprise that he'd arranged and paid for, a surprise and joke thrown together just to discomfit me at my first final night of competition.

But then a wave of excitement washed through the room. Something fabulous was on its way. This was patrician, low-key excitement, without screaming or a crush of people or even a lot of head-turning. The wave, which involved a subtle realignment of everybody's attention, rose up and came our way, and Scott Scovell Hamilton rode straight at Don Laws, surfing on the crest of a wave of appreciation. *He* was with us, and now things could really start to happen.

Don flashed his delighted teeth and put his arm on Scott's shoulder, and Scott said he wanted something to drink, maybe a Coke.

The Junior ladies' final event was almost over. Scott wanted to watch. So he rode his wave of adulation out of the snack bar, quipping, giving strobe-quick smiles of recognition, patting people, but all the while imploding in dark self-absorption.

The fire doors opened and the Champ and his coach walked along the boards, at the base of the great upward-sloping carpet of skating fans. "That's him!" people hissed to each other, in the momentary madness of seeing a face familiar from TV. "That's him!" Kids came at Scott with programs, planting themselves dead in his path, so Scott had to stop. And Scott signed when he had no choice but to sign, with complete indifference, sometimes not even looking at what he was signing. Scott signing autographs was like a horse slapping at flies with its tail.

"This is ridiculous!" Don was saying. "These people won't let him alone."

The crowd watching the skaters, like the crowd in the lobby and snack bar, had come to full power. A Princess skated out and presented herself, a very popular Princess, and a wild sound hit our eardrums, a feral frequency so high and wild that you knew it couldn't be coming from humans, particularly not from those pretty athletes cheering for their peer. Impossible. No, this sound was coming from another dimension. What we heard could only be the sound from beyond of the death agonies of all the little animals killed to make the fabulous Morristown coats. All the minks were screaming.

Scott: Don can tell when I'm going to be on. He knows, because of my concentration. My focus is about six inches in front of my face. There's a little wall, a little field, and nobody can penetrate. When I get like that, almost trancelike, I usually have a pretty decent performance. When I just totally put myself in my own little world, and just think about what I'm doing. It's kind of self-hypnosis. You think about everything in a positive way, and you see yourself landing everything before you step on the ice. And you feel the ice, and you think of nothing else but each jump. Knowing you *have* to land something usually helps, too.

Scott's wall was going up. After Junior ladies, he was incommunicado, but incommunicado with a lot of talking. He paced in the back corner of the arena, beyond the stands, near that absurdly isolated cosmetics display. The people loitering back there were skating people, Senior competitors mostly, a few coaches, everybody more or less intimate with Scott. He went bouncing among the little groups and individuals like the steel ball in a pinball machine, fast and random. He'd come at somebody with something to say, as if it were suddenly important to have a talk, but his attention to the words coming out of his own mouth was destroyed the instant he started saying them. The hole in his inner wall, through which Scott had begun to send a message, was instantly sealed shut, every time, and Scott was gone. He was gone because he walked away, or quit talking. Sometimes he stayed where he was and kept talking to you, and he was still entirely gone.

Scott: You know what I was thinking about last night during short program? Living in Malibu. I said to myself, "This has got to be clean or I won't live in Malibu." My back hurts tonight.

9:28 P.M. Kitty and Peter joking around with Scott. This was the deal: If Scott did a perfect program, Peter had to drink four double shots of Jack Daniels bourbon. Kitty would become Scott's slave. If Scott blew it, he had to be Kitty's slave, and he had to drink the whiskey. They came up with the bet in pieces—"Yeah!" —and the one talking would rapid-fire what he wanted to say with hypertense delight, as if this silliness was the funniest thing in the world. They laughed and laughed.

Long program was taking over Scott's mind. He'd started dancing through it, lost to everything. Then he'd come out of the program and grab one of the women or joke around. But then he went back into the program. Ceaseless motion.

9:45 P.M. Don testy. Angry about the kids coming to Scott's corner and bothering him for autographs. Don cordoned off part of the floor space, the part back toward the entrance to the girls' lockers, a cul-de-sac. Don manned the cordon himself, driving away strangers.

One by one the World-level skaters at Easterns came to Scott Hamilton and spoke. "Paid their respects," is the phrase that wants to be used, because these brief visits were ceremonious and formal. Scott's sanctuary became, for the period of the other skaters' visits, funereal. Scott played the bereaved, and the skaters the guests who each delivered a sympathetic phrase and then listened to the chief mourner's acknowledgment. Like a funeral, this was an occasion that made impossible any real exchange with the man hardest hit by events, Scott Hamilton. But the occasion demanded that you say something.

What you said was, "Good luck, Scott."

And what he said was, "Thanks."

Among Scott's well-wishing fellow skaters, Elaine Zayak spent the most time with him. For something like five minutes Scott stopped his pacing and ghost-skating. He and Elaine, deep in Scott's sanctuary, spoke seriously and intently. Scott got a hug at the end of this talk, and Elaine was gone. What passed between them is lost forever—they were out of earshot, and Scott's memories of that night did not include what he and Elaine said. It can be said, though, that Scott's wall could not keep those two from talking, because Elaine, more than any of the other skaters at Easterns, was on the same side of that wall.

Elaine, a sixteen-year-old blond-and-blue-eyed singles skater from Paramus, New Jersey, was the only American amateur figure skater whose competitive success approached Scott's in January 1982. She was 1981 National Champion, and 1981 World silver medalist. At Easterns her celebrity stood as tall as Scott's, maybe even taller. She was, at the least, the undisputed Sweetheart of the East Coast, on her way to becoming a real coast-to-coast Sweetheart in time for the 1984 Olympics. So when Scott and Elaine talked, the king and queen of American figure skating were talking.

The audience with Elaine concluded Scott's ceremonial visits. The Champ went back into his kinetic trance.

\* \* \* \*

10:16 P.M. Kitty, attentive and even wifely in these last minutes, rubbed Scott's back. All the while she had been standing at the boundary of Scott's private floor space, with a silent Don still blockading fans. She held the Champ's coat. Not a great deal passed between Scott and Kitty—mostly she faced away from him, watching guys do their programs—but Kitty was a tree. Scott, caught out in the nerve hurricane, could tie himself to Kitty.

The people in the stands were becoming Scott people, you could feel it. Scott's corner was empty because those people had gone to their seats.

Time to go to the lockers.

Scott: The only thing I don't like is skating first after warm-up. That's poor, that's really poor. You're a little tired and your muscles are tired. So you start out tired.

The last group, the scared boys in shiny, vivid-colored costumes, stood where you go out on the rink, nowhere to go now but the ice. Then they swooped away from the floor that you could stand on, where your coach stood ready to pat your shoulders and put comfort and courage into your ears, telling you things to remember and think about. They left all that and went out on skinny blades riding on frozen water, with two thousand people screaming and looking.

When Scott went onto the ice, the minks screamed again and again. They screamed for his warm-up waltz jumps and his doubles and triples. He hadn't done any real skating, but already he was killing them.

He wasn't killing the jumps, though. The warm-up was a disaster. Scott's triple Lutz, the very first jump in his long program, broke down. Scott missed two triple Lutzes.

Triple Lutz should have been a friend, a piece-of-cake jump at the beginning of things to get Scott going and give the crowd a

166

squealy thrill. But the friend betrayed Scott, putting unexpected fear and doubt into the Champ's head. Then came another surprise defection, the triple Salchow. Two triple sows went bad in warm-up, with Scott popping and then scraping down into messy landings, barely hanging on. Later he would call this the worst warm-up in his competitive career. I went out scared, he would say. I was scared the whole program.

He looked scared, too. Not messy panic, but cold soul fear showed when the other skaters got off the ice. Scott skated flattened figure eights in front of his coach. Don put a few last words into Scott's ears. He grinned and crooned to his skater as if skating in front of a couple of thousand shrieking people and seven judges, after a warm-up that had shattered faith in the easiest jumps and therefore smashed confidence in *everything,* were the most delightful possible way to spend Friday night, a privilege, a lark. Don acted as if Scott's palpable terror was momentary silliness, out of which Scott could be jollied. Don't worry, he was saying. Just do it. Just do it and everything will be all right.

Time to do it. With the speakers saying Scott's name and home club, the ungodly death shriek of every fur coat in metropolitan New York daggered the ears, and Scott skated to mid-rink and smiled for the people and then stretched himself into the opening position.

Everybody hushed momentarily, listening for Scott's music. Then came crackling and the opening fanfare notes, the brass sound bleared and muted from overmodulation on the tape and the brutality of rink speakers to orchestral sounds. It came out like the sound of a gramophone, hand-cranked, but very loud. Of course nobody cared how the music sounded. The point was how Scott skated to the music. If you gauge the performance by crowd noises, Scott did fabulously at Morristown, better than anybody ever. The stabbing shrieks came almost continuously, with powerful detonations of voices and applause for each of Scott's jumps and spins. Triple Lutz went up and came down just right, quelling the first fear raised in warm-up. Triple toe loop was good. So was double axel. But then Scott popped the triple Salchow into a double, a disappointment for Scott but not, apparently, for anybody else. Since this was competition, Scott managed to sell the popped jump to the audience just as if it had been a triple. He came down clean and presented it and kept going, and they exploded as they had for the first three jumps.

Everything was going all right. The popped triple Salchow would turn out to be Scott's only glitch in his long program at Easterns. But then again everything wasn't going all right—you could tell sixty seconds into the program. What, exactly, was going wrong was hard to say. The Scott watcher of five weeks found the performance dissatisfying, thin, with no idea what was missing.

The crowd went into Scott Hamilton madness, as crowds always do. But Scott's face, even while he was giving those people such a whopping good ride, showed discontent. Until the very end of long program, he kept an unhappy, self-absorbed pout. His face flashing by in all the bodily pyrotechnics was oddly still, as if Scott were sitting somewhere far from the ice, alone, thinking very hard about something that pleased him not one damned bit. Someone, you could tell by this face, was going to hear about whatever it was that fell so far short of this man's expectations. Heads would roll.

No, Scott was not winning this one. This wasn't victory with the big screaming V. It was only not losing. There was no zing and no wham-bam in Scott's stuff, because Scott was occupied pulling every second of his program out of the jaws of defeat. Every last jump, spin, and line of footwork had to be fought for and rescued. Disaster loomed, and for four and a half minutes of the world's hardest skating, Scott stayed a stroke ahead of disaster.

This isn't to say that Scott skated poorly. Even this lackluster long program was overwhelmingly better than anybody else's at Easterns. It was probably better than anybody else's skating in the world. Scott's only failure on Friday night in Morristown was the failure to do as well as he could do.

And failure looked out of his finishing smile, which didn't open up until the last few seconds of the program. A white stripe started showing in the blue-and-flesh-orange blur of his final scratch spin. When the spin slowed down, the stripe turned into Scott's teeth. The teeth were part of the smile that said, as Scott himself said a little while later, "Thank God it's over."

His presentation of himself to the two thousand people going absolutely wild over Scott Hamilton included another smile more meek and apologetic than it was triumphant. Then Scott didn't have to smile for anybody, particularly not for Don, on whose shoulder he put an arm at the edge of the rink. "That sucked," Scott was saying. "That's the worst I've skated," when the wracking breaths let him say anything. Speech sobbed out of Scott, in erratic bursts, not because he was crying but because he had to fight the fast breaths to make words. Don said nothing. Instead of saying anything he put an arm on Scott and the arm carried all the world's love and sympathy. Once more Scott was the star of a funeral scene. Everyone he knew had died, everyone but Don. And Don silently comforted him.

The sorrow of skater and coach was idiotically mismatched with the happy kids crushing at Scott for autographs, and the Scott-mad crowd. Nor had the judges seen anything sad about Scott's skating: 5.8s and 5.9s for technical merit came over the speakers. Then more 5.8s and 5.9s, for artistic presentation.

In the throng around Scott, still near the boards, two little-bitty ice princesses in costume, silver if memory serves, came at Scott Hamilton with two bunches of roses. Scott, barely up to this cuteness, crouched and kissed each kid, gray and shaking like a man up for the first time after surgery. Then a swarm of autograph kids was on him. Scott tried to sign a program, but his hands trembled too violently for writing. Scott gave an apologetic shrug, but the kids kept coming. His invalid tenderness with the Morristown little ones was gone. On his way to the boys' lockers, Scott Hamilton smashed a hand into each side of his head and howled as if the kids were bayoneting him, an absolutely chilling sound to a Scott person. But Scott's genius for public relations hadn't failed him, even in this worst possible moment. The howl was a smidge overacted—it could have been a joke. So the bystanders took it that way. Scott, of course, was not joking. He was hiding behind the thin possibility of a joke.

Out of the public eye, he collapsed in silent despair, his respiration slowing. "It sucked," he said. "It really sucked." Don stood over Scott and filled the wretched locker room with fondness for his skater, silent balm. "The trance didn't come," Scott said. "I had to *think* my moves all the way through." Scott compared that night's long program to Saint Ivel's International, in England, in the fall of 1981. That, he said, was another night when his skating trance hadn't come. Saint Ivel's was the only competition after the 1980 Olympics where Scott had been beaten. Saint Ivel's was one of Scott's words for defeat.

"I'm glad I came," said Scott Hamilton. "Now I know what I need to do for Nationals. This is going to drive me."

Five minutes later, and it might have been five days, or even five weeks. A lot of time should have gone by for that tragic Scott to be the Scott saying all that upbeat stuff to the television cameras. Don and Scott walked out of their chamber of despair under the stands. Scott got up on Don's back and Don carried him piggyback all the way to the top of the stands, where Dick Button and the cameras were waiting. Everybody who could see this split their sides. Don and Scott grinned and hammed it up.

You might have thought that this was the outcome of some sort of a bet—if Scott won, the coach had to carry him around. The real reason was that Scott had lost his skate guards, and he couldn't walk on concrete without skate guards. Scott could hang onto skate guards for maybe ten minutes, at the most, so Don piggybacked him.

Dick Button thought that Scott was skating great. Scott did not say, as he had been saying since he got off the ice, what he appeared to have been saying all the while he was on the ice. He did not say, "It sucked." Scott opened his mouth and in fluent televisionese said that you learn things from each competition, and that this week he had learned a great deal.

Dick and Scott went back and forth. Scott told the cameras, "I'm *happy* with the way I skated here. It's just that it will help me. . . . It will help me toward a better performance at Nationals. Just the fact that I skated here."

So Dick asked Scott what was going to make his skating different and better this year. Scott said his comedy sketch was going to help. And he said his spins were better, which was true and also was a way of needling Dick, who had told Scott in 1981 that he needed to work on his spins. And he said he wanted to put in triple flip for Nationals, Worlds for sure.

"What can I say?" one of the TV people asked. "Let's do it again until we get it right." He meant, of course, that Scott Hamilton, as usual, had been just fabulous for the cameras.

"We'll see," Scott was saying to Dick Button. "I did my combination for the first time. I was so happy. That's why I didn't make Worlds in 1979."

Some hours later Scott was back from the inferno to which the long program had taken him. There were no cameras to make him speak sports celebrity-ese, which he spoke so well. He gave his own postmortem on Morristown.

Scott: I was disappointed, but I got good marks, and I won, so I can't be too disappointed. . . . You see, Easterns is an everything-to-lose, nothing-to-gain competition. Thank God it's over.

Then Scott was being funny again. Everything is wonderful, he said. Skating is my life.

# 17

# Jaws III:
# Shark Lunch at the Park Lane

A new monster, scarier than all the horrible ice beasts put together. This one was swimming. The *Jaws* movie music would go just right here, sinister deep plunkings with an orchestral convulsion when the thing's fin cut the surface coming straight at—Scott Hamilton!

No, the image isn't quite right. At noon Monday in the dining room of the Park Lane Hotel in New York City, we were on a tropical reef, colorful and quiet, and the thing was swimming overhead. You couldn't really see it, but every so often its shadow would come over our table for four, and the fear for Scott Hamilton, and every other poor jock the thing wanted, would grip. Nobody at our table but Scott was in danger. Don and I had absolutely nothing the thing would eat, and the guy in the suit at our table was the shark's pilot fish and its intimate business contact.

The shadow and the gut fear for Scott would come and go, and when it went, you could appreciate the grace of the setting. Below us a school of taxis swam in a yellow band around Central Park. Far away there were coarse New York fish in their vicious lunch-hour feeding frenzies, but our piece of Manhattan reef was hushed and dignified. And, like a warm ocean, it was absolutely heaped with delightful things to eat.

But the point of all this was not to marvel at the deliciously tony surroundings, where Scott's fresh-fruit-and-cottage-cheese plate cost more than prime rib back in Bowling Green. Nothing was cheap here. A dish of mousse went for four dollars. When you wanted pepper in your soup a man in a tuxedo with a pepper mill the size of a softball bat would run up and do the work for you. And the really great thing about all this was that the pilot fish, who had a fabulous suit and a pocketful of excellent cigars, was buying. Anything you wanted.

Pay attention. The point wasn't the lunch from heaven, but another lunch, which was going to take place just over two years from that day, after Scott Hamilton skated in the 1984 Winter Olympic Games in Sarajevo, Yugoslavia. The Big Lunch. In 1984, the great white fame-and-fortune shark was going to eat Scott Hamilton. The shark couldn't eat amateur athletes, but the figuring went that Scott was going to turn professional—edible—after the Olympics. The point of the Park Lane lunch was that the pilot fish, who made his living on scraps from the shark's mouth, wanted to arrange for Scott to be consumed in the most attractive and lucrative fashion. He wanted his agency to represent Scott. His was the largest shark-feeding company in the world, an international concern so rich and powerful that it actually owned and controlled many of the shark's teeth.

The fish in the great suit ticked off some of the megadollar possibilities: television specials, guest appearances, ice shows, movies, books, product lines, endorsements, commercials.

He paused to give his next pronouncement drama. "We're talking about a lot of money," he said, with another short pause to make the kicker just perfect. "Seven figures. And I don't necessarily mean with ones in front."

For all the reaction this got out of Scott, he could have been offering seven bushels of cucumbers. Most of us, hearing that we might be millionaires in twenty-six months, would say, "Gee, really, me . . . ?" and drift into Rolls-Royce fantasyland. Scott was not moved. He pushed a desultory fork around in the fruit and cottage cheese. He didn't have an appetite that noon, not for lunch and not for big-dollar talk. The work of talking to the fish fell mainly on Don, who was enthusiastically interested in listening, without necessarily being enthusiastic about what was being said. The Silver Wolf, that infinitely crafty and controlled creature, was just perfect for business like this. He loved it.

The pilot fish, flashing a stunning lunch-and-money talk and meganames like Bjorn Borg and Billie Jean King, was trying to dazzle Don and Scott. The whole artful presentation was meant to suggest that everything in the world worth having belonged to the pilot fish, and Scott, if he was smart enough to say yes, could be cut in. This was flimflam, though. The thing worth having was the sullen little man who wasn't hungry. If he kept going the way he was going, he would surely be worth a fortune. An all-American guy who skated in a way that drove people crazy and was personable and lovable on and off the ice, a potential Olympic gold medalist figure skater who was obviously and publicly heterosexual, straight as an arrow. A pilot fish's dream. A groaning board for the shark and at least one lucky pilot fish and other, lesser creatures. The point of lunch at the Park Lane was to put Don and Scott into the best possible frame of mind for hearing good things about the pilot fish's international athlete-marketing company. High-tone, oblique salesmanship was going on, and it was all very pleasant except for the Champ, who would not come out of his self-absorbed funk. He responded now and again in conversation, even laughed a little, but you could tell it was forced. The fork went on making disinterested stabs at the fruit plate.

The fish was telling about his company, which, like Scott himself, had been born in Ohio, with a lawyer from Cleveland who made some minor business deals on behalf of Arnold Palmer. That had been almost twenty-five years ago. From the small beginning grew an eleven-company group best known for selling golf and tennis stars, but with an interest in all sorts of big-dollar athletes and athletic events. Different branches of the company worked together to make each other rich, by setting up spectacles and professional competitions, and then booking its own clients. Scott could, for instance, if he signed up with the pilot fish, count on appearances in the television Superstars competitions, where ultrabig name athletes competed against each other in events other than those that gave them big names.

The big company offered absolutely comprehensive services for making book and movie deals and getting onto the right TV shows and everything else you needed for long and remunerative fame. Besides promoting the star athletes and controlling some of the markets where star athletes are in demand, his company offered complete financial management, disbursing and banking money for clients. Certain superjocks, he said, were profligate to the point that they needed somebody to keep them from throwing away their megadollars.

Things slowed and stopped and all eyes followed the pilot fish's eyes to Scott. The pause was to see if Scott was going to bite on any of the bait that was being trolled in front of him. Not yet.

The pilot fish angled some more, and then there was another expectant pause. We were too absorbed in the pilot fish's patient, expert casting for Scott Hamilton's attention to notice that the tableau we made was ridiculous. Three grown men dressed to the teeth, in a dressy restaurant, waiting like Lhasa apsos for some sign of recognition and approval from this other man who was roughly half our various sizes and dressed like a ninth-grader called out of school to come to the Park Lane. Scott wore his usual jeans, T-shirt, and running shoes. His underdressing was so phenomenal, and his self-absorption and self-assurance so complete, that the effect was regal. He might have owned the Park Lane. He could have come to lunch in his underwear if he wanted to. We had to put on ties just to sit in the same room with him.

"I don't want to be a carny." The statement was quiet and directed at the plate in front of him, but it was emphatic. Scott seemed angry. He wasn't angry at the pilot fish, who was, after all, just doing his job. The quiet fury was provoked by the very idea of carnyhood.

That, for the moment, was all that was going to come out of the Champ's mouth. So the pilot fish tried different kinds of bait. Eventually he had Scott's interest. What worked was when the fish stretched and changed speaking modes to the corporate getting-down-to-brass-tacks voice. These, he started saying, are the sorts of things we'd do if Scott belonged to us. One of the things was arranging for Scott to be seen and photographed around the right places with hot models and actresses and other image-enhancing women, to establish a playboy image for Scott and crank up his glamor and salability.

For the first and only time in that long lunch hour, Scott had heard something that dragged him out of his gloom. "Yeah," he said, and went into what were obviously high-temperature daydreams of himself and all sorts of gorgeousness hanging on his arm, having guys from *People* take his picture and then getting into who knows what. Sooooo fine. "Yeah," he said from deep in dream ladyland. "I can see it. That would be great."

Every man, the fish must have been thinking, has his price. I have just found this skater's price.

Of course you can't sit around and talk all day. The dishes were gone, the coffee was cold dregs, and everybody was telling each other what an enjoyable lunch that was. Learned a lot, lot to think about. Good to start considering this sort of thing before the last minute and on and on. The fish pressed business cards on us, and everybody shook his proffered fin. Then Scott Hamilton was walking from the shadow of the worst monster of all.

Three in a cab. Scott was cheerful as could be, obviously relieved to be done with all the business talk. He was about to knock off for the afternoon and meet a soap opera actress and her boyfriend and maybe some other people. The plan was to go ice skating at Sky Rink. This was to be the only instance in the 1982

176

season when Scott Hamilton went skating just for fun.

The cab seemed like a good place for talking about the lunch, which had been my initiating experience in the waters where men and women are food for celebrity sharks. The sensation brought on by the shark's shadow was terror, a protective terror for Scott Hamilton. The impulse was to bundle him out of New York to somewhere secret, where he'd have a head start. Run, I wanted to tell him, run while you have a chance. No, that's not right. The mental video showed Scott skating to safety. Nothing could catch Scott Hamilton on skates, not even the shark. Two days earlier an ice rink on the last night of competition had seemed like the world's most dangerous place. But the Park Lane reef made it clear that Scott Hamilton was safer by far doing ice impossibilities in front of judges and screaming maniacs—he was safer by far on the ice than among the people eaters. But of course that was no answer. Scott's artistry on the ice made the shark ever more ravenous for Scott. There was no sanctuary for Scott—the big lunch was his fate. Nevertheless, the impulse was to try to save him from butchery by seconds and minutes and hours, however lavishly the shark was willing to pay for all the Scott cutlets and Scott burgers. Scott's life, as lives are lived back in the Mudlands, was lost by that time anyway, hopelessly lost. Still the impulse was to fight for that life.

But Scott was entirely unbothered. You could tell he thought my fussing about his soul and the horrible evil represented by the agent was overwrought, if not just stupid. Guys trying to get him to sign away his time and talent and image were commonplace in Scott Hamilton's life. They spieled, and Scott listened and forgot. Don was the one who had to pay attention to this stuff, anyway. Scott was the skater. Some day, when the time came, Don and Scott would sign with somebody. That day, however, was impossibly far away in January 1982. And when the cab was hurtling through the Arctic sunshine toward the Statler, Scott could not have cared less about the agent and his message. He was liberated from that tedium, on his way to see some people he wanted to see. Gonna have some fun.

More music now, show music. The perfect tune for now was part of Scott's 1982 repertory of exhibition numbers. Besides long and short competition programs, Scott had a few ready-to-skate exhibition programs, which he performed at USFSA-sanctioned shows. Exhibition programs were not so much technical *tours de force* as they were skating entertainments. They were relatively easy for Scott, and great fun to watch. When the nonskating world thinks of figure skating, it thinks of something a great deal more like exhibition skating than competitive performances.

So Scott skated to the perfect music for this snippet of 1982. The song was "New York, New York," sung by Frank Sinatra, which Scott interpreted on the ice wearing a black and white costume that suggested a tuxedo. "New York, New York," dated to the 1981 Worlds, in Hartford. The World Championship meant that Don and Scott had to dream up a new exhibition program, right then, for the medalists' tour of American cities. Out of one day's on- and off-ice brainstorming came this fabulous melding of showy Broadway music and Old Blue Eyes' voice singing grandiose words about getting to the top of the heap and Scott Hamilton's A-Number-One flashiest skating. The New York audience went mad for Scott, as did the crowds everywhere, except, as we shall see in a later chapter, in Oberstdorf, a little town in West Germany, in the Bavarian Alps.

The music, at any rate, was perfect for this slice of Monday night, when Scott was dancing up Broadway. He should have been wearing the tuxedo outfit, but this was real life, nine above zero, so he was wearing his down-filled coat with tan outer shell. His head was turtled down into the collar because of the hideous wind, damp even at that low temperature, which was keeping everybody indoors. The Mudlands were having one of the worst

178

nights in history, way below zero, with blizzards, so in comparison to Bowling Green the night on Manhattan Island wasn't so awful. It was bad enough, though, particularly in city clothes and no hat.

"I love New York," Scott enthused. "It's so alive, so exciting."

He had a hard time reining himself back to walking speed. Sheer kinetic enthusiasm would get hold of Scott and he'd trot a half block ahead of his companions and then wait for us to catch up. Or he'd turn and trot back. His spontaneous happy running was a peculiar half stride, up on the balls of his feet. It was fake running, like a dancer's, but Scott went fast. Sometimes his feet pattered out a facsimile of a line of skating footwork, and he went skittering ahead of us that way. The running and footwork might have been because of the cold, but it wasn't. Scott did the same thing, regardless of weather, whenever the high spirits of a night on the town got the best of him. There was no temptation to succumb to the same giddiness and run alongside Scott. The person jogging next to Scott felt absurd, a water buffalo capering with a gazelle. Ridiculous.

So Scott's ecstatic feet took him, all by himself, into a setup that looked like a scene in the movie version of a musical about Scott Hamilton. He danced through Times Square. Since nobody was on the sidewalk and the murderous wind bleared the vision, the illusion was that Scott was performing on a big sound stage set up to look like Times Square. Frank Sinatra really should have been singing while Scott hoofed.

The illusion faded when Scott ended the scene with a peremptor left turn that took him off the sidewalk and into a huge video-game arcade. The place was cacophonous and filthy, with unwholesome neon light falling on unwholesome characters feeding quarters, no doubt unwholesomely gained, to the latest video games. Scott was delighted. He put his quarters for the first time into now classic games such as Tempest and Missile Command, and played with a connoisseur's appreciation. The high scores on games already known to Scott were very impressive, he said.

Obviously the world's better quarter feeders haunted that place. Scott played, Don looked over his shoulder and gave him quarters, and the two of them shared the giddy release of a night nowhere near a skating rink and nowhere near the money monsters that haunted Scott's future. They were just Scott and Don, jokin' around and playin' games. Scott's extraordinary aptitude for the games showed in instant mastery. One quarter and he comprehended rules and patterns of play that were mystifying to the video illiterate.

The final virtue of that sleazy arcade was that nobody in there pointed and said, "Oooooo, you're Scott Hamilton!" We were a long way from Sweetheartland.

The idea had been to go out and see a show, so our group committed itself to the horrible cold and steered toward the theaters where all the big musicals were playing. The obvious choice was *The Best Little Whorehouse in Texas.* And there we were, in twenty-five dollar seats. On the way in, at intermission, and on the way out, people tugged and asked him, "Are you Scott Hamilton?" Pardon us, they'd say, but we just had to ask. Women did the asking, and they were polite about it, even pleasant. Scott didn't seem to mind saying that yes, he was indeed Scott Hamilton.

The wake-up call obliterated sleep on what you could tell, even burrowed into blankets on a rollaway in the Statler Hotel in Scott's room, was a Siberian morning. Scott talked to the phone. Then he sighed, stood up in the blue-gray gloom, and walked to the bathroom. The door shut. Water ran.

The call, from Don next door, had awakened Scott early in his fifth hour of sleep. But Scott had failed to do what most of us would have done just then. He didn't make himself cozy for a last baby-delicious snooze. He didn't moan and ask the universe why he couldn't stay in bed. He performed not one of the theatrics that say becoming conscious is awful, and that sleep, the stepchild of death, is sooo much nicer than wakeful life. No, Scott awoke and got up as if he had no particular attachment to bed and sleeping, and no particular terror of what the next day would bring.

Watching Scott rouse himself in the Statler Hotel was then, and remains, one of the most striking experiences in all those days on the 1982 World Championship trail. The instantaneous acceptance of being awake, the matter-of-fact standing up, seems to hold many, if not all, of the secrets of Scott Hamilton's World Championship and his fabulous, exemplary pace of living. Maybe having been so close to death cured him of the infantile, womb-regressive, death-loving adoration of oblivion that so many of us act out at the beginnings of our days. Study is needed. There is no doubt in my mind that the way Scott Hamilton got out of bed has a great deal to do with his extraordinary skating and everything else about him that is extraordinary.

The cab rolled through yellow-blue monochrome dawn toward Sky Rink, an oblong of ice high in a homely skyscraper on Thirty-third Street. We got in an elevator that should have been taking us up to office suites. The doors opened and we were in a rink with meat-locker air and warehouse light, just like hundreds of places across our land where kids make dawn sacrifices to the Ice Gods. Nobody made much fuss over Scott. It could have been that the hour was too ungodly for Scott madness, or maybe the Manhattan princes and princesses were too sophisticated. So Scott had comfortable privacy for a very so-so hour of freeskating. Not awful, but not good.

The day's real business was at hand. Scott had to do voiceover commentary for a CBS presentation of Superskates, an exhibition held in Madison Square Garden back in November, which the network had taped for showing on Super Bowl Sunday. The place for doing the voice-over was an independent studio that was doing the tape editing and sound for the Superskates video.

A taxi took us across the city and up a sidestreet to a small

181

anonymous building. Absolutely any sort of business could have been carried on behind its blank facade. Even inside it wasn't too apparent what went on. The sound studio where Scott had to say things for the CBS audience could have been a showroom for the best audio and video equipment, or a playroom for some billionaire's electronic toys. It was carpeted, everything in deep tones, with an ambiance much more intimate than institutional. The opulent hominess of the place was furthered by the arrival of a tray of fabulous sweet rolls and coffee. The Danish materialized at the perfect moment for a sociable light knosh, just after Scott had been introduced to the producer, a few other studio employees, and Jack Whitaker, a longtime network sportscaster who was then newly arrived at CBS. Whitaker and Scott were going to add their voices to the Superskates tape, which had already been edited into a television-ready form—close-ups, long shots, dissolves, and views from different angles, all segueing in a satisfying moving picture, which the studio guys showed us on a big projection-screen television. Then it was time to get down to business. Scott and Jack Whitaker went into a small sound-proof room with a color video monitor, and the producer worked his control board.

Jack Whitaker was on the screen in a tuxedo, welcoming us to Superskates at Madison Square Garden. Here with him, he was saying, was Scott Hamilton, who was standing next to Jack at the Garden, also in black tie. That was all the appearing and announcing those two did at Superskates, but studio magic was going to make it seem as if they went up to a booth somewhere and talked all the way through, with Whitaker introducing skaters and Scott giving insider's color comments and talking back and forth with the sportscaster.

The producer started rolling the tape, the sportscaster got going, and Scott tried to think of things to say. Voice-over didn't seem to come naturally to Scott, so the producer had to stop the tape, rewind, and get Scott to make the right sorts of remarks in the right places. The studio electronics laid the voices over live skating music and audience sounds from Superskates, giving a perfect illusion that Scott and the sportscaster were there, in person, watching everything happen and giving us their immediate thoughts. The illusion preserved itself even when Scott's remarks were pieced together in three or four run-throughs. Sometimes he made good remarks, but left too much dead air, so the producer would rewind and tell him to add a comment at such-and-such a place. The replay would sound absolutely natural, even though Scott never made utterances in the order in which they played back.

Everybody started out that morning with high hopes and enthusiasm, probably born out of Scott's great performances in off-the-cuff interviews after his competitive performances. More than most skaters, he managed to sound fresh, intelligent, and often witty when somebody stuck a microphone in front of his face at rinkside. Ice athletes, athletes in general for that matter, usually don't come off well in interviews, but Scott was very good at coming off. The problem that Tuesday morning was to get him into the same loose mode as his improvisations for the camera at competitions. Scott was clearly nervous. His facility for quipping broke down. His voice was shallow and unnaturally high. He sounded like a jock trying to say something when he could think of nothing to say.

Don and I had to go. He'll loosen up, we were telling each other in still another taxicab. He'll get the hang of it. No problem.

After lunch we were back in the studio. The scene belied our foolish optimism. Scott wasn't just nervous anymore; he was angry, damned mad, on top of being nervous. And the studio people were nervous and worn from trying to foster a little spontaneity and fun in the sullen skater sitting next to Jack Whitaker in the sound booth. Everybody was sick of everybody. But in spite of the phenomenally bad vibrations, the finished product didn't sound that bad. It was acceptable.

The last piece of the tape didn't have Scott in it, because he was skating and the illusion of the tape said he couldn't skate on the screen and talk at the same time. No, he'd gone downstairs from the imaginary broadcast booth some minutes earlier.

So Scott skated on the gigantic projection-screen television, to "New York, New York," in front of thousands of berserk New Yorkers, one of his glossiest performances ever.

Scott's failure to come across while sitting in a booth watching a television monitor didn't matter then, anyway. Everybody, even the annoyed producer, was transfixed by the guy on the screen skating to Frank Sinatra's song about New York. Nobody with skates on his feet could do what he was doing.

Jack Whitaker's voice on the tape said what everybody was thinking just then: "The incomparable Scott Hamilton."

# 18

# Scott Agonistes

A late-afternoon nap can make a quiet cavern in the day. A half hour's sleep kills whatever happened before the sleep and leaves the just-awakened with—nothing. This momentary blankness can be shaken off and the action of the interrupted day picked up again. But always there is a hole. Five o'clock found Scott supine on his bed in room 639 of the Statler Hotel, entirely awake but lingering at the edge of his sleep, staring into the hole. The room wasn't cold, but the cold of another Arctic night was pushing in. The closed curtains dimmed and became another black wall. Tuesday was ending quietly, but the stillness wasn't as peaceful as it was empty. The things that kept us warm and lighted seemed flimsy and unreliable, as if the Statler were a tent, and the bed lamp a burning rag in oil, and any accident could leave us frozen in the night.

Coming back from short slumber as night falls can bring the waker terrible insight. The mind at such moments is unmerciful. At five o'clock, Scott was caught in just such a clear, merciless moment. We spent the forty minutes before my flight back home talking. The stillness and sense of peril wasn't broken in this talk. Scott flipped on the tape recorder and spoke without once using the voice of the giggling, endearing, self-consciously appealing kid:

Recorder, I'm tired.

*The recorder wants to know why you're tired.*

Because I sat with those stupid little earphones on all day. And tried to do something wonderful. Something instrumental for my career.

*Which career?*

Professional, after I'm done. See, maybe if I had a good commentary thing, maybe I'll have a job after I turn pro. . . . (Muses.) Why am I disgusted with myself? Am I disgusted with myself? Yes. Because I've been doing too many other things besides skating. You see, skating is my life. (Breaks up laughing.)

*What's the joke?*

It's a joke among skaters. Some kids during interviews say, "Skating is my life." (Scott thinks again, becomes serious, sighs.) I guess I'm disgusted because last year and the year before and the year before I spent more time just trying to work to be good and to succeed and now that I've succeeded I'm kind of resting on my laurels and not improving. I'm spending more time being the World Champion than being the best skater. How's that? Heavy? Heavy duty. I've betrayed my direction. . . .

*What will you do about it?*

I'll bust my frigging rear end.

*Think in ten days you can pull it off?*

Well, I don't know. I've never had to do it like that before. So I don't know if I can do it or not. I probably can. But I'm worried. I want to go to Nationals and feel like I did last year. Mean and lean and skatin' machine.

*You don't feel that way now?*

I feel tired and burned out, like I can't jump because my legs aren't strong enough, like I can't land because my back and upper body aren't strong enough. I went out tonight and did my program, and I'll be doggone if I didn't feel sloppy through the whole thing. Last year I felt like the program was easy. One unit. Boom, I started it and I ended it. I'd get a little tired at the end, big deal. But I'd hit everything pretty much every time. Now, I go in with every jump thinking, "Oh my God, how am I going to do this?"

*Mad at Don about all this?*

It really isn't his fault.

*He seems to be encouraging you to get into things like the commentary.*

Yeah, he just wants to make sure that I have something after I turn pro. (Thinks for a minute.) Maybe it would be better if I just turned the whole thing over to him and said, "Don't talk to me about it." Huh? The most important thing is to be the best skater for now.

*Did you two talk about that this afternoon?*

No, at CBS I told him about the offer for me to do the commentary at Europeans, and he blew up! He said I should be worried about other things. And it seemed like a double standard. Like I should be worried about this when he wants me to, but, you know . . . And I was upset enough to begin with because I didn't think I was doing a very good job on the commentary. And everybody was fussing and fuming and getting into it, and I just really didn't feel like going through all that just then.

*You weren't flattered by all the attention in the studio?*

That wasn't attention. It was a professional whatever. I mean Jack Whitaker's a professional. He makes a living out of working with people who have no idea what they're doing. And I'm one of those people. He's trained. He's gone through broadcasting. He's done everything. I've never had to do that much talking and make sense unless it was an interview. Those I can do. I know more about me than I do about anything else. So, I guess I was a little nervous and uptight about talking today. (He pauses.) You know, the first thing everybody does when there's a commentator or something on television is to cut him to shreds. I don't like being put in the arena of being criticized except in skating. I can handle that.

*So why did you agree to do this?*

Well, they called me about it last September or October. And I said, listen, I'm going to talk to Don about it at Skate America and I'll let you know after. And I was scared. Even then I thought, "Uh-oh, this could be trouble." But it was such a good opportunity.

*Are you sorry you did it?*

Not sorry I did it, no, but I wish I would have been more prepared. You know, learn about it, go to class. I was nervous. If I don't ever do it again, I'm not going to be worried about it. Maybe I'm not following in the tradition of the great superjocks of this century. The Kurt Thomases. I don't care about television. I just want to go out and have a good triple Lutz. I just want to know that I skated the best performance possible.

*Was lunch at the Park Lane pleasant for you?*

No, I was very uncomfortable. . . . They're talking money. Money's fine and good to think about. But it'll probably never happen. You know, if it does, it's wonderful. But why talk about it if it's not for two years? Why are these people telling me how to make millions of dollars when tomorrow it could all collapse in my face? I'd rather not hear it.

*What do you need?*

Self-satisfaction.

*Where is it now?*

I left it scattered among the last seventy-five shows I've done. It's like somebody handing you a million dollars and you spend it.

*More shows after Nationals?*

Yeah. Day after, exhibition. Day after that, city exhibition, and the day after that another city exhibition. The third day I go back to Denver. Then I go to New Haven for a dinner. On the thirteenth I do a show in La Jolla. I just might make that one hard on me. I might do my long program there. That might be fun. On the fifteenth I go to the Sullivan Award banquet. The eighteenth I go to Europe. In Europe that'll give me two and a half weeks.

*Why do you do all this stuff?*

I don't know. I guess because I have the opportunity to do it. (Shift of mood. Upheaving lower lip and a rising out of the sad collapse.) I've still got it. Now it's coming down to delivering the goods.

*Nationals. Do you feel these guys Santee and Wagenhoffer breathing down your neck?*

David's not skating well from what I hear. Maybe the pressure's cracked him. Wagenhoffer I hear is injured, but in my opinion I don't think he works hard anyway. He's just twice as talented as everybody else. . . . It's fifty-fifty whether I'll come out of it with my short.

*You give yourself fifty-fifty to win?*

No, I give myself seventy-five/twenty-five to win. Fifty-fifty to come out with a decent performance. You see, David's gonna have to *beat* me to get the title. Wagenhoffer's gonna have to skate better than his best to get that title. I have to skate without making too many mistakes.

*You feel like you don't deserve to win?*

Yeah. But I don't know who does. It's not like anybody else deserves to win, either. When you're coming down to righteousness, who deserves to win?

*The best skater. You still the best?*

I think so. I think I'll be ready for Worlds. I *know* I'll be ready for Worlds.

*That's your mindset now?*

(The conversation wanders back to the starting point, Scott's frustration.) Well, I'm just ticked. I'm ticked as hell because I made a commitment to myself and skating and to other people. If I were in second, or third, or fourth place, and the guy who was in first place was out there playing Joe Hollywood, doing diddly-squat as far as training, getting by by being mediocre, I think I'd be pretty ticked off. I went through that myself when I was coming up, so I'm angry as hell at myself. For being such a goddamn idiot. Such a self-important egomaniac. The fact that

189

I'm doing all this other stuff. I don't need this. It may be a good career move, but big deal. I've let more people screw me around.

*Who?*

Anybody who has anything to do with me making career moves. You know, back when we supposedly had an agent, that other guy, I was never so happy. I thought we'd finally got rid of this and I'd never have to worry about it anymore. You know, I thought I'll get to hear about this stuff from somebody who knows what he's talking about. I've got somebody working on it. Fine, I'll have my money in the bank when I turn pro. And then Don gives me this "Don't make any commitments to anybody because you don't know who you're dealing with." I thought we were going to go with that guy, for sure. We pretty much gave him a verbal agreement. Then Don says we're not going with anybody. You've got to give to get, right? You've got to take chances. . . . (Phone rings. Scott talks about supper arrangements, then hangs up, puts the heel of his hand against his mouth, and makes a ripping flatulent sound.) That was Don. We're going downstairs for sandwiches. Do they have salads downstairs?

*What else do we need to know?*

I think this anger will be the best thing in the world for me now.

*Angry with anyone besides yourself?*

I'll confide. All right. I'm a little disappointed in Don. I thought he had the same beliefs I had. The best skater always wins. The best skater is always the one who trains hardest. This year we've been worrying about business more than we have about skating. I can really see that now. I did something every month and that can drive you crazy. And it did. I wasn't ready for one competition yet this year. Easterns was the closest I've been to being ready for a competition. . . . (Reconsidering.) I don't know. I think Don is excited about the whole thing.

*Maybe he's out of his depth, too.*

I'd really like to put it all in somebody's hands. Wouldn't that be nice? You know, I'd like to get something on paper and worry about the skating. . . .

*You're going up for sale. They're going to start marketing you one of these days.*

I'm not the first. I won't be the last. I'm in the limelight now. It's going to fade soon, I realize that. The only thing we're doing —this is the distracting part—is adding a couple extra volts to the limelight.

*What about the rest of your people? Mrs. Camp—are you mad at her?*

Not really . . . well, she means well. Everybody means well. She's being extraordinarily nice and so is Mrs. O'Laurel and so is my father. It's just now I think a lot of people are more concerned about the win. When I got to Philadelphia back in 1979, everybody was concerned about skating. "Let's skate! Let's be good, let's be happy! Let's show everybody it can be done!" Now, it's "Let's write down the marks. Let's compare. Let's see who's going with whom. Why didn't you win this judge?" I don't think it matters how I win anymore as long as I do. We're getting away from the pure and getting into business. It doesn't matter how you win as long as you have the title.

*Closing thoughts.*

You know, this is really going to sound corny and stupid, but I really relate to *The Rose*. Did you see that movie? It's about a self-destructive rock star. She burns herself and she burns herself out. She keeps on going just because she's supposed to. And at the end she's so screwed up about whether she wants to get out, give it up for something she really cares for, go her own direction. Her manager just keeps pushing, pushing. It's not Don so much that's pushing—it's the atmosphere. The Rose finally overdoes it in the end and dies in the middle of a concert. I told Don about needing a year off. I need a month off, anyway, and I need to gradually get back into it. So I'm not sick of it. So I'm hungry for it.

191

*You're not hungry?*

Not now . . . Next year I plan on having the best year I've ever had. I've already turned myself into a roadie next year, but there's one thing I'm going to do, and you can take this to the bank. Next year I'm going to disappear for three weeks, and nobody's going to know where I am. I might even try to grow a mustache. I'm not even going to see ice. I'm going to see sun and fun and for three weeks I'm not even going to go to an ice arena. I'm going to stay with friends. I'd like to do like the Russians, take twenty-eight days at the Black Sea, come back in August, September, get ready for the next season. You know they're going to be ready.

*This is really a turning point for you, today?*

Yeah, it hit me more today, but I've kind of realized it for a while. Underlying realizations. I'll tell you one thing. I won't win Olympics if I keep going on the way I am now. I want to be so good that nobody can deny me anything but straight sixes.

*Maybe you'll be that good.*

But I don't know how. I know I want to and I have the desire and I know I have the gift to do anything I want to in skating.

# Indianapolis, Indiana

*January 25–31, 1982*

1982 United States Figure
Skating Championships

# 19

# Indianapolis

On the morning of Monday, January 25, 1982, three inches of snow had fallen—the first of many inches that would fall on the capital of the Hoosier State during the 1982 United States Figure Skating Championships. The snow imparted prettiness to the walk from the Essex Hotel, where I was staying, to the Hyatt Regency in Indianapolis, temporary home of Scott Hamilton and the temporary location of Sweetheartland.

The Mudlands at the latitude of Indianapolis usually have relatively gentle winters. But in merciless 1982 Indianapolis was the recipient of weather that should have gone to Duluth or Sault Ste. Marie. The mental video from Nationals shows a week of continuous blizzard, seven days and nights not fit for man or beast. But this is mnemonic overstatement. It didn't really snow all the time. It did, however, fail to get warm enough between storms to cut down the feet of snow that piled up. By the time Nationals ended, the scene was like one of those apocalypse books where the New Ice Age comes and destroys civilization as we know it.

The Hyatt Regency was a gigantic brick box that was as new and snappy-looking as many of downtown Indianapolis' other buildings were old and sad. Cars pulled up, and doormen took away the cars and parked them for people who got out of the cars and went inside. Following them through the glass doors you entered a world as much like the lonely snowy streets as Palm

Springs is like East Berlin. The place had its own sky, a shaft of summer air soaring up above the lobby. It had its own climate. Tropical trees and plants displayed fat green leaves, and unfrozen water trickled. We were a long way from Indianapolis in January.

But the hotel's smartness was merely an enhancement of the far more potent stimulation of be-all-and-end-all Sweetheartland. At eight in the morning on the day before Novice ladies' and Novice men's figures and Junior men's figures—Scott wasn't going to compete until his figures Thursday morning—the Hyatt lobby had already reached excitement levels approaching readings taken at the Eastern Sectionals on the final nights of competition. The moms and teenage royalty and ice professionals were up and cooking, moving through the hotel's core to a side entrance where buses waited to take the skaters to their practice rinks. Scott had to go to the Fairgrounds Coliseum, about six miles northeast of the Hyatt, for figures. So, if I kept lookout, I'd see Scott going to the bus, which would be a great place for quick questions and answers, a light breakfast for the tape recorder.

Princes and princesses went by, queen mothers, ice major-domos and functionaries, coaches, judges, everybody went by. Everybody but Scott. The procession quit coming, the buses were going to go any minute. But then there he was, moving from left to right across the narrow field of vision. Blue jeans, running shoes, a short red jacket, a type given by some company to top U.S. skaters, so you saw a lot of them at Nationals. He walked with a slight lean to counterbalance his lumpy skate bag, like a mailman with his satchel, but mailmen don't walk that quickly. And no mailman would wear that expression of bottomless, black, all-encompassing fury, unless the mailman's wife had just left him for someone else, on the day he got a layoff notice, after a terrier had bit him, while it was sleeting. Scott's gnome face was set in cold anger, his jaw jutting and his lower lip swelling. He looked neither to the left nor right. Even that brief view of Scott was unnerving. His ability to project his moods, the way opera singers project their voices, sent a wave of freezing wrath through the Hyatt lobby. All impulses to call to him vanished. Scott's "Leave me alone!" lights were flashing, no doubt about it. The best idea at that moment was to skip that bus to the coliseum and spend another half hour with coffee in a cardboard cup.

But then after patch Scott came charging out of the coliseum, still mad as hell. Barbara Camp was with him, obviously trying to soothe him, or to keep him out of trouble if he couldn't be soothed.

Bam! He hit a door as if the idea were to knock it down, not open it. "I'm finally going to bitch!" Scott snarled.

"Don't do it," Barb said.

This went back and forth, Scott saying he was going to go to somebody and complain about something and Barb telling him not to do it, that he'd just be making trouble for himself. Barb finally offered to go to Don about whatever it was. It would be better, she said, if Don tried to do something and Scott stayed out of the picture. But Scott kept reiterating that he had absolutely had it, that the time had come for him to open his mouth. He wasn't going to take it anymore.

The problem, it developed, was that Scott had been assigned end ice in figures practice. Senior men practiced figures all at once, with each man getting his thirteenth of the rink and nothing more. Who got which patch of the rink was predetermined by competition officialdom, with each skater's assigned ice changing every day. End ice was bad, Scott explained later, because the Zamboni, the gasoline-powered mastodon that ate old ice and left a sheen of water for new ice, passed over a rink's ends more often than its mid-section. That closing hemisphere at each end of a standard oblong rink meant that the machine was going over and over the same ice. More ice eating and ice watering meant valleys in the surface and puddles in the valleys and bad, bad figures. Monday morning was an absolute waste, Scott said. He had been assigned more end ice on Tuesday, and he was furious. The fury was compounded by the fact that Don, who could have gone on Scott's behalf to the right people to *do* something, had missed that practice.

It wasn't a bad scene. The Champion raved and threatened to do rash things that would bring him harm. His poor worried ice mother counseled against his tragic rage and tried to put out the fires of wrath with mother love. At the time the scene was quite compelling. You wanted to get involved. A few more weeks following Scott Hamilton and months of listening to and studying his utterances to the recorder suggested that Scott wasn't really angry about end ice and Don. The end ice was, of course, a reason for some pique, but the monumental snit that Scott entertained Monday morning was all out of proportion. Barb Camp, for all her melodrama at the coliseum, knew that Scott's fit was part of his inner agenda. "Oh," she said somewhat later, "Scott's about where he should be right now. He always starts competitions on a sour note."

But you would not have wanted to make light of Scott's anger scene while it was being played. No sir. The Champ would have highly resented any suggestion that his bad temper was mostly causeless, transitory, and shallow. The rules of his psychodramas said you had to immerse yourself in the moment and *believe,* and the rules said that the Scott people had to believe as fervently as Scott himself. So it wouldn't have done any good to pooh-pooh Scott's ire in front of Barb, not just then. Irony and lightheartedness were not part of such moments. The thing to do was to keep your mouth shut, put on a respectfully serious face, and listen.

The bus going back to the Hyatt was there. Senior men, coaches, a scattering of mothers and other post-youths who had things to do at Nationals. The doors sighed and squeezed shut and the big thing was skating southward through one of the poorer sides of Indianapolis.

Scott took a seat and gave himself over to silent brooding. A bunch of Senior men in the back benches jabbered about Japan.

Some of those guys were four or five inches taller and much more heavily muscled than Scott, who occupied a size class all his own at Nationals. But the same differences that pertained when Scott skated also applied on the bus. Scott was unmistakably the bull skater, the tough guy, the old man. What, exactly, communicated his Alpha maleness was hard to divine, with only his head and hands showing out of the winter clothes. But the message came through. The kid had weight and strength. There were teeth in this skater. He was dangerous.

The skaters had a way of talking about the distinction between veteran competitors like Scott and guys just coming up, like the guys talking and joking about Japan in the back of the bus. The kids were puppies. The veterans were dogs. Skating puppyhood went back to a *Time* magazine article about 1980 Nationals, when Scott had regained a position in the top three after his year of agony, 1979. *Time* said Scott skated like an exuberant puppy, an excellent expression, really, for how he skated back then.

Scott's words: "So I started this thing where people who are first-year Seniors and are really hungry and like to compete are called puppies. They really enjoy competition. Where people who have been in it for a while don't enjoy competition—they're dogs. The puppies think of us as dogs. We think of them as puppies. A puppy has to do twice as much in a program to win as a dog does, because dogs were there first."

Puppyhood and doghood were prevalent subjects for jokin' around at 1982 Nationals. One puppy who trained at the Broadmor in Colorado Springs had a "Puppy Power '82" T-shirt made. So the older guys bought "Cycle-4 Training Team" T-shirts, after the name of a dog food specially formulated for old dogs. More guys got puppy shirts, and the puppy who started the shirt business sent a dog shirt to Scott.

The puppy and dog business had to do with standing and experience in Senior-level competition, and the concomitant attitudes toward skating. But it also said a great deal about what distinguished Scott from the jocular group talking about Japan on the bus. They might be bigger, heavier, stronger, and better-looking than the Champ, but their deportment had a certain feckless, goofy good cheer that was adolescent and, yes, puppyish. You'd think of a litter of six-month-old Irish setters clowning around and in their midst a prime bull terrier, scarred and fight-wise from the pits. No question who would defer to whom, and who could bite harder.

Scott maintained his gloomy self-absorption. The pups enjoyed each other's company. Mrs. Camp and the mother of the previous year's Junior National Champion warmed the same seat. Both women had passed figures practice doing needlepoint.

There was something about the way the budding Senior men carried on, strikingly different from a bunch of, say, twenty and twenty-one-year-old college football players riding a bus together. They were, after all, highly trained athletes, as tough and nervy and disdainful of pain and injury as any other college-age athletes. They had worked and hurt and honed killer competitiveness for years. If each didn't have a big dose of the right stuff, he wouldn't have gotten to Nationals-level competition. You might have expected some sort of gruff, macho wisecracking and horseplay in such company, the kind you would get on a college team bus. But these ice jocks failed to act jockish. Something supercilious and sweet came through in those voices, a sort of girlish restraint.

This isn't to say we were riding with a busload of sissies. Not at all. The absence of sweat-sock machismo and four-letter words spoken with a lot of hoarse testosterone had nothing to do with whether or not these guys were gutsy and male. They were, absolutely. And it had everything to do with Sweetheartland. Your mom and the place-kicker's mom don't ride on the team bus at the Cotton Bowl. And you cannot moon people on the sidewalk and break wind when somebody's mom is on the bus. You can't, for that matter, act like a guy who would do those sorts of things if Mom wasn't around. These skaters had been training and competing in close proximity to their own mothers and everybody else's mothers for a decade and more. They had, consequently, been thoroughly conditioned to act the way mothers want their boys to act. Their public personas could be too, too nice—sometimes disquietingly cute and clean for young men. The poor skaters had to hole up in hotel rooms and otherwise hide from Sweethearthood and the eyes and ears of Mother before they could let the old testicular savagery rip.

This is the Oedipal sport, a woman's sport much more than a man's sport, and Sweetheartland was a woman's world. By necessity the men in Sweetheartland were somewhat womanized— they had to be womanized to survive. Scott Hamilton got away with more overtly virile coarseness than the others. The reason seemed to be that he was small and therefore, in the eyes of the Great Skating Mother, cute. And Scott, when circumstances dictated, had an amazing knack for becoming just the right happy and nice little guy. Awww, they could coo then, isn't he something!

So in the areas of dominating gender and gender-identity, skating really is different from other sports. This, perhaps, is why our ostentatiously he-man sports press so far has failed to embrace figure skating as a "real" sport. And, if skating is popularized and masculinized, Scott Hamilton will be largely responsible for the change. One of the Champ's dreams was to make United States sports fandom look at him the same way it looks at a world-winning boxer or gymnast.

A few more words on this delicate subject of skating and men and women, boys and girls: the light conversational style of the guys talking about Japan was conditioned by forces much more complex than the ever-presence of mothers. In a profound way, skating *belongs* to mothers. The matriarchal character of the sport is acknowledged in the often-used designation Skating Mother. The caricature Skating Mother is a pushy, ambitious, child-destroying beast like a Stage Mother. Never, not once in my weeks with Scott Hamilton, did I hear anyone say anything about Skating Fatherhood. The concept doesn't exist.

The idea of Skating Motherhood points up something about how skaters start skating. Little boys can pick up the basics of baseball or football or basketball without parental involvement. They can play at school. They can play sandlot ball after school. Even if a kid's parents won't pay for getting him into PeeWee League, he can play tons of baseball. It is entirely conceivable that a kid with parents indifferent to sports could grow up to be a great star of the diamond. He could get training and encouragement from high school and college coaches, virtually for free, all on his own. But there is absolutely no casual, cost-free route to figure skating proficiency. The decisions to start spending big dollars on training could never be made by the eight- or nine-year-old with fuzzy ideas about being in the Olympics or the "Ice Capades." A child at the age where children start to skate is equally unable to commit himself to a quest as long and painful and demanding as the journey to Sweetheartland. No, somebody else has to dream the big dream, has to spend money for ice time and coaching and costumes and travel, and has to keep the kid working. Mom. A kid without a Skating Mother, no matter how gifted and how fervent his skating dream, won't make it. If a skater does make it, his triumph in large part will be owed to what Mom did for his skating when he was a kid.

There are a few Skating Fathers, who perform about the same functions as the SMs, but the role is somehow awkward to a man. Most fathers I encountered in the 1982 season were insubstantial, almost ghostly visitors. They generally were late arrivals at competitions, the work week keeping them at home until Friday. Sweetheartland is not a natural setting for dads. The vibrations are all wrong. The dreams dreamed in Sweetheartland are not a guy's sort of dreams, unless, of course, the guy's mother did some timely gardening in his brain so the Sweetheart Dream would flourish.

Cause and effect: why, and how, figure skating in America became the province of women. Perhaps Sonja Henie. Or the fact that the American stars of the last two decades have been women. Peggy Fleming. Janet Lynn. Dorothy Hamill. Linda Fratianne. Dick Button, of course, popularized figure skating while he skated, and afterward, when he became the voice, and face, of the sport on television. Without him skating wouldn't be what it is today. But it became what it is mostly for women stars. And if the sexes ever divide figure skating glory fifty-fifty—if dads are going to brag about sons growing up to be great spinners and jumpers—the new alignment will be owed to Scott Scovell Hamilton.

So it was Mom who made those guys talk the way they talked, skating's Omni-Mom, omnipotent, omnipresent. Mom on the bus. Mom when you were eight. Everybody else's Mom. Mom forever.

Then we were there. Scott went upstairs to get rid of his stuff and came down to the Porch, the Hyatt's coffee shop. We were in the giddy honeymoon period with the food. The sandwiches cost a lot, but they seemed to be worth it because they were so uniquely good. This, of course, was a temporary effect of the hotel's fiendish brain warfare. Everything in a place like that would seem fabulous and worth the money the first few times around.

The sandwiches, uniquely good as they were, failed to cheer up Scott's lunch with Barb Camp and me. He ate half of a gorgeous turkey club as if the white meat and bacon and great veggies turned to ashes on the tongue. He then regarded the remaining half of the sandwich, which still looked very good, as if he'd found bugs in the half he ate.

Scott said he felt like a fool. He said he felt like he was really being dumped on.

Barb said he probably had some reason to be annoyed. Don

should have been at practice. She again offered to talk to the coach, on Scott's behalf.

The sullen lunch ended quickly.

"I'm going to prowl in the lobby and brood," Scott said. "I've got to cool down before practice."

Coach Don Laws demonstrates a turning fine point during a figures practice before competition. *(photo courtesy Laura L. Keesling)*

cott runs through e figure. *(photo urtesy Laura L. eesling)*

oach and skater dge the results. *hoto courtesy Laura . Keesling)*

*(Above):* Washington, D.C.,
December 1981. Scott and Don
Laws, right, headed for a lunch
break. *(photo courtesy Laura L.
Keesling)*

*(Right):* Washington, D.C.,
1981. *(photo courtesy Laura L.
Keesling)*

*(Above):* Scott in an exhibition program.
*(photo courtesy David Leonardi)*

*(Right):* Scott Hamilton skating to "New York, New York" in an exhibition program at Havertown, Pennsylvania, 1981. *(photo courtesy Laura L. Keesling)*

*(Left):* Scott in the Landis backyard, Denver, Colorado, 1982. *(photo courtesy Laura [ Keesling)*

*(Below):* Bournemouth, England, July 1982. Scott in Stars and Stripes exhibition costume designed for the Olympic year. *(photo courtesy Donald E. Laws)*

# 20

# New Person: Ricky

A scene from *Alice In Wonderland* here, played backward:
When the Cheshire Cat vanished, he started disappearing at the
tail, and then everything else went. The grin lingered. With
Ricky Harris, Scott's choreographer from Los Angeles, you started
with a grin and no woman. The overpoweringly wide smile lingered alone for some minutes, saying it was glad to meet you, it
had heard so much about you. Then the woman faded in, a
woman as ostentatiously womanly as the smile was wide. Ricky
Harris was indisputably the best-dressed female in all of Sweetheartland, an absolute cumulonimbus of fur, from neck to floor.
The storm cloud of fur flashed lightning from the load of gems
on her fingers. The whole arrangement moved with the speed and
force of squalls storming over the summer Mudlands. And there
you were, caught out in the weather, immobilized by Nature's
grandest display of teeth, state-of-the-art coiffure, pelt sewing,
haute couture, gemology, and the salubrious effect of hard exercise on a middle-age woman's rear end and legs. Good heavens.

If the visuals weren't enough to knock you down, there was this
woman's astounding level of bubbly, vivacious energy. She didn't
just meet you, she scooped you up, stunned you first, and then
kidnapped and hauled you off to wherever she was going just then,
which was going to be fabulous good fun but even more delicious
because you could go along, too. Her voice came out raspy con-
tralto, somewhat overmodulated, and full of enthusiasm almost

childish in its giddy intensity. Ricky was always carried away with something.

The first response was incredulity. Nobody could be that bubbly. Come off it, I wanted to say. But the idea that Ricky was a sham vanished within an hour. This really was one of those people that newspaper features call "human dynamos." Nobody could spend time with Ricky and not be won over. The only person encountered in 1982 who had something less than sensational to say about Ricky was her son, a drop-in visitor in Germany and Denmark. He allowed that it had sometimes been a trial to have a mother who sparkled as brightly as Ricky sparkled. But then familiality breeds a certain skepticism, and no son sees his mother in the same light in which the world sees her.

Ricky's celebrity in Sweetheartland had been shot up by the 1980 publication of her *Choreography and Style for Ice Skaters*, a definitive text, the first to explain a system for designing competitive programs, and an explication of Ricky's own system of expressive body shape and movement for skaters. The tone of the book is thoroughly gung ho, and it ends with a chapter about what makes a great skater.

"Champions are not average people," the book says. "They are superhuman beings. In addition to conscious and subconscious minds, they have superconscious minds."

Ricky on discipline: "Successful skaters are tough! By that I do not mean someone who is hard. Hard gives the connotation of being brittle. By tough I mean resilient and recuperative; having the ability to bounce back when the average skater has given up. . . . It is more profitable to use time and energy toward a particular end so that time and energy become the means. You will benefit from this type of discipline if you are prepared to accept it."

Strong medicine. And Ricky took her own medicine every day. No matter where she was, she put herself through a regimen of strenuous dancing exercises and then burned her waking hours as brightly as possible, giving complete wide-awake attention and enthusiasm to whatever she was doing. Among other things, she ran her own studio in Los Angeles, for teaching dance principles to skaters, and she took her act on the road, giving week-long workshops at rinks across the U.S. Only once in the author's acquaintance with Ricky did she slow down. Pneumonia flattened her for a little while, but as soon as the disease loosened its grip on her, Ricky was up and sprinting again.

Scott's first encounter with Ricky took place in the summer of 1979, at the Squaw Valley Olympic Training Center. Don, who had been coaching Scott for just a few months then, wanted his skater to learn what Ricky taught, so he brought them together. "We went to a little room, away from everybody," Ricky recalled. But the Champ, Ricky told the tape recorder, was not receptive to her ideas about energy balls, showing feeling, and expressing dynamic articulations with the music. "He was embarrassed and intimidated, doing things that to him seemed really weird."

Ricky went to Denver. Choreographer and skater still failed to hit it off, a failure that persisted for the next several sessions in which Scott was supposed to be getting new bodily ideas, to extend and polish his artistic expression. Ricky told Don that it might be better if Scott worked with another choreographer. Maybe the chemistry would be better. But Don said no, keep trying and it would work out.

Don took Scott to Los Angeles. One day Ricky gave up on a hopeless session of working on steps in her studio. They went to the ice. But being in Scott's element failed to rescue the session. The Champ went around the boards, where nobody could see, and kicked the boards. He was that frustrated.

Scott told somebody that Ricky intimidated him, and Ricky heard, so she took another tack. She communicated obliquely, telling Don what Scott ought to do, and with Don telling Scott. The system worked. "New York, New York," was the result of such communication. Don and Ricky would talk about how a certain section of the program should go, and Ricky would work out how it should go on the floor. Don would watch and then call Scott over and show him. On other occasions Ricky whispered choreographic advice into Don's ear, and Don would tell Scott. The system of using Don as a telephone worked, apparently, because Scott trusted Don implicitly and absolutely, and Scott knew Don would never tell him to do anything that would make him look silly. The fear of silliness seemed to underlie Scott's resistance to Ricky. He hadn't known her long enough to entrust his skating image to her.

The year 1981 was the year of the big thaw between Scott and Ricky. Finally the sessions got easy. The big icebreaker was a collaboration on short program. Said Ricky: "Where Don really wanted me to work was short program. And Scott really knew he needed to work on short program. He finally asked me to work with him on short program. I said okay. And I was very careful how I worked with him. All of a sudden everything clicked. I'd tell him what I thought something should be, and he'd do it, and I'd say yes, that's just right. We worked. And when I finished the short program, Scott told me he had a program that he really felt was artistic. And he felt good doing it. I really feel that Scott and I have a much closer relationship now, just this past year. He doesn't feel intimidated any longer, and he's more open. He trusts more."

Ricky's contributions to Scott's skating at Nationals were restricted to minor bodily adjustments that made his programs look better—detail work. Indianapolis was far too late to change the substance of short or long program. Her contribution at the long-program practice Tuesday was the suggestion that Scott relax his left hand in the opening pose of long program, where his right arm soared upward, and his left arm went down. Scott did what she said and his hand in the opening pose looked that much better.

Mostly Ricky stood next to Don at practices and spoke her half of a dialogue about Scott's skating that ran continuously. She provided commentary and feedback and seemed to take part of the load off Don without overtly having a great deal to do with Scott and his skating. The running dialogue rather often ran off the tracks of serious skating talk and dumped the two of them, Don and Ricky, into frivolity. At least once a session something would crack them up, and they'd laugh and laugh.

Probably that laughter, not the tidbits about hand position and centering spins and so on, was Ricky's chief contribution to the Scott Hamilton Victory Team. At Nationals, and at Worlds, she wasn't so much a choreographer as she was a psychiatric nurse and social worker for the Scott people. It's hard to picture them getting through all that bad competition craziness without Ricky. Ricky constantly buoyed up the others and kept everybody moving. Her infectious, madly energetic good cheer was put at everyone else's disposal. And, of course, good cheer was sorely needed. It is very easy to picture Scott and Don getting lost in precompetitive dementia, and never coming back. Bad things, for sure, were possible. But they were much less possible with Ricky around. Tall, dark, with short black hair like cat's fur, Cadillac breasts, and Rolls-Royce legs, Ricky Harris was the entourage's emotional buffer. She neutralized the nasty acids that could have pickled them all like herring.

Don and Ricky made quite a couple. Other coaches dressed for the ice simply, but those two went around all moneyed up, with Don in his WASPy country club ensembles and Ricky dressed to kill—dressed, that is, to massacre. They were similarly set off from other ice professionals by their hilarity. They lit up in each other's company like sunlamps. They'd come into a rink arm-in-arm, convulsed with some secret joke. They'd carry their mirth to the rink's bang boards and lean, attached to each other like Siamese twins, watching Scott and talking through the practice except when laughter got the better of them again.

The delightful illusion resulting from this was that Don and

Ricky were frivolous billionaires who owned the rinks in Indianapolis and were paying everybody else to be there. The competition was an elaborate stunt, a very funny one, so funny they couldn't keep straight faces for more than a few minutes. It was all for their amusement, theirs alone, the F. Scott and Zelda of skating.

Ricky held a position of leadership among the Scott people, and her work kept her with Scott, but Ricky was not really a Scott person. Unique among the women in Scott's coterie, she could take Scott Hamilton or leave him. Yes, she liked the Champ. But her affection was not a mythic bond. She did not want to destroy everybody on earth but herself and Scott. She absolutely did not worship him. She was, indeed, annoyed with those who had become so madly overinvolved with Scott Hamilton. She stayed outside all of that. And when she talked to the tape recorder about Scott, the voice spoke from a great distance, detached.

Scott acknowledged Ricky's separateness. But he didn't say anything about it. The acknowledgment came from what he *didn't* say. Scott's intimate hours with the tape recorder at these competitions featured lengthy, overwrought diatribes against various members of his surrogate family. At one time or another he denounced Don, his sponsor, his ice mom, his girlfriend, and his father, for mostly imaginary failings, insults, and betrayals. Conversely, everybody got at least one heartfelt tribute, where Scott spoke about how good that person had been, how generous. In 1982, Ricky got neither damning nor praising. The tape recorder, playing back Scott's voice, barely speaks her name. Ricky seemed to play no part in the Champ's chapter-a-day psychodrama.

This isn't to say that skater and choreographer had not formed personal impressions of each other. Ricky, for one, seemed to have given a lot of thought to Scott's psychology. She had ideas about what made the Champ tick. And she had ideas about what ought to make the Champ tick. The first set of ideas did not equal the second set of ideas. Like everyone else, Ricky measured Scott with her own yardstick, marked off in units of discipline, drive, the will to constantly expand the range and variety of artistic expression, to strive always. And on Ricky's yardstick Scott wasn't as tall as he should have been.

Scott's choreographer seemed enchanted by Scott's physical genius, his body built for skating, and his physical line so clean and forceful that all he needed to do to be beautiful on the ice was to skate. His proportions were perfect. When he jumps, she said, the whole bodily unit goes up and comes down in one seamless piece, nothing lagging behind the jump and nothing ahead of it. Somehow, Ricky said, Scott developed a dancer's total body control and poise without being trained as a dancer. Was Scott's flawlessness just a physical accident? No, Ricky said, the physique was only part of it. Scott's body was a precondition, but the body alone would not have been enough. At the core of Scott's beauty was a steely perfectionism, a resolve to bring every muscle and bone under the control of his mind. And from the mind came the will to weld everything into a perfect machine for skating.

But having said all that, Ricky expressed a general disappointment that Scott hadn't done more with his perfect skating. She said, more or less, that Scott was failing to measure up to his own abilities. Ricky saw Scott, in 1982, as a young man in crisis, caught between a wastrel persona she called, with disdain, "just a kid," and the skating adulthood that would take him to the aesthetic heights he was capable of reaching. Scott was being pulled both ways, she said.

Ricky was a particular enemy of the mother-love faction of the Scott people. Nothing could make her wilder with anger in 1982 than the sight of Barb Camp fussing over Scott. That sort of thing, she averred, threatened to trap Scott in perpetual dependence and kidhood. There were, on the other hand, encouraging signs that Scott was going to make the jump to adulthood, quit screwing around with his genius, and do something of permanent value. Ricky, in 1982, had no prediction as to the outcome of Scott's crisis. That was still a question.

Ricky: Where are you going, Scott Hamilton? What are you going to do to improve yourself in life?

And this cryptic observation: Scott, I think, has to learn to look at the world with quiet eyes. If he could learn to do that, it would be helpful to him.

How, I asked, would he learn quiet looking?

Ricky: By thinking. I don't think Scott takes the time to really sit down and think.

Of course a woman looking into Scott's mind and saying what he needed and what was bad for him sounded a great deal like one of his inner corps of Hamiltonites; but Ricky maintained a coolness, a detachment, simultaneously liking Scott and giving herself over to her work with him, but resisting all those twisted black alleys of Scott involvement. She stayed in the open, far more immune than any of the rest of us to the neurotic Scott-mania.

So there was Ricky, diamonds and furs and teeth, huddled with Don at the boards for Scott's afternoon freeskating session, the hour for short program. Don was saying something that had her howling. And Don kept it going.

The joke turned out to be that Don was telling Ricky what Scott was going to do, in advance of Scott's doing it, and Scott, who was lapping the rink and then warming up pieces of his short program, did everything Don said.

"Okay," the coach said. "He's going to come around and say something."

The Champ on his next pass did make a slow swoop at conversation distance from Don and offer an indistinct wisecrack. He did another piece of his program.

"Now he's going to circle around like a shark in front of us, then give us a look, and crack his knuckles."

Actually Scott did a flattened figure eight, a holding pattern going back and forth in front of his coach. Without saying anything he shot a level deadpan look at Don and cracked his knuckles.

Ricky was delighted. "Is there anything you don't know about Scott?" she asked.

Don replied, "Anybody who is that highly trained is a person of habit, with habits he doesn't even know about."

# 21

# Defeat Clouds Gathering

Tuesday, 8:00 A.M. To get from downtown Indianapolis to Carmel, Indiana, you drove north on a street that took you into open countryside, which on Tuesday morning was stark snowy naked under the sun, burning bright even though the temperature was zeroish.

This was the first day of competition at Nationals. Nothing involving Seniors yet. Novice ladies' figures in the morning and Novice and Junior men in the afternoon, all at the coliseum, which had been specially prepared for figures. Figures competition meant that nobody could practice at the coliseum all day, which in turn meant that Senior men's figures practice started at six o'clock that morning. After patch the bus was going to take the men up to Carmel.

That Carmel freeskating session was an absolute must-see because it was going to be the first big showdown between Scott and David Santee, skating's self-styled Rocky, the guy who had fought Scott very hard for the 1981 National Championship. He had almost, pretty close to it, knocked Scott out of first. And he had finished second to Scott at the 1981 Worlds.

The town wasn't big enough for these two skaters. Every practice, now that Santee was in Indiana, would involve tricks to destroy each other's composure. The big psych-out was about to begin, no-holds-barred brain warfare on a slab of ice right there in peaceful little Carmel.

I arrived at the Carmel rink in plenty of time for the freestyle practice. The Senior men and coaches and parents and aunts who were there to watch drank coffee from the rink's snack bar. Scott was feeding quarters to a video game. Everybody's just-removed coats made big woolly mounds on islands of benches in the rink's foyer, which featured a picture window giving a grand view of a very nice skating rink. To the right, doors went into another rink, full-sized, but without windows looking in on it.

Some pacing while waiting for coffee to cool took me through the doors to the windowless rink. A young man was about to jump rope on the concrete to the left of the doors. He was all alone in there, which was probably his goal when he went into the windowless rink. It would have seemed silly to jump rope out in the lobby, where the group was milling and socializing in a way much like a cocktail party and reception, except of course they had no martinis, just coffee. It would have been worse still to jump rope in the other rink, where all those gossips and rumor-spreaders and politickers could watch through the glass and say whatever came to their ill-disposed minds. The one and only place where David Santee could with any dignity jump rope and otherwise prepare himself for freeskating practice was the place he had chosen. Somebody coming through the doorway gave him momentary pause—he was just about to start twirling the rope and jumping —and he looked up, startled and even wounded by the intrusion. Momentarily, rope in hand, David regarded me with the hurt indignation you see when you walk into the wrong room at a hospital, catching some stranger in a pose of pain or immodesty that was not meant to be seen. But this was just a flash. The eyes unmet and the rope and feet started doing their stuff. This guy was an impressively good rope jumper. He meant business.

That was my first close look at David Santee. Tuesday was his second day at Nationals. What we had seen of him Monday in short-program practice, the same practice where Don and Ricky laughed and laughed about Don's knowledge of Scott's ice habits, was not supposed to count. He was punchy from flying into Indianapolis, and tired on top of being addled by jet travel—and his skating reflected it. So the Hamilton camp did not comment extensively on David's inauspicious arrival on the Indiana ice.

So soon the defeat clouds gathered over poor David. In January 1982, the ice gods were designing an ignominious final fall for David, who had risen and fallen so many times, always beginning his fall the moment when permanent skating glory—a National Championship, a World Championship—was just within reach.

It sounds, perhaps, like an abuse of hindsight to foreshadow events with a defeat cloud over a skater's head a week before he was defeated. But the signs appearing in David's vicinity that said his skating dream was in bad trouble were unmistakable, and they were almost universally recognized. The whispering in Sweetheartland, before he got to Indianapolis, chorused a dirge for David's dreams: I hear he's skating badly, the whispers said. Why didn't he get out last year, when the getting would have been so good?

Sweetheartland was not overly kind to this twenty-four-year-old who had made a long, long career of excellent skating and almost, but not quite, winning championships.

Tough stuff, winning and losing. Each trip to competition ice was, ideally, a fresh chance for the best man to win: a new toss of the skating dice. A man only thirteen months older than Scott, and who had challenged Scott a year earlier, might have expected to challenge him again. Anything can happen, they like to say in Sweetheartland. Sometimes anything does happen. But not all anythings can happen. In January 1982, David Santee's anythings were gone. And Scott Hamilton had anythings to burn. He had them by the million. It showed, on and off the ice. There would never be a rematch of the great skating National and World title fights of 1981, which had been classics.

From the beginning at Indianapolis, moral exhaustion could be discerned in the brown-eyed and brown-haired Santee, who was five and a half inches taller than Scott, and about thirty-five pounds heavier. Physically he looked great, his beefy musculature sculpted into manly power. The baby pudge and hippiness of his boy-wonder years on the ice were gone without a trace. But weariness and fear lurked, furtive, in David's features. He fought back with strident messages of confidence and resolve. David seemed to be cheerleading himself, trying to convince a body and will that were hurt and tired to give it one more try. To go for it, as David would have said.

David told the story of his life on the ice about six weeks after he and Scott started firing shots across each other's bows at Carmel. Although he didn't identify it as such, the story he told was mostly the story of how his anythings were spent at the wrong times, and how, just when he needed them most, he never had enough. Comparing David's career to that of Scott Hamilton, you can see why our Champ was rich in promise in 1982, and David was going bankrupt.

David, the elder of two sons of Neil and Rose Mary Santee, started skating when he was five, at the old Michael Kirby ice skating school in his Park Ridge, Illinois. David stayed home and skated locally until 1976, when he moved in with an aunt in Janesville, Wisconsin, and trained there. He didn't move away from the Midwest and his family for the sake of the ice gods until August 1981, when he went to Colorado Springs and began skating under Carlo Fassi.

David was one of Sweetheartland's more mature, articulate speakers, free of nervous giggles and cuteness. He spoke frankly, without rancor, even when he talked about things that in their time had brought him horrid pain.

David had been a skating prodigy. At age thirteen he became the youngest Junior National Champion in history. (Scott won the same championship when he was seventeen.) David was thrust into Senior men's competition when he was fourteen, with few years of sub-Senior maturation. "You know, I was just a little kid," said David. "I was forced to grow up in Senior men."

He grew up quickly. His mastery of school figures took him to third at Nationals the second year he competed as a Senior. That year only two men were on the U.S. World Team, so David was an alternate. Sweetheartland expected big things of its new skating whiz—he was expected to break into second place the following year, and go to Worlds. But David was fifth at Nationals in 1974 and fifth again in 1975.

In 1976, David was again hot, second behind Terry Kubicka at Nationals, sixth at the Olympics in Innsbruck—his first experience with Olympic pressure madness—and fifth at Worlds in Sweden. He was, at age eighteen, in exactly the position in which Scott Hamilton would find himself in the 1980 Olympic year. When the U.S. Champion graduated from amateur competition, David Santee would be the heir apparent to the U.S. title, and in a strong position in subsequent Worlds, with four years to groom himself for the 1980 Olympic medal.

Sweetheartland was betting on David, but Charlie Tickner won, beginning a four-year U.S. Championship reign. At Worlds that year David did what he was supposed to have done at Nationals. He finished ahead of Charlie, in fourth place. In 1978, when Scott for the first time was third at Nationals, David was second. But David skated poorly at Worlds, finishing sixth. David: "The worst long program I've ever skated. I just made a lot of mistakes. I skated last, and I was totally psyched out from the time I got on the ice. The first jump I did, I fell, and it was downhill from there."

Scott's year of agony, 1979, was also a disaster for David. Nationals wasn't too bad—David placed third. But at Worlds he went from third after figures to thirteenth in short and tenth in long program, finishing eighth overall.

David was hitting an all-time morale low in 1978 and 1979. After 1979, there was some question whether he could place high enough at 1980 Nationals to make the U.S. Olympic Team.

During David's great depression, a friend took him to see this movie about a second-rate boxer from Philadelphia who through sheer guts and determination transforms himself into a first-rate boxer who challenges the World Champion. David made his celebrated connection with *Rocky,* identifying himself with Rocky Balboa and skating to the movie's theme music.

In 1980 the Rocky-fied David was up and fighting again. He was second at Nationals. At his second Winter Olympics he came within hundredths of a point of beating Charlie Tickner, who won a bronze medal. David was fourth, Scott fifth in Lake Placid. They held the same places at the 1980 Worlds.

So David had once again cheated skating death. A fall in placement from one year to the next can easily turn into a fatal, final plunge out of high ranking and out of skating altogether. But David in 1981 was still alive. There was no heir apparent in 1981. San Diego was a toss-up, everybody said, between Scott Hamilton and David Santee. Anything could happen.

And for once David Santee had his anythings together. He skated gloriously, the best in his life. Such skating would have won him gold at Nationals, possibly World gold, in any year but that year. David skated, in Scott's words, "as if he demanded to win." He skated as if he deserved to win. Just David's luck that he had to compete against one of history's richest anything-men, skating's Croesus, Scott Scovell Hamilton.

Skating excellence is only part of the story of who wins. The stories of Scott and David suggest that victory includes a knack for winning per se, distinct from how good you are. David had none of Scott's talent for winning when he should have won, none of Scott's talent for doing winning things at winning times. Scott possessed a special efficiency for victory. By rights David should have been a retiring champion in 1980, never having to grapple with the killing efficiency of Scott after 1980. The timing, something, was wrong. And too many years of wrongness had taken a toll on David.

219

"If it wasn't one thing," he said, "it's been another. If it hasn't been a competitor, it's been confidence. And if it hasn't been confidence, it's been injuries. I've always had to battle something. I think it's a never-ending battle to prove to myself that I'm not just another schmuck. And when I think that for so many years, I thought I wasn't that good. Like I wasn't that good a skater. And I wasn't someone special."

In spite of the defeat clouds and weariness and shaky skating, David Santee had not resigned himself to losing. No, he came to Indianapolis to fight, to give it all he had. His position was particularly thankless. He had to do battle with skating's ultimate weapon, with the inner and outer momentum running the wrong way. And Sweetheartland did not necessarily admire the old ice warrior. His own milieu seemed to be getting tired of him, but David was still going to give it a shot. You had to admire him.

Scott Hamilton, of course, could not admire him. He had to hate him. But, on the other hand, Scott couldn't hate him, because David was a really nice guy, and they were good friends.

The relationship of Scott and David was as contradictory and complex and twisted by the exigencies of skating as the relationship of Scott and Kitty. Scott and David were rivals for the skating crown. Now and again they were rivals for the attention of Kitty Carruthers. You could imagine them at skating weigh-ins screaming and trying to get at each other like boxers wild with bloodlust. But of course Sweetheartland did not allow such forthright expressions of the killer spirit of competition.

And yet Scott and David would seek each other out for companionship. Even at Indianapolis they'd talk in each other's rooms. And Scott, in 1983, would be an usher at David's wedding.

These contradictions are not necessarily signs of the two skaters' personalities. They are signs of the crushing forces of Sweetheartland, a place so small that your friends are your enemies.

Tuesday morning was a time to be enemies. Scott coasted past

Don at the boards on the rink with the big windows, where the shooting was about to start. Scott, the blood drinker, the dream-killing machine, spoke to Don, indicating the enemy and his coach, ten yards or so to the left. "I want him," Scott said.

# 22

# The Good Witch; Bad Ice

Jo Jo Starbuck was a professional skater who figured in distant but significant fashion in the story of Scott Hamilton in 1982. Her part was like that of the moon, faraway and silent, dime-sized in the sky, but exercising tidal pulls on Scott in Sweetheartland.

A movie scene is right for Jo Jo coming into the story Thursday morning in the coliseum, when the men were competing in compulsories. We need footage from *The Wizard of Oz:* the arrival of Glinda, Good Witch of the North. The Good Witch came in early in the film, immediately after Dorothy's house fell on the Wicked Witch of the East. Dorothy was looking at Oz for the first time, the Munchkins were hiding in the bushes, and this golden bubble came out of the sky. The bubble contained Glinda, blond and radiating light and goodness. She coaxed the Munchkins out of hiding, gave Dorothy the magical ruby slippers, and started her following the yellow brick road. Then she took off in the bubble. But she watched Dorothy, from afar, sending help when needed.

Jo Jo Starbuck did all of these things. She came to us in her own golden bubble, shining in a golden aura of goodness and beauty. This former Sweetheart—she and partner Ken Shelley were the U.S. National Champion Pairs team in 1970, 1971, and 1972—worked absolutely paralyzing magic with her sweet good looks, warmth, and humane, soothing manner. Yes, she was the Good Witch, and everyone else was a Munchkin. Had there been big plants growing around the benches at the end of the coliseum rink, we would have hidden in the leaves until Jo Jo coaxed us out. We would have giggled, like the little citizens of Oz in the movie, awestruck and delighted by the gorgeous practitioner of good magic.

What was it about Jo Jo? She had something that can only be expressed in inane combinations of sickly-sweet words. Scott would try to express her special qualities by saying things like, "She's so *genuine.*" That wasn't bad. She seemed, after just a few words, genuine, free of vanity, falseness, and all the idiosyncrasies that being a minor celebrity for all those years might have developed. She seemed, moreover, truly good, in real and full possession of the generosity and innocent, universal goodwill that so many others in Sweetheartland pretended to have. She was a prize. She was something else.

Everybody was susceptible to Jo Jo's charms. Even the most jaded, catty characters would sigh and fog over when her name came up. "Oh, Jo Jo," they'd say sweetly. "She's sooooo great."

There, on Thursday morning, newly arrived among the Scott people, was a medium-sized blonde with a ski-jump nose and a coat that represented a large loss of life in some species of dark brown animal, probably mink. The contrast between blond angel hair and shiny ebony fur was divine. Scott was fabulously happy to see Jo Jo, and he broke away for some time from his murderous competition-day trance so the two of them could share a bench and talk. At one point the Champ nuzzled into the furry sheen of Jo Jo's coat, gazing up at her with an ingenuous smile of adoration. His look was that of a four-year-old infatuated with a good-looking grown-up woman—"Ooooh, pretty lady . . . " Scott could have been saying.

Those of us in the rink that day were seeing a friendship that had been formed in December, when Don had gone to Washington, D.C., to judge a competition for professional skaters, and Scott had accompanied him. Scott met many of the luminaries in professional skating, all former greats in amateur competition, among them Jo Jo and her partner, Ken Shelley. Jo Jo turned out to be the ideal conversation-mate and friend for a World Champion suffering the tortures of preparing to defend his title, simultaneously besieged by people and yet lonely. Jo Jo, who had turned thirty-one that January, was having a bumpy year herself, finalizing the end to her marriage with star quarterback Terry Bradshaw.

So the two had a lot to talk about. And they did, in phone calls between Scott's hotel rooms and Jo Jo's house in Marina del Rey, or wherever skating had taken her. The Good Witch's name came up regularly in Scott's monologues for the tape recorder. When things were really rough in 1982, Scott would want to talk to Jo Jo, and if he was unable to, he sorely missed their conversations.

It had been a decade since Jo Jo had competed as an amateur, so she had no connections in Sweetheartland. But her veteran status gave her a deep understanding of Scott's temporary skating neuroses. She was able to provide an ideal, therapeutic combination of knowledge of Scott's world and distance from it—the perfect confidante. Combined with Jo Jo's golden aura of goodness, you had a guardian angel, Scott's particular guardian angel, reachable by phone day or night.

One last *Oz* image: the poppy field, Dorothy and the lion put to sleep by poisonous plants, a trap set by the Wicked Witch. Glinda materialized and woke them up with an unseasonal snowfall. Jo Jo did this sort of thing for Scott, working her saving magic by sending him, from far away, things he couldn't get in Sweetheartland.

Jo Jo told a yellow legal pad about her and the World Champion while Scott warmed up for the second figure, the paragraph double three. He had won the first figure, the inside rocker, with a nice spread of numbers, from 4.2 to 5.2. David was close behind him. Figures was David's strongest event. He had been considered one of the world's best figures skaters, possibly the best in

America. The year before, in San Diego, David had been a close second, behind Scott's first. David had beaten Scott at 1981 Worlds. Figures re-moralized the Santee people, parents and others, who were at least as numerous as the Scott people. It seemed as if the spectators belonged either to Scott or David, except for a small cadre of reporters, who seemed bewildered by their first contact with compulsories. David people, Scott people, and the press—but this, no doubt, was a false impression. Other skaters' people must have been at the coliseum, too.

David's defeat cloud had burned off considerably that morning. He looked terrific, solid musculature trimmed back by hard training, like good steak trimmed for economy, encased in a figures costume that did what figures costumes were supposed to do. It made David look like a target arrow. The outfit featured a navy blue top with chevrons. David even wore gloves to add to the streamlining.

Scott, as he had at Easterns, wore his blue outfit with vertical white stripes and piping. It still failed to put a good edge on Scott's frame. Scott also wore a pout of concentration, gettin' down to business, that took you back to Bowling Green. He went to work slightly angry at his work, angry in general, like a little mud country mechanic about to tear into a big, expensive, and delicate job on his own van.

Meanwhile Jo Jo went on about Scott. "I think he's like steel," she said. "Tremendous control of his nerves, his abilities."

She said Scott and his skating initially caught her attention at his first Worlds, in 1978, in Ottawa. "He was so cute. And unique in that everybody else was nervous and he kept calm through it all."

Jo Jo, it turned out, seemed flattered that Scott in his crucible year would lean on her. She was overawed by his skating, the way a mature concert pianist would have been overawed by a young Horowitz or Rubinstein. Her attitude toward him had none of the worldly superiority that would figure in the attitude of most women in their thirties for most men in their early twenties.

"I think I just make him laugh," she said. "Plus, I'm not really in it. I don't know what's going on. He can tell me what's going on. He can sort of let it all hang out. Or maybe I give him a third eye, to look from the professional point of view. And maybe I make him recognize there's a big world out there."

Watching the skaters took Jo Jo back to her combat years in Sweetheartland. "Nothing is normal," she said. "Extremes. Everything is done for them, but everything is demanded. You don't know who your friends are, really. Your real friends get jealous. People who didn't use to be friends want to be."

She talked about skaters' humility before the fickle fortunes of skating. "With the pressure, you're never sure how you're going to do. You're only as good as the next performance. Nothing's in the bag," she said. And about being on top: "Everyone's thrilled that you're champion. But then everyone's out to dethrone you. It's not getting the title that's hard." But, said Jo Jo, "I think he'll hang on to it."

Scott was about to do some hanging-on. All eyes went to the mechanic in blue pajamas.

Something was funny about Scott's first trip around the big forward-and-backward-switching figure eight. The first tracing looked shaky and slow. The second was near-disaster. Scott flowed as he should have flowed in the first part of the tracing, but then he stalled in the top circle. His skating foot wobbled as he slowed almost to stopping. The spectators, seasoned skate watchers, murmured and gasped and craned to see what was wrong. For a few horrible seconds, it looked as if Scott would stop altogether before he got to the figure's center, where he could push off and get going again.

Scott, obviously rattled, finished the paragraph double three. Flushed, he walked a tight oblong around the figure. He talked to the referee. Words were spoken out on the ice, judges examining Scott's figure. Don looked as if he were going to jump over the bang boards. He was horrified. Looking back on that moment, he said, "I needed a change of linen."

"Because of ice conditions, Mr. Hamilton will reskate the figure," the loudspeakers said.

Scott skated another paragraph double three, earning nine numbers that were lower than the numbers earned by his first figure. He still looked unnerved by what had happened. He came off the ice. Everybody was sensationalized by the incident.

David Santee was incensed. "If it would've happened to me, I wouldn't have gotten to reskate," he told the air. He was furious for the rest of figures competitions. "Talk to me in an hour," he said, "after I cool down." David wanted to protest the reskate, a notion that was not shared by Carlo Fassi.

David's anger and dismay, which seemed plausible at first, turned out to belong only to that moment. He had, it developed, similarly asked to reskate a figure when he ran into bad ice two years earlier, at the World Championships. The reskate was granted. Scott had been thinking of David's reskate when he asked for a second chance Thursday morning.

The problem, one of the judges said later, was a patch of bad ice. A flaw. No question about it. And no, the judge said, the decision to grant a second chance had nothing to do with the fact that Scott was an incumbent National Champion, Champion of the World, and the brightest skating hope of the United States. Anybody who asked would have gotten the reskate. She also said that Scott had showed presence of mind when he asked the referee for a reskate. Not everyone would have had such presence of mind.

David won paragraph double three. Scott was second. Five judges gave better numbers to David for the figure. One judge gave the same number to both. Concern lined the foreheads of the Scott people. If the loop went bad, Scott might be number two in figures and Santee number one.

Everybody was in the bleachers to watch the change loop. A

reporter from *The Washington Post* interviewed Ernie Hamilton, but everybody quieted and looked when Scott went rolling through the three-lobed curling little figure that would have fit inside one of the circles in the first two figures. Scott rolled like a diamond tool guided by invisible machine linkages, his free leg swinging in counterbalance through the quick little loops.

The first indication that Scott had done a great loop came from Don Laws, who brightened immediately, the happiest coach in the world. The numbers were good, too. The Scott people's brows smoothed. Don patted Scott coming off the ice, beaming.

The numbers for the loop said that Scott had beaten David. So he won figures, which put him thirty percent of the way to winning Nationals, a good way to begin.

"I was so scared," he said later. "I didn't think I was going to make it through the second tracing." Yes, Scott said, he was happy about getting another shot at the figure, but the one on bad ice was probably as good as the one he subsequently did on good ice. The wrongness of the first paragraph double three broke his concentration and his confidence. Thank God it was over.

With one obstacle to happiness out of the way, the Scott people inflated with relief and good cheer. Time for lunch.

And sometime late that evening, after Scott held Ron Ludington's arm during Kitty and Peter's winning free program, their final event, the golden bubble that brought Jo Jo into Sweetheartland took her away. Scott and the friendly skating angel had one last earnest conversation, leavened with laughter, and the bubble went west, to Jo Jo's coastal California, and thence to the next television commercial or network special or acting class, whatever was calling her onward.

# 23

# Dad, Poor Dad

In figure skating's most intense hours of competitive craziness, one role became thankless. The lot of a parent of one of the top-ranked skaters was hard. The skaters were completely twisted by pretending to be human marzipan for all the judges and USFSA bigwigs and reporters and Sweethearthood at large, in the same hours when they were trying to bring themselves to killer edges, praying to the awful inner spirits of competition. The stress of getting ready to gamble their whole existence on how much nine judges liked their triple toe loops would have been bad enough. But that stress, coupled with the stress of acting like a dream of youthful innocence and good sportsmanship, could not be borne. It could not be borne, that is, without somebody getting blasted with the powerful un-nice counterforces conjured up by all that being nice.

The kids *had* to have angry fits. But they couldn't have them in public. So they had them in private. And the objects of the tortured ill will of those crazy days were the very people who sacrificed money and everything else for the sake of the kids skating. Mom and Dad. Tragic, but inevitable. Who else could a kid scream at?

Even Jo Jo Starbuck, that angel, said that she had flamed off competition brain poisons in her mother's direction. She said, moreover, that she imagined a mean scene or two behind closed hotel room doors was a normal event for most skaters and their families at all big competitions.

Dr. Ernest Hamilton—Ernie to Scott and all the Scott people —was about to get his. And in this case son-father rancor was particularly unfortunate, because Ernie was the most inoffensive and universally well disposed member of Scott's entourage. There were people around Scott who might have deserved sharp words, or worse, from the Champ; Ernie was not one of them. But because he was Scott's father, he was going to suffer for the excesses of others and the excesses of Sweetheartland in general. Ernie, characteristically, took his son's outbursts on Friday afternoon in stride, with tolerance and good humor. He seemed to understand the inevitability and impersonality of Scott's venom. And so he declined to take any of it personally.

Ernie had shown up in Indianapolis on Tuesday night. He went out to dinner with everybody, and joined the decorous tagging-along of the Scott people. He alone in the group maintained steadfast nonpartisanship, taking neither side in the controversy over whether Scott needed mother love or a kick in the meta-physical rear end. He ate lunch and chatted and liked and enjoyed all the Scott people equally.

And they were equally generous in their opinions of the pleasant professor. "Have you met Ernie yet?" each one would ask before his arrival. "Ooooh, you'll love Ernie. He's fantastic. He's so relaxed and so nice."

Ernie squinted at the world, much in the manner of the near-sighted cartoon character Mr. Magoo. He was small, and trim, with the beginnings of an abdominal pot that told of slight overin-dulgences in life's good things. He had just the right mildness and accommodation to keep company and get along with just about everyone. "Easygoing," is how Ernie was almost universally de-scribed. People who said it spoke as if Ernie were immune to the horrid nerve pressures of his son's skating. But if you talked to Ernie you'd learn that he was as nervous as anybody else. At times he was more nervous. The difference was that Ernie did not wear his nervousness outwardly. He particularly did not inflict his nervousness on others. He inflicted very little at all on others, except his soothing good nature. So the impression given by Ernie was that of a man easygoing in all dimensions.

Ernie would have liked to see more of Scott, but Scott's phenomenal success had virtually destroyed the chance for father-son intimacy. Scott's trips to Bowling Green had gotten to be hometown celebrity-media flea markets, with a crush of reporters, local fame grubbers, and people with endless things for Scott to do. So Bowling Green wasn't like coming home. Besides the relatively short and infrequent visits to Ohio, Ernie and Scott would see each other mostly at competitions, the worst possible places for celebrating kinship.

Togetherness at competitions forced the familial communications of the Hamiltons into one-sidedness, and a reticence on Ernie's part that one year earlier had been spectacular. At Nationals in San Diego, on short-program day, Ernie woke up feeling as if he'd suffered a stroke. "Well," he recalled, "I got up, and my left side wouldn't work as well as it should have worked. I tried to use my hand, and it was like slow motion. The leg didn't want to work right. This side of my face drooped. And I knew what it was."

Knowing what it was, Ernie had breakfast and went to a practice rink, up in La Jolla, and then went to see short program that night. After the short program he went out to dinner with Scott. He went through a daylong charade of normalcy so his son wouldn't be distracted from his competitive skating.

"I had a feeling it was his year," Ernie explained.

On long-program day Ernie's condition was the same. He began to worry about whether flying home the next day in such a state would be all right, so he got hold of his doctor back in Bowling Green. The doctor told Ernie to get to a hospital, and absolutely forbade him to fly home. Ernie went to long-program practice and then got two Scott people to take him to a hospital. At that point Ernie hoped he'd be free to watch long program. But the hospital kept Ernie, and he swore all the Scott people to secrecy.

Ernie said, "Everybody kept telling Scott, 'Oh, I just saw Ernie over there someplace,' when he would look for me. I didn't want him to know where I was. He just did not need that on his mind."

So Scott was fooled into thinking his dad was perpetually "over there someplace" on long-program night. He won, and got his medal, and then a doctor told Scott what had happened. Meanwhile, Ernie was supposed to have taken a sedative, to put him to sleep, but he refused until he heard from Scott himself how the 1981 Nationals had come out.

With Nationals won, Scott could afford to be properly filial once more. He stayed in San Diego, skated, and visited his father every day at the hospital. Barb Camp stayed in town, too, to help out the Hamiltons.

The San Diego stroke did very little permanent damage to Ernie, virtually none. But the fatherly forbearance in the face of what could well have been a crippling or killing episode is still very impressive. It's hard to imagine an equivalent incident in nonskating families. What could be so vitally important that a son would be spared immediate information about his father's hospitalization for something that might have been the beginning of catastrophe? In most lives, nothing is that momentous, and that sacrosanct. But Ernie never doubted for a moment that his son's psyching-up to skate was sacrosanct. You can picture him giving the final measure of devotion, with the worst possible thing happening, and Ernie, as long as he was able to talk, saying that Scott should skate long program before he heard any upsetting news.

Parental heroism does not endure in the minds of the beneficiaries of that heroism, particularly in those moments when proximity and privacy force a kid to take out his frustrations on his father. So there was Scott, on Friday afternoon up in room 1722 of the

Hyatt Regency Indianapolis, pitching a nasty fit. The subject matter of this fit was Ernie's insistence that he and Scott go to the post office that afternoon and apply for a new passport for Scott, whose current passport had expired. Ernie was saying that if he didn't see to it that the passport business got done, it probably would not get done, and the day for going to Germany to get ready for Worlds would roll around and Scott wouldn't have a valid passport. Ernie, like the rest of the Scott people, had doubts that Scott by himself could take care of his own detail work, his passport and airline tickets and so on. There may have been another dimension to Ernie's concern. Disease and figure skating had long kept Scott out of fatherly reach, except for brief encounters such as 1982 Nationals. And in Sweetheartland Ernie had to compete with the rest of the Scott people to do for Scott. Here, at any rate, was an opportunity to be fatherly. There weren't many such opportunities. Ernie took it.

The whole thing incensed Scott, who was storming around his room, looking for something. He pointed at a chair and told Ernie, "Sit!" as if his father were an Airedale who had just chewed up the boots on the skates he had to use that night in short program. "Just sit there!"

Ernie sat there. Being a witness was terrible. Other eyes weren't meant to see this, but there was no escape. Actually, being a witness was probably a good deal worse than being Ernie, who treated the episode as if it didn't involve him at all, as if he were helping Scott to rehearse a scene for community theater. Ernie did not seem to be paying attention.

More aggrieved shrillness from Scott: "Cool your jets! You do this to me every competition. I've got to make sure I'm going to Europe before I worry about this passport."

Scott had found whatever it was he needed. All right, he said, let's go. So the Hamiltons and I plummeted earthward in the Hyatt's see-through elevator and found out where the post office was.

The post office was on the fringe of downtown, on the other side of a railroad viaduct. After some back-and-forth with a civil servant it became apparent that Scott couldn't apply for a new passport at that post office. The application would be processed too slowly for the new document to be ready by the time Scott needed it. The civil servant said that even if Scott went to a bigger city's passport office, with faster service, there was some doubt that Scott would have his passport by the time he required it, which was just two weeks from that day. Scott said he'd have to try Denver.

The bad news about the passport seemed to cheer up the Champ, by giving his fit-throwing legitimacy. There, this new nuance of aggrievance seemed to say, I told you so.

"If you want anything done right," Scott snorted, "do it your-self." The remark in that situation was nonsense, but it fit the inner drama of the moment.

Just to add variety to the walk, we went back to the Hyatt on another street, which went under a different viaduct. Water had run out of the roadbed gravel and concrete overhead, its flow slowed and then stopped by the miserable cold. Some of the water hung in a fat icicle along the viaduct's cement wall. The icicle pointed down to the resting place of more water, a puddle frozen perfectly glassy, with a sugar-coating of cold-weather snow on its surface, a surface far icier in treacherous slip than the rink at Market Square Arena. The clear hazard of the miniature ice rink caused the three walkers to cross it with elaborate caution, one foot at a time. But—wham!—in spite of that caution, Ernie Hamilton went down, flat on his back.

The fall looked injurious, but Ernie was all right, not even shaken. Probably his winter clothes kept him from breaking any-thing. But the mood set by Scott's quiet nastiness was multiple-fractured by the fall. And it would not come back. Scott, you could tell, did not want to let his short-program-day nastiness go. But it wasn't possible to be nasty to Ernie anymore. He hadn't really been mad at Ernie anyway. The now targetless anger expanded into an amorphous cloud of blue funk, directed at the world in general. And the clouded-over Scott walked, still pouting, back to the hotel.

# 24

# Falling

A note from earlier on short-program day: At the 11:30 A.M. practice session, Scott blew his combination. He made a mess of it. He actually fell.

Practice had started with Scott fussing. His ankle hurt.

"Yeah, yeah," Don told him. "Shake it out and loosen it."

After Scott's combination failed, he went back and studied the ice scrapes left by his crash landing. He made a pass by Don, asking the coach silent questions.

"Put your shoulders back," Don said.

Scott was loose and cheerier when practice wound down.

Scott explained after practice that blowing his combination on short-program day was probably a good sign. He always messed up his combination in practice on short-program day. The bad jumps and subsequent crash seemed to relieve Scott. The idea, apparently, was that bad luck and falling should be gotten out of the way in practice and not carried into competition.

The following went unnoticed at first in the Hamilton camp. On Thursday night in practice, the second of two freeskating practices Thursday in which Scott skated immaculate run-throughs, David Santee had an accident.

The ice was dirty because Scott and David's practice group skated second, and the rink had not been Zambonied after the first group. David did a spin, an everyday bread-and-butter spin, and a rut grabbed one skate. One foot went one way, and one went the other. The pulling apart strained an eight-inch-long adductor muscle in his groin.

But even before the muscle strain David's skating had looked like it was in trouble, and Scott's worrying had turned much more toward Robert Wagenhoffer and Brian Boitano. Those guys, he said, were sure to skate clean short programs.

The ladies rode the same practice bus as the men on Friday, which was the ladies' long-program day. They were thoughtful and somewhat withdrawn, victims of last-day nervousness made even more acute by a growing feeling that funny things could happen that night. Something, everybody would later agree, was in the air.

Elaine Zayak, the previous year's National Champion, had yet to take the lead. She was second after short program, behind Priscilla Hill, a twenty-year-old skating veteran, old in comparison with the other Senior ladies, who did fabulous compulsory figures. Elaine had been second after figures, behind Priscilla, in a fine position to win short program and move ahead. But Elaine caught a rut and placed third in short, beaten by Rosalynn Sumners and Vikki de Vries, Carlo Fassi's Senior lady. And Priscilla Hill had a very good short program and came in fourth. Since short program counted for less than figures—twenty percent to compulsories' thirty percent—Priscilla was still ahead of Elaine. Rosalynn, the short-program winner, had been fifth in figures. Her first in short moved her to fourth overall. Vikki de Vries was third overall after short.

Savvy skate watchers said that Priscilla Hill would not win long program. She was going to drop. Arithmetic said that the best free skater would win overall. Anything could happen. Elaine was by no means the hands-down favorite to win at Nationals that Scott was. Vikki de Vries had vanquished her at Skate America, in October 1981. Elaine also had been beaten at the Ennia Cup, in Holland.

Rosalynn, fifth in 1981 Nationals, had skated very well in the fall. This seventeen-year-old from Washington State was skating on an injury in Indianapolis, a pulled muscle in her hip. All week she had been getting ultrasound, heat, and physical therapy. But being hurt did not diminish this consummate Sweetheart's star quality, on or off the ice. Rosalynn was a hot property, with big moments about to happen. She was a Sweetheart's dream of Sweethearthood, a green-eyed blonde, a porcelain skating heart-throb whose performing presence on the ice overshadowed that of all her competitors. Don Laws, talking about all the madness that would come that night in ladies' long program, said that the improbabilities occurred because the three leaders looked over their shoulders and saw Rosalynn Sumners coming. If you aspired to National Sweethearthood, the sight of a natural-born Queen Sweetheart like Rosalynn would be unnerving, a nightmare.

For the time being, emanations from the near future notwithstanding, the lady of the hour at midday Friday was Priscilla Hill —Prill Hill to Scott and other affectionate fellow ice veterans. She was still leading the ladies.

In 1982 Priscilla was one of skating's competitive antiquities, in her eleventh year among the best and oldest women. Twenty is an advanced age for a Senior lady, and Priscilla had started Senior competition earlier than anyone in the annals of skating. She passed her gold figures test when she was nine years old, the age at which Scott Hamilton first took skating lessons. She first skated at Nationals in 1973. She pioneered triple loop in ladies' competitive freeskating in 1976. In 1978 she made the World team and finished ninth at Worlds. But 1979, as it had been for Scott, was a year of dashed hopes. She hurt her leg so badly she couldn't skate that year. After that, injuries made Priscilla's skating future uncertain, but she stayed in. And she wasn't doing badly. In 1981 she was a silver medalist at Nationals, and seventh at Worlds.

Priscilla's forte was skating figures. She was first at figures at Nationals in 1981, and she beat the reigning ladies' World Champion at 1981 Skate Canada. But of course being a genius at figures brought very little glory. Priscilla competed for the love of competing, for her own reasons, with very little hope of mining National Sweethearthood for ego building and money. The other skaters, talking about her, would marvel at how much she had given to her sport.

On the bus going Hyatt-ward, just before it got back to the hotel, Priscilla rested her elf face on her hands, which lay on the back of the bus seat in front of hers. She had a seat to herself, near Scott's. Heavy fatality hung over poor Priscilla. A moment of truth was stalking her, closer and closer. Scott kidded her about long program, and she kidded about it, too.

The bus went by a large building that was half torn down, one side of it ripped away so we could see the insides of the entire structure. The arrangement of components in place and skeletal parts hanging in disarray was perfect, a very artistic depiction of man's efforts coming to ruin, of the vanity of building big things and believing in those things. The spectacle was made even sadder by the cold and snow against which walls and windows now offered no protection. The sadness of the place was so complete that it struck the skaters as funny, and jokes about it came from all parts of the bus.

Priscilla made her own joke. She spoke wistfully, pensive and looking quite seriously at the wreckage.

"Yeah," said Priscilla Hill, "that's where I'm going to live if I do a really bad long program tonight."

Another new plateau of nervousness, where the Scott watcher was high above mere noise and jumpiness and fear for the poor little guy who had to go out there and skate. The physical sensations brought on by Senior men's short program were a great deal like the flying-rock-and-thin-air giddiness experienced by Mudlanders going for the first time into the mountains over Scott's Denver. This, you could say, and breathe deep, is what I came to see. The real thing.

The tension of the moment transformed the Market Square Arena. America's Sweethearts and the sleek adults of Sweetheartland, along with an excited segment of the general public, had peopled over the arena's coated-aspirin-orange seats. Looking upward from the bang boards where the skaters went onto the ice, you saw a vast glacial valley. The blinding white glacier spread out in front, and on either side the eyes climbed steep slopes bouldered with wool, goose down, mink, and pink Caucasian faces. Gone entirely was the intimacy of the near-empty arena on Tuesday night, Scott's last practice in there. It was *huge* on shortprogram night. The view from the boards was spectacular, with a vast sense of scale that brought on disturbing illusions. The ice, burning with a zillion candlepower of excellent illumination, pressed upward. The speakers and scoreboard and flying saucer–like paraphernalia hanging over the ice hung so low you wanted to duck. (Peter Carruthers had earlier said that he felt all that machinery pressing down on him when he skated in Market Square.) But then the illusion went the other way. Standing at the boards brought on vertigo. You wanted to step away and hang on to something reassuring, the way you want to hang on to a tree looking over the lip of a gorge. Television cameras looking and thirty thousand eyes looking and the great things about to happen kicked the whole place and everybody in it to a higher plane.

You got to the boards through a wide chute, a flat-bottomed gully at ice level, which went back under the stands to a highceilinged concrete hallway. Here there were dressing rooms and a little area for television interviews and plenty of open floor space for the men to do their hypertense running-shoe skating.

Out in the chute there was a raised platform where the ABC coverage team had field headquarters, electronics and cameras, and the familiar "Wide World of Sports" meganames—Jim McKay, the veteran anchor; Dick Button, video voice and face of American figure skating; and Peggy Fleming. The charged particles from the team's microphones and the cameras, which swept every square inch of the great frozen bullring, were conducted via cables to command trailers out on the street. The meganames were going to interact with the millions of dollars in seeing and hearing equipment to make tape that would subsequently be reduced to a creation about twenty minutes long. That crystallization of Friday night would be shown the following afternoon, in tandem with a surfing tournament from Hawaii. Ice dancing and Senior men's final event, on Saturday night, would be taped and similarly edited for America's viewing the next Saturday afternoon. Delayed coverage and radical reductive editing was the rule for skating coverage on network television.

Somebody up on that platform was an astounding eater. A network lackey ran almost continually, bringing the stars pizza, popcorn, and other delights. One of the network people explained that on-the-air talent went into a binge of manic gluttony when there was work to be done.

So they were getting nervous up on media mountain. The crowd, too, was starting to cook. Ten thousand high-pitched voices warmed up on minor Senior men. Now and again the adults shouted, giving the crowd sound more low-end presence than the awful shriek of Easterns.

Short program was the first men's event to come to a climax. Skating order in figures was random, with big names and minor players mingled indiscriminately. In short program, the leaders after figures (a group that almost always included the best free skaters) competed last. And the leaders after short program competed last in long program. Skating order was not a precise reflection of overall standing. The skaters were divided into warm-up groups of four or five or a half dozen men, depending on the size of the field, and skating order was also random within the warm-up groups. But the effect was still a dramatic climax—you had to wait until the end to see the men who had the best chance of winning. This arrangement also gave the feeling of head-to-head competition, like the final heats in a footrace, or the last games in a tournament, but that was largely an illusion, an illusion the skaters used to develop their competitive frenzies, and which the crowd used to enhance an evening's skate watching. A win in one event, no matter how decisive, or surprising, merely represented a number, which was added to other numbers. The winner at the end of everything was the skater whose numbers added up to the winning number. So you might see fabulous things in short program that had very little to do with the final results.

But numerical mental detachment was not part of the drama of in-person skatesport. The point Friday night was that minor men led up to major men in a slightly less than major event, which in turn led to minor women leading to major women in their ultimate event, the selection of the 1982 Senior Ladies' National Champion. Two big deals, with the first made a good deal bigger than it might have been because Scott Scovell Hamilton, Champion of the World, was going to skate. So the crowd was practicing to be electrified by Scott.

And Scott was practicing to electrify. He had been gone, totally gone, for several hours. Sometime in the late afternoon, short program took over the major portion of Scott's conciousness, occupying most of those surfaces of the Champ's frontal lobe that made him recognizably human. We were left with an android facsimile of Scott that seemed to need readjustment, badly. If somebody didn't turn down the Scott robot's voltage, you would have thought, it was going to overheat and melt. A grilled microprocessor in the machine's head kept telling it to do little pieces of short program, kinetic snippets that stopped and started abruptly. Now and again the droid's sociability program would kick in, but the instant the face showed recognition and friendly words came out, the program would quit working. So the face would go into its blank test pattern and the body into simulated skating.

A half dozen skaters similarly off-world gave our concrete vault under the stands a fascinating aspect. It was like a ward for the extremely insane in the days before drugs made crazies sit still. All those boys, blind and deaf to this world, dancing to music nobody else could hear. The scene also brought to mind fringe-group Christian meetings, where brains go to heaven and bodies dance in the Holy Spirit.

Odd, very odd, but it was all familiar stuff to Don and Ricky, who stood in the center of the floor, facing toward the curtained chute leading out onto the ice. As usual they looked perfectly Cos Cob. The effect at that moment was that those two were touring a sanitarium that was one of their philanthropic projects, for tax purposes. They were indifferent to the circulating skaters and paid no more than passing attention to Dick Button, skating's best-known TV pundit, who had a piece of popcorn clinging to the side of his nose, and had come down from the headquarters platform. He might have been on his way to the chute, to get ready for instant interviews when the first-rank skaters came off the ice. Obviously, the guy was keying up. He grabbed Ricky, went into a ballroom position with her, and they danced a few steps. Then he stuck wires from his headset and microphone into his ears. He made a face. In pancake makeup he looked like a corpse reawakened by bad magic. Dick Button was in working garb, which was evening dress from the waist up, and a pair of blue jeans. He could wear jeans because the world saw only his face and upper body.

Dick Button went away. Don and Ricky rocked on their heels, waiting for the big moment. Scott danced around wearing still another Malibu T-shirt, the top of his one-piece maroon short-program costume turned down at the waist. Down at ankle-level you could feel the cold, wet exhalation of all that ice. And back-stage in the arena, on the third night of competition, things were getting messy. Derelict cups and results sheets and all sorts of detritus had collected back there. The look of brand-newness that Nationals wore initially was gone.

Carlo and Christa Fassi sat on folding chairs, with cups of coffee, chips, and sandwiches. They lounged with coats split open.

All the hate had gone out of Nationals. The ice adults and skaters in the concrete cavern, from which the rest of the world had been barred, were enveloped in a moment of intimate community. The grown-ups showed each other smiles of greeting,

"Here we go again" smiles. In those minutes they stopped being adversaries and congregated as fellow humans before the inhuman thing they all faced.

The coaches, as they had done all their coaching lives, prepared themselves to play the big-stakes ice game, to toss their skaters like dice and see how the numbers came up. The skaters prepared themselves for the roll on the big frozen table.

But there was more to the feeling in the cavern than shared risks and shared understanding. In that world, a night such as that night was one of life's landmarks, a point in time they all shared together. Time passed in review—a whole skating year and then many years marching by in those minutes when the last few men waited to skate. The shared momentousness was like that of a faculty at a graduation, or New Year's Eve among sober people. There was melancholy, sad intimations of time going and gone, auld lang syne.

"Oooo," Ricky jittered to Don. "I wish it were all over."

"No," Don said. "Don't wish your life away like that."

There followed a moment of shared sentimentality, nobody saying anything. In all my weeks in Sweetheartland no moment approached this one for overwhelming, gooey sentiment. Supermarket greeting cards try, and fail, to express the sort of feelings that moment held. A susceptible person would have cried. Unforgettable. Odd that it occurred on that night, which was far from being the most momentous night in Scott's 1982 competitive season.

The Champ was talking, standing in front of the Fassis.

"Damn!" he said. "Damn that combination! I've done a million of them in five minutes. All I can think of is this . . . Bam! Bam!" He made his right forearm act out what he meant. Bam! It fell from upright to the right. Bam! It fell to the left.

Scott, his face back in the robot test pattern, walked up to his coach. He lifted each foot and shook it, with more than human quickness in the shaking, a cat shaking water off its back feet. Don imitated the shaking, wigwagging his 10½ Ds. The effect of a man wearing a trench coat wagging wide feet in leather shoes was much more gooselike than catlike.

Warm-up. Pumping past Don, who stood with the other coaches at the boards. "Hazardous," Scott said. "This is hazardous."

Scott may not have heard Don's answer: "Jesus Christ, just *standing* on the ice is dangerous."

Scott pogoed on the floor in the chute, head down. He stopped jumping and limbered as if he were about to start fighting with somebody.

He was back on the ice, for real. Quick circuiting, talking to Don, scared to death about holes in the ice.

"Don't be concerned. You checked them all out before," Don reassured.

The mad screaming began. Scott was in crucifix position. The opening chord whined, and the percussion behind it spidered. Scott was skating. No time for anything but the short-program mental checklist.

First the big one, combination. Whammo! Scott nailed combination.

Flying camel. Fine, just fine.

Double axel. Looking very good on the way up . . . No. Scott Hamilton was sitting, legs flat out in front, on the ice. The double axel that took him upward so nicely took him downward very nicely until his landing foot slipped out from under him and he went down tail first.

From *The 1981–82 Official USFSA Rulebook:*
On falling, excerpted and adapted, from Skating Standards Regulations.

From SSR 1.325, on marking falls in freeskating [a statement of a principle that applied also to marking short program]: "A fall, in itself, is no bar to winning or passing."

SSR 1.434, on marking short program: "Every failure in the required elements must be reflected only in the first mark (technical merit) according to the importance of the element failed or omitted and the gravity of the mistake itself, since there is no direct relationship between the first and second (presentation) marks. However, marks must be deducted for failures in the second mark if the harmonious and artistic aspects of the program are involved."

SSR 1.435 specified point deductions from the technical merit for missed required elements in short program. A missed double jump costs from 0.3 to 0.5 points.

The great slopes of people went "Oh!"

Kitty screamed.

Dick Button commentated for the following week's "Wide World of Sports," words machine-gunning: "There it is. Watch him step, lift with the arms, two-and-a-half revolutions . . . Oh! And a spill! A very unusual situation. He can do that jump any time of the day or night. A simple jump for him. Yet it's always treacherous because of that forward edge. Never quite secure."

Scott did everything to make sure the fall cost him as little as possible. As soon as the fact that he was sitting down registered, he was up and gone, smiling and skating superbly.

Ricky grabbed Don and hung on.

Don started saying that the fall wasn't going to be much of a problem. It didn't hurt his presentation, so the second mark would still be high. Probably a minimum deduction on the first mark, just three-tenths of a point.

All the short-program questions after the double axel got emphatic, double-underlined yesses.

Then Scott was coming off, with the million animals dying again, just for him.

"Donald," he sing-songed. "I'm mad. I'm really mad. I'm not accident-prone."

The judging came up like this. Technical merit:

5.3  5.3  5.3  5.3  5.2  5.3  5.4  5.4  5.2

Presentation:

$$5.8 \quad 5.8 \quad 5.7 \quad 5.8 \quad 5.8 \quad 5.8 \quad 5.8 \quad 5.9 \quad 5.6$$

The high marks, particularly the 5.9, made the crowd squeal in happiness for Scott.

"I've got to cool down," Scott said, and vanished.

This is how short program came out:

Robert Wagenhoffer bobbled a little on his double axel—a jump as easy and everyday for him as it was for Scott—but he saved the jump. He won short program, with eight of the nine judges marking him the highest among the skaters, eight firsts.

Scott was second.

Brian Boitano's very solid short took him to third place in the event. Four of the judges scored Brian higher than Scott in technical merit. But Brian's presentation marks were not nearly as high.

David Santee, who had skated wearing an elastic football player's girdle, was fourth in the short. His program had been the effort of a hurt man, minimal and cautious. He skated trying not to do anything wrong.

Overall standings after the short:

Scott Hamilton.

David Santee.

Robert Wagenhoffer.

Scott's finishing two places ahead of David in the short put a little more numerical distance between them. David and Robert Wagenhoffer were quite close. Robert could pull ahead simply by placing ahead of David Santee in the long, which seemed very likely. But it seemed highly unlikely that Robert could unseat Scott. To do so, Robert would have to beat the Champ by three places, an eventuality that would involve not only brilliant skating on Robert's part, but also a complete beginning-to-end debacle for Scott in the long program. After the short, it did not seem reasonable to worry about David beating Scott. Before new ice was made for the ladies on Friday night, Sweetheartland was whispering that David was going to have to fight to stay in the top three.

Robert Wagenhoffer treated his unexpected triumph as a very, very funny event.

"Can I get a big head now?" he asked one of his friends back in the cavern. About his rescued double axel: "I just have this thing about falling in front of seventeen thousand people." And his delightful calm: "I don't like getting nervous."

David, aggrieved, asked no one in particular—asked the air after the short—if Scott was going to get another chance to skate the short program, the way he got another chance to skate his paragraph double three.

In street clothes and all cooled down, Scott Hamilton sat on a shelf in front of mirrors in a dressing room that opened into the cavern, holding an impromptu press conference. Newspaper reporters and a guy with a little tape recorder, who may have been newspaper but seemed more like radio, listened and scribbled.

The first issue was what happened, the name of the jump on which Scott fell, and what a combination was, and so on. Most skating press talk had to start like this, with Scott giving elementary information. Sportswriters who knew as little about football as was generally known about figure skating in the United States in 1982 would have begun post-game interviews by asking how many men played on each side, what the players were supposed to do with the ball, and how the game was scored. But Scott never seemed to mind his from-the-ground-up interviews.

Scott reviewed for the reporters his hard luck with double flip, triple toe loop, his injury on it in 1979, when he got dumped off the World Team. The combination he had just done, Scott said, was by far the best double flip, triple toe loop he'd ever done in competition. "And so for me to come back and do it after all that trouble in 1979 and be able to land it so well, that's really important," Scott said. "Double axel was just a silly little error. I have one tomorrow night in the same place in long program. I'm not going to take it out."

Somebody asked about that pet press subject in 1982: quadruples. People were talking about the first quad ever in competition happening Saturday night in long program. Was Scott worried? Was he going to put quads into his programs some day? No, Scott said, he wasn't particularly worried, and he wasn't on the verge of doing quads. "That'd be great if somebody did a quad, though," he said. "It'd make the record book."

A reporter on his way out thanked Scott and wished him good luck. Another reporter thanked Scott for finally talking. He was sorry he'd been so insistent.

"No, that's all right," Scott said. "I was out trying to get something to drink. I was really thirsty. And I was trying to get my head straight."

One reporter, a knobby old guy from one of the Indy papers, remained. Could Scott remember when he last missed double axel in competition?

He answered instantly. "October of 1977. At Skate Canada." Scott thought about what went wrong. "I think I relaxed a little too much. I felt really comfortable after combination, and I felt really relaxed. I was going to do a little axel. I wasn't going to go all out for a big huge double axel. I did kind of a weird takeoff. But it felt good until I landed. And I really wanted to come up and present. And I just slipped off a heel. I was shocked. I went down. I couldn't believe I went down. But then I felt fine. It just took me a second to find out what happened. And what I had to do to make up for it."

First, the reporter said, you had a little glitch in figures. Then you fell tonight. . . .

"In figures it was an accident. Here it was an accident.

249

Whether this kind of luck continues—I hope not. Long program has been pretty solid for me. I really shouldn't do anything stupid tomorrow night. We'll see." The words weren't flowing anymore. "That's it. What can I tell you? I wish I could give you something more interesting."

The old reporter reassured him that the interview was fine, thanked him, and was gone.

So now Scott was alone and unmuzzled, talking to the tape recorder. He sounded angry.

"I hate being accident-prone. I'm not accident-prone. If I hit combination there's no way in the world I should miss anything else. I guess I was still a little worried about David."

Was he sure there hadn't been anything on the ice?

"I'm sure. It was dumb. It was stupid. I really think I was kind of worried about David. He did such a disappointing job, and I just let down. I still wanted to skate clean, though."

Scott wasn't sure he could nail long program hard enough to give Nationals real authority. "But Worlds," he declared, "I'm going to kick butts at Worlds. If they haven't lost respect for me."

Then he added up the scores, to see how he'd have to be beaten to lose Nationals. "I'm kind of scared about tomorrow night. I really wasn't that nervous about short. I just blew it."

Scott looked at the opening door and brightened. "There he is!" Peter Carruthers had a new pair of boots. "Hee-haw! Frye boots!" Scott shouted.

Don was at the door. "Do you want to do an interview?" he asked.

This one was for the "Wide World" camera. Scott told Dick Button more or less what he had told the newsprint men, that combination felt so good he got overconfident and too relaxed.

Dick Button: "A forward-edge jump like the double axel is always treacherous."

Scott: "You have to look where you're going. In other jumps

you can just say, 'It's back there and I don't have to look at it.' When you're going into double axel, you're looking at all this wide open ice, and you've got to jump over it. . . . It was just a silly error, and I'm going to redeem myself."

It was very hard to tell on Friday night how deeply Scott had been shaken by the fall, if he had, indeed, been shaken. Even his private remarks that night had the tone of press statements, issued for himself. They acknowledged falling, but emphasis was put on Saturday night, getting on with things. Some sort of interior damage control was going on, with Scott isolating his ice accident in his mind, refusing to reflect on it, starving out doubt before it could rage out of control.

Scott's fall opened the door to the wrong side of the figure skating world. And the door, ajar for the rest of Friday night, let in swarms of jump gremlins and edge devils and all species of malevolent ice entities that can wreck freeskating. The nightmare creatures were loose. Even the world's best skaters were terrified by those things. Friday night would show why they were scared.

From "The Wide World of Sports":
Jim McKay: "Very strange things are happening out there, Peggy. Think there might be a problem with the ice again—ruts or anything?"
Peggy Fleming: "Well, I don't think so. . . . I think it's just one of those crazy nights."

Prill Hill was the first of the four leading ladies to skate. She accepted her applause, and began a figure-skating reenactment of the Charge of the Light Brigade, a massacre of a long program so complete that it became a spectacle of fatal glory, a triumph of the will to keep going.

The opening axel crashed. Her next jump, triple toe loop, was also a casualty. Reeling from the opening mishaps, Priscilla charged onward into the mouth of skating Hell, strewing the ice with dead and dying jumps. Game, always game, she skated away from each casualty, and tried something else. Virtually nothing worked.

The defeat was particularly cruel considering Priscilla had for accompaniment music from the movie *Chariots of Fire,* a lugubrious electronic anthem to victory in amateur sport that was very popular in 1982. The music went with the opening scene of the movie, a herd of young men running in the surf, training for the Olympics. It was meant to be, and was, an inspiring theme that made you think of imaginary sacrifice and work for imaginary moments of triumph and gold medals. It was heartrending, awful, to hear music intended to accompany a screenwriter's myth of athletics while watching a real athletic heroine gamble years of sacrifice and training, and lose so disastrously.

The four minutes ended. Coming off the ice, she had to face the camera and try to tell Dick Button what had happened.

"I don't know," she said with an airy giggle that threatened to become a sob, a Sweetheart's giggle of agony. "Just wasn't there tonight."

Dick Button: "Just one of those nights."

Priscilla: "Just one of those nights."

DB: "Is this the biggest disappointment in skating you've had?"

P: "Probably. I don't know."

So Dick Button looked up and machine-gunned off the judges' scores for artistic impression, which went from 4.6 to 5.2. He told Priscilla he thought she'd done much better than that. And he told her how beautifully she'd moved, how much she'd improved in that respect.

Awwwww, went Priscilla.

Good, good luck, he said. And she thanked him.

The debacle in long dropped Priscilla like a stone. She would place eighth in the event, and finish sixth overall.

Time warp to the next night. Back view of a woman wearing shining golden stretch pants, in a pose of leaning, one leg straight and one bent, one muscled Sweetheart bun riding over the other. Priscilla Hill was outside the big closing bash at the Hyatt, which featured great food and an ear-damaging band and ran to all hours. Everybody went, at least for a little while. Party sounds from inside. But she was outside, leaning against a railing, looking down toward lobby level. The festivities sounded far away.

Standing next to her you could see that Priscilla was in a condition on the far side of despondency, in a reflective emotional vacuum.

"I really don't know what I'm going to do," she said, the first of a half-dozen times she uttered a sentence that carried this meaning. Priscilla was absolutely bereft. Happy words about how she was only twenty and could go to school or do anything else she wanted to do did nothing to make her less bereft.

Sure, she said, she could do those things. "But this has been everything, my whole life."

Elaine Zayak skated after Priscilla.

Momentarily it looked as though the craziness had been used up on Priscilla. A triple toe wally, the first of seven triples she had planned to do, went up and came down perfectly. All those voices howled with relief to see something go right. The arena was ready to see success. But the dastardly craziness was back again. A triple Salchow crashed and took Elaine down with it. Then she fell again on a Lutz-toe loop combination.

Elaine tried to save the program, but the craziness ran rampant, knocking her to the ice, wobbling jumps, scaring her and wrecking her presentation. Elaine went straight to the dressing room, too stricken to say anything at all to Dick Button.

Elaine's performance earned her a very so-so set of marks, not as low as Priscilla's. She was going to be third in long program. But of course nobody just then knew how she was going to place.

The thing to do was watch Rosalynn and see what would happen. It wasn't at all clear in Sweetheartland where Elaine was going to finish in the top three.

And Sweetheartland hoped mightily that the craziness was gone. The noisy sixteen thousand hoped as one that Rosalynn would come through.

And she did. She skated a cautious program, somewhat less technically demanding than usual because of her injury. But she made a show out of what she did, working her Sweetheart magic. The crowd was getting crazy over Rosalynn. Everybody hoped together that nothing would mess up the shrinking stretch of seconds to the end. And nothing went wrong.

All the spectators made their loudest noises. There, in Indianapolis, a new and beautiful American Sweetheart had materialized. But nobody yet knew which Sweetheart would be picked by the numbers. Only the numbers would tell who was National Champion. And they wouldn't tell anything until Vikki de Vries skated.

Vikki was in a position, in numbers, to win. But the psychological moment, skating after Rosalynn, was not right for triumph. The crowd had already given its heart to Ros.

Besides, Vikki caught the tag-end of the craziness that had savaged Priscilla and Elaine. Jumps bobbed and popped. She went down on a triple toe loop. But, all in all, her long program wasn't that bad. She got marks that put her behind Rosalynn, and ahead of Elaine.

The result was the skating equivalent of a photo finish. At first nobody was sure who had won. Everybody was doing arithmetic, with widely varying results, all the time wild with impatience to find out what the computer said.

This is what it said: Rosalynn was National Champion. Vikki was second overall. Elaine placed third.

One of skating's most dramatic nights was over. The crowd went home charged up by the fabulous plot reversals and gorgeously happy surprise ending of ladies' long program. Surprise is not normally a part of watching competitive skating.

But Scott, brooding in the emptying arena, was not so pleased. What had happened, particularly what had happened to Elaine, bothered him. He said so later. He couldn't enjoy the upset because he knew Elaine well enough to be pained by her misfortune. And there was something else—a message to him, an expansion on the message he had been given thirty seconds into his short program. Accidents *can* happen, even to Scott Hamilton, the first message said. And the new and just as sobering message said what might happen if more than one accident happened. Accidents could join forces and synergize into unstoppable disaster. And disaster could see to it that the 1981 National Champion did not become the 1982 National Champion.

# 25

# Unfalling

12:15 P.M. Saturday. One last bus ride north through Indianapolis and the New Ice Age to Carmel.

Onlookers packed the lobby, autograph hounds, kiddie skaters, Sweethearts free to watch Senior men because their own events were over. Talk ran around and around Friday night's surprises. The suspense of the night before gave Senior men's long program an atmosphere of suspense that it probably didn't deserve. The ladies' numbers going into the final event had been wide open. Anybody could have won. And anybody did win. But Scott's first in figures and second in short gave him a comfortable lead over the other men. The erratic performances of the others in the first two events—the ones high in figures were low in short, and vice versa—kept them close to each other and relatively far behind Scott. The Champ was really out of anybody's reach, barring a disaster on the scale of the disaster that had struck the leading ladies. That's what the numbers said.

But the numbers only said who was going to win at Indianapolis. Winning, just winning Nationals, would not be enough for Scott Hamilton. A win with a second or even third in long program, which the numbers said Scott could pull off, would hardly constitute success. Such a win would show the rest of the world a United States Champion who might be beatable. Dangerous whisperings would spread in the international Sweetheart community.

If Scott failed to win resoundingly, the whisperings would cross the eastern third of North America and jump the Atlantic that night. Oooo, the people would be saying in all Sweetheart languages, I hear he didn't skate very well. He almost blew his own Nationals. Bzzzz bzzzz bzzzz; and to the already considerable burden of skating better than anyone in the world would be added the burdens of stilling the whispers and burning off the defeat cloud that would darken his arrival at the World Championships in Copenhagen. Scott and every other skater feared the awful power of whispering. But long program was giving Scott a chance to stifle whispers that might have already been started by the repeated paragraph double three in figures and the fall in short. Scott was mortified on Saturday about his whisperability after the first two events.

The Scott people on Saturday seemed not to be shaken by the Champ's fall the night before. The guessing went that the disaster might bring him into focus. Insiders had sensed before that things had been going a little too easily for Scott's good, what with the injury and demoralization of David Santee. Scott himself had said that David's collapse contributed to his concentration failure in short. But the fall, which might have been caused by a competitive letdown, had cured that cause. Scott now had to unfall. And he had to beat the freeskating heavies from California—Robert Wagenhoffer and Brian Boitano—both in their contrary ways dangerous skating machines, both of whom could be counted on to do clean long programs.

So David was off Scott's enemy list. The Californians were causing enormous anxiety, but they didn't become enemies in the same all-encompassing sense in which David had been an enemy. Scott had elaborate reasons for the difference, which had to do with who deserved the respect and who had tried to win the wrong way and so on. But the real reason seemed to be that the threats posed by the Californians were relatively limited. One, or both, might embarrass Scott in long program, if something went wrong for Scott. That was all either could do. David, on the other hand, had just one year earlier given Scott a hard fight for both his titles. And 1982 Nationals had been widely seen, before it started, as another Hamilton-Santee confrontation.

The theory that falling down in short might have brought more good than bad was borne out by Scott's face. He went through the mob in the Carmel rink like a military vehicle, absolutely no-nonsense, as steady as he had ever appeared. No one would want to see someone coming after him, or her, with the look Scott Hamilton wore at noon Saturday. He showed absolutely no nervousness, no fear, no anger—nothing that could be worked on to his disadvantage. No skin for getting under; the face was a war mask.

The passing of Scott Hamilton caused the usual stir. Little princesses approached Scott and offered Nationals programs for him to sign. Somebody pointed out in wurbly Carmelese, "See, he's that little sucker over there."

Meanwhile, David Santee was wearing his own war mask, girding for a fight that seemed to appeal to him, a fight like that of his Hollywood alter-ego, Rocky. Goin' the distance. Winning, in his case, was not losing. In the best space and privacy that the crowded Carmel rink afforded, he jumped rope and went through elaborate stretching exercises.

While David Rockied, Scott was feeding quarters to a video game, warming up on evil Gorfians from outer space, who ridiculed him in hideous robot-talk when he got hit.

The Scott people, Kitty among them that day, were all there, polite and serious, as if the rink at Carmel were a funeral parlor. The occasion was not right for too much smiling or joking.

The Silver Wolf showed lupine unease. The effort of bringing himself and his skater to competition readiness, and keeping at readiness, kept him in an irritated condition of half attention. The shrinking percentage of Don's mentality that paid attention outwardly was just enough to want to pass the empty time before practice by talking. But the effort of talking and listening to what other people were saying irritated the rest of the brain. Difficult to tell what was going on inside the wolf skull. It must have been something like pre-blastoff at NASA, with computers talking to millions of electronic sensors and strung-out technocrats worrying about everything. Scott was the rocket, and Don was the Space Center.

Talking to Don in the last hours of competitive countdown was scary, but irresistible. His distant-sounding utterances could be fascinating.

On Saturday Don said, "I don't exist when Scott skates." His prognostications were all optimistic. "Oh, he'll do fine," the coach would say. "No, I'm not worried at all." But that was his grin talking, the grin that always said everything was going to be fine. The real level of concern, or unconcern, was impossible to assess.

Everybody else was saying the same thing. "Well, we'll see."

But then there was ice for skating. Scott wore a Pepperdine University T-shirt. Pepperdine was in Malibu, he said. On the ice he looked, as he had looked most of the week, great. Just great.

And where did Saturday go?

The hours vanished, Scott exiling himself in his room, nobody else with anything to say but "We'll see." A very lean day for the tape recorder.

There we were again, in the Market Square Arena, sixteen thousand people in restless percolation. Saturday night was a twin bill again, first Senior dance finals, then Senior men.

Ice dancing was gorgeous, as ice dancing always is. Even the worst ice dancers had style and polish on a level you saw only in the other events' medalists. The rules deprived dancers of the acrobatics that could rack up points in singles and pairs skating. Dancers had to stay on the ice, in contact with each other, moving in synchrony. The result was an event that emphasized the beauty and flow and showmanship implicit in skating on ice. If you had to choose to see only one event at a competition, ice dancing might have been the best choice. The blemishes on a so-so singles or pairs program were too easy to see, so in those events things didn't start to look good, and become truly entertaining, until the better skaters performed. Then, of course, things could get *gurr*reat.

The skating order: Brian Boitano. Scott Hamilton. David Santee. Robert Wagenhoffer.

Scott would tell me after everything had ended that he spent his last hours in an anxiety fit that had to do with skating after Brian. He had to look good after this kid who was getting to be a freeskating legend, still a bit rough-looking, but a powerful, clean jumper, a technical whiz.

Mark Cockerell, a Californian, tried for the record books. Third after figures, fourth after short program, he took a long shot that might have moved him up in final standings and earned him figure skating immortality by making him the first skater in history to execute a quadruple jump in competitive performance. A valiant effort, the quad crashed.

Just one more skater before Brian Boitano. Time to get a seat. The corridors under the arena's vast, peopled slopes were quiet. All but a few were up where you could see the ice. Ernie Hamilton, of all people, was hurrying around the far end of the rink.

"I've got to walk." He chuckled.

Yes, he was nervous, he said, nervous as hell. Maybe he would go up and look, but maybe he'd walk. The worst part of this moment, Ernie said, was that Scott had gone to a place where Ernie, his own father, couldn't do a thing for him. He walked on.

Brian on deck. The press section was packed, as was every other section. Then you saw how Brian could give other skaters jitters. His skating in 1982 was hardly stylish, but the jumps were killers.

From the mouth of Dick Button ("Wide World of Sports"):

"Brian Boitano has that wonderful quality of the youthful challenger. He's not restricted. He's loose. He's free. And along with it he has some marvelous technical ability. Coming up we see a triple axel—three and a half revolutions. This is the most difficult rotation jump done. . . . He has it secure enough, even though there's a slight problem at landing, to step into a double toe loop. Now that's quality control!"

That high-and-mighty triple axel—high as the boards, Scott would say in Europe—brought animal screams of delight. Those kids in the audience knew skating quality.

And so Brian made a very solid bid. Good, but not great, numbers came up. The numbers left plenty of room for higher scoring.

The sound was worse than animals dying. It shrieked like jet fighters flying low over the ice because there, on the ice, was Scott Scovell Hamilton.

"From the Philadelphia Skating Club and Humane Society, Scott Hamilton," the speakers said, the cheers drowning out the Champ's name.

The man in electric blue with flashing gemstones on his chest took his opening warship position, waiting for the music. The dark fanfare sounded and crashed. Wham! Scott scored a direct hit on the opening triple Lutz. The orchestra crashed again and Scott shot off a triple toe loop that exploded and cut like chain shot. In those opening seconds Scott and all his sixteen thousand Scott watchers established connections tying his jumps and spins and the rest of his tricks into the pleasure centers of all the attendant brains. The watchers bellowed and howled as Scott nailed the elements of his long program, like people going wild on a roller coaster. But the man causing all the pleasure didn't seem to be sharing it, not yet. The face of Scott Hamilton showed inward-looking blank concentration. He was working too hard, thinking too hard, to smile. He had to drive the big pleasure machine.

261

So the crowd swam through the slow section, roller coastering again at the climactic jump. The futzy part killed them. But the laughter didn't go on for long because the ice jester vanished into another triple and came down throwing off skating stuff so quickly the sixteen thousand voices went up into a continuous screaming thunder of approval. Scott went into the great skating giveaway smiling widely, delight spreading across his face into the final spin. He blurred and unblurred, transformed by joy. The crowd broke new noise barriers and stood as Scott bowed to both sides of the wide, ice-floored valley.

"That's the best I've skated," Scott breathed to his ecstatic, embracing coach. Everybody where Scott came off the ice was suffused with the general happiness.

The numbers, all 5.8s and 5.9s, with a total of seven 5.9s in both scores, brought one last sonic concussion from the crowd.

Even before the numbers came up, Scott was talking to Dick Button for television. "I couldn't be happier. I hit everything as clean as could be hit," Scott said.

Dick Button told Scott he was sensational, better than ever. Scott by then had caught his breath. He started a TV-jock, off-the-cuff improvisation, explaining what went right.

"I definitely think that's one of the finest performances I've ever done," he said. "Everything felt big. Everything felt controlled. I didn't have a low hip on anything. And I really just felt clean."

But he couldn't keep it going. "Oh, who cares?" he said. "It's over. . . ." Laughing stopped him from saying one more thing.

After Scott, David skated a performance that was technically rather lackluster, because of his injury, but still a hit with the crowd. The girls squealed, as they always squealed, when the bells in the Rocky music started pealing in the last part of David's long program. The final smile was a triumphal grimace, victory over pain.

Robert Wagenhoffer breezed through a technical *tour de force*, laying down everything with his West Coast insouciance. The Man Who Didn't Like to Fall Down. The Man Who Didn't Like to Get Nervous. He was the last skater, and he might have gotten a little less ice ecstasy than he deserved. You can only scream and clap so much.

Scott was first in long and first overall.

Robert was second in long and second overall.

David was fourth in long, third overall.

Brian was third in long, fourth overall.

The wrung-out but happy Scott people congregated down in the backstage cavern. Mrs. O held Scott's silver cup and the armload of rose bouquets that Scott had gotten after he skated.

It was well after midnight, but Scott had to stay and skate for the TV cameras, demonstrating jumps for a technical sidebar to go with future skating coverage. Peggy Fleming would work on-camera with him.

2:00 A.M. Sunday. Sweetheartland had long since lined up with plates and pillaged the fabulous buffet. The band was making a din louder by many decibels than the government would allow in a foundry, so talking to other worn-out adults was impossible. The kids had a great time, dancing and carrying on up by the band. It would have been a great party if you were a Junior-level competitor, in your fifteenth January. Even the Seniors seemed superannuated there.

This was how final events at Indianapolis ended. This was, in fact, how most figure skating competitions ended. A midnight bash in a hotel ballroom, which was really a tremendously expensive high school dance with too many adults watching, and the adults not having fun. You didn't realize to what extent the skating world was peopled with kids until you went to see one of these post-competition hotel parties.

For people older than seventeen who wanted to party there were sociables of all stripes going on in hotel rooms. Officials' parties. Coaches' parties. Parties thrown by convivial skating moms and dads. Soft partying and hard partying that screamed on until dawn. Parties where kids threw up, and secret parties—undoubtedly mythical—where mystery skate people performed unspeakable acts in groups. The latter stalked the hotels of Sweetheartland like Bigfoot, with everybody whispering and believing even though nobody whispering had laid eyes on the object of belief. But the prurient myth added atmosphere to what was already an atmospheric situation—a carriage-trade hotel full of gorgeous people unwinding after a week of winding up.

The Senior skaters' partying could be superb, the very best that a roomful of young adults with high-priced libations and rock and roll pumping out of a pricey Japanese boom box could give. Behind locked doors with brass numbers these skating Mouseketeers would get as cranked-up, mean, horny, unhinged, and hilarious as the rest of the post-teenaged U.S.A. on Saturday night. The rooms would rip themselves out of their hotels and roar down the highway to where all young America was going, gettin' ripped.

Tremendous events were unfolding high above the ballroom party, no doubt about it. Not an epochal party night like the one after Dortmund Worlds in 1980, where part of a very nice German hotel got wrecked, a supreme night of international fun. Far from equal to the partying known in other years right there in Indianapolis. The problem seemed to be that men's finals had ended so late that people got sleepy before the bacchanalia could be fully realized. Still, though, there were things upstairs worth checking out. And Scott in certain moods would have been delighted with the big room cooking with hundreds of people he knew, which would lead him upstairs to craziness among his peers. Scott, when the competitive pressure was off, could be as sociable as the next skater.

But Scott, in the wee hours Sunday, failed utterly to harmonize with the rest of the Hyatt. He was a figure apart, stalking solitarily up to the entrance of the noisy ballroom, looking for some minutes into the throbbing gloom inside. He had very little to say. What little he said was tired and sad. Reluctantly, he entered the grotto of people and noise, making an appearance that his station in Sweetheartland obligated him to make.

Victory had brought Scott Hamilton to a condition that looked a great deal like the condition brought by defeat to Priscilla Hill, who not fifteen minutes earlier had been looking over the walkway edge outside the party, wondering what was next. At two o'clock on Sunday morning, with skating festivities booming in the background, the winner and the loser were twins.

# 26

# The Victory Rose

"Champion Scott Hamilton receives a victory rose," it said under the two-and-a-quarter-by-four-and-a-quarter-inch photograph at the upper right-hand corner of the Indianapolis *Star*'s last twenty column inches of ebullient booster city newspaperese about the 1982 United States Figure Skating Championships.

The picture froze Scott forever as he took a flower from a teeny-tiny skating princess—six years old at the most—who had walked and slid on skates all the way to mid-rink while seven-thousand people said "Awwww" all together. Scott was taking his last bows after his show program, the finale to the "Exhibition of Champions" Sunday afternoon. The rest of the fifteen thousand people who should have been watching Scott and the Senior-level medalists and Junior and Novice champions do their show numbers were kept away from Market Square by one more foot of snow. But the half house was enough to reach an appreciative emotional critical mass and charge the sight of the U.S. Champion and a skating pixie with the proper all-American goo that the moment deserved. A very cute thing was happening. Scott gave the little girl all the overacted, big-brotherly tenderness—he skates like a demon, but, gosh, he seems so nice—that the moment required. Our hearts were warmed. Aw . . .

The picture doesn't show the girl, just Scott leaning forward with a flower in his right hand. At that moment, we in the arena were blinded by the Champ's virtuoso corniness with the moppet.

But the camera saw through, and the truth appeared stark naked in ink tones and halftones in the *Star*. He looks terrifyingly tired in the picture, his eyes pulled back into three-inch sooty circles, his features so drawn with fatigue that he positively resembles "E.T.," the reptilian outer space creature that stole America's heart in a movie exactly the same way Scott was stealing it on the ice.

It is a tribute to his art that Scott didn't look that way to his audience. His vitality is dazzling, so what we saw was the usual five foot three inch "dynamo" (the *Star*'s words). "The little man on the flashing blades with the phenomenal footwork."

Before the exhibition Scott's weariness was not quite as stunning. Still, it weighed on our final interview. We huddled, intent and serious on what was being said, in the room that had been used for after-program press conferences, strewn now with the wreckage of a major event: handouts and results-sheets and foam coffee cups. Scott had a great deal to say, but fatigue seemed to control his speaking, pushing him in and out of subjects, pulling him on and off lines of thought:

Except for long, I haven't really walked away from anything and felt really good about it. Figures were okay. First and third were good, but the double three was kind of scary. That was kinda weird. Short program was bad, because of the double axel. So I haven't really been able to take pride in anything I've put down, except the long program.

*Angry Friday night?*

I was just mad, because I wanted to win short. I wanted to win all three aspects of competition. Because it's gonna get to Worlds, or Europeans, that I was second in short. Because I fell. You know? And that doesn't look good. You want to go there and have them say that they've never seen you skate better, ever.

*Will the Europeans hear about you taking the double three over?*

Oh yeah, people will talk. It should have been boom, boom, boom. You want to convince everybody that you can't miss. That you're so talented and good that these things are a breeze for you, and really easy. That you're that much better than everybody else who has trouble with jumps.

*Before short you were joking with Carlo and Christa about falling on the combination. Was that a genuine premonition that you were going to fall?*

I don't know. No, sometimes it just feels good to get that sort of thing off your chest. I was really worried about the combination. I did it great on Sunday, great on Monday. Good on Tuesday. All right on Wednesday. (Giggles, mimes panic.) By Thursday they were kind of sloppy. Friday they were a mess. I didn't think I was ever going to be able to land it in the program. But I never thought I'd miss a double axel. Never, ever.

*Thought that business with your dad might have had something to do with the break in concentration in short, the fall.*

No, not really. But that was frustrating. I just didn't want to spend the whole day walking around worrying about a passport. You know? I mean, I've got other things to think about than worrying about a passport. And walking all over the city and trying to get that settled. Oh, Ernie was kinda following me around a little bit. Well, you see, he wants to help, and I understand it, I love him to death, but during competition he makes me nervous. Because I always feel I should be spending time with him, but there's nothing to talk about. I gotta get my head straight. You see, there's been so many people around all the time, and it's getting more and more and bigger and bigger and bigger. It's getting a little bit overpowering. "Oh, you want to have dinner tonight? Sure, let's all eighteen of us go out to dinner tonight." Wonderful! Gee, this is fun, you know? At a competition I like to go up to my room and watch TV. Worlds is a lot of fun. Because Michael's there. I'm there. I go up to the room and watch TV, be relaxed, go to practices. I'm usually practicing for most of the day, and if not, I'm with one of the kids.

*Michael Seibert, the U.S. Dance Champion?*

Yeah, he's my roommate. Always at all Worlds, Internationals. Every time I've roomed with him, I've won. He's a really good guy.

*What did you do for companionship here?*

I just saw a lot of people. The most I spent with any one person was probably Jo Jo. I tried to stay away from my father and Mrs. O and Mrs. Camp as much as I could. Mrs. Camp is usually pretty stabilizing. Mrs. O, she's great, but I get antsy when I get around her. So, I kinda stay away from everybody. Jo is so good, because she doesn't talk about skating all the time. And just spending time with her is really fun. She's great. It's hard to dislike Jo Jo because she's so genuine.

*Then you have to shut everybody else out.*

I just want to build my little wall and get my concentration settled. I get really scared. I don't want to get so distracted. . . . Skate Canada one year, the last time I missed my double axel in short program, I was, like, messin' around and really relaxed and jokin' around, and huggin' and kissin' everybody. Warmin' up, I warmed up my legs fine and everything else, but when it came down to the competition, I was just—my concentration was just blown out of my mind. I had no idea what I was doing. So I was gone. There was nothing I could do.

*Has this been different for you than other competitions, the preparations before the programs, etcetera?*

I was the same. I haven't had as much rest as I usually do at competition. I had about five or six hours of sleep, which is ridiculous when you're trying to be competitive. But I felt kinda weird. Because I felt Robert was gonna skate perfect. And I knew Brian would. [A break while we get coffee, then talk turns to Saturday night, before long program, when Scott talked to Dr. Bruce Ogilvie, the sports psychologist]. . . . Because I was a little paranoid, so Don went looking for Dr. Ogilvie. And Don goes, "Oh, look who I ran into!" And I looked at Dr. Ogilvie and I go, "God, how long did it take Don to find you?" Don looked at me and walked away. I go, "I know my coach." He knew I was a little upset and paranoid before long last night. Don wanted me to talk to Ogilvie for about twenty minutes. So we just talked. About what it's going to take, and whether I'm ready to skate a good performance. Yeah, I was scared to death. Because I had to skate after the best freeskater in the world. I didn't want to look bad skating after Brian Boitano. Because I knew he wasn't going to be in the top two.

*Why wasn't Brian Boitano in the top three?*

Because David Santee's been there all his life. Because Brian got ripped off.

*Boitano was good, wasn't he?*

Damned good. I thought he should have made World Team.

*Is he really a better freeskater than you?*

No, I realized last night that he skated perfectly and got a standing ovation. And he did a triple axel—and that was great. But I did three different triples clean, and I repeated two of them. And I guess my program was better. I guess the results mean not only who can jump the best, but who's the better skater, too. I did the first triple Lutz in short program. In the United States. When I was doing triple Lutz consistently in my long program, nobody else was. Charlie Tickner wasn't—he never did. David Santee wiped out on the boards every time he tried one in competition. Like Boitano's doing now, I was doing in '78. Okay, I had three different triples. Solid, boom. Every time in the program. He has six, which is double, right? Which is really hard. But do more triples make that much of a difference in the program, where he can pull over and beat me? That depends on the judges. I had to wait for Charlie Tickner to get out. He'll probably have to wait for me to get out.

*Maybe you needed Brian to nail his program?*

I wouldn't have skated as well as I did if Brian hadn't skated that well. It's weird. I'm beginning to think that's the only thing that can make me skate well. Because last year David skated the performance of his life. And I skated the best I'd done up to that point. I was scared to death last year. I was wantin' to nail it. But it was much easier last year. Because I knew if I lost, big deal. Who cares? If I lost, it was something I could live with. If I lost this year, it would've been something that was kinda, "Oh my God, I've been dumped! Last year I was National Champion, and this year I'm second, or third, or I didn't make the team!"

*Afraid of Brian for the future?*

Well, I'm only gonna have to compete against him two more Nationals. Next year will be his first World Team. So he won't beat me, he shouldn't. Unless I bomb. See? That'll be his first one. In 1984 they're not gonna want to dethrone me. Because I'll be going in as World Champion, and Olympic medal opportunity. So I don't think he'll beat me, really.

*Wagenhoffer?*

Robert's all right. There's a lot of things that I don't respect about him, competitively. Like, "Oh, I just started doing run-throughs last Monday." Or the fact that he smokes a pack of cigarettes every day. But it's his way. Some people have to do it that way.

*You said Boitano's never missed an element in short program in competition.*

Ever. He's great. I think everybody knows it. They're all trying to come up with reasons why he's not on the team. Excuses: "Well, he's still kind of rough." His triple axel's gorgeous! Every jump he does is perfect. European's don't care if he's rough. Look at their skaters. They've got Norbert Schramm, who skates like he's about to take off. He looks like a Concorde jet. He can do triple axel, but big deal, he's so hazardous. I hope that when Brian wins Nationals—which he will, real soon—I hope he looks at me and respects me.

*You're the one who started all the falling on Friday night. What did happen to you in that double axel?*

The other night? I lost some concentration going into it, and

271

I was just too cautious. I don't know. I thought I landed it until I was sitting on the ice. I thought I had it. It makes me paranoid that I'm gonna do it again. But, you know, accidents can happen. But I'm not accident-prone. People like David are accident-prone. He's not usually, but he can be. Charlie Tickner was very accident-prone. There's no reason for it.

*Does a fall like that cause problems in the next program?*

It can, if you let it. It will, if you focus on it too much.

*What goes through your mind out there?*

Sometimes, you just kinda go through, and sometimes you notice things, and sometimes you don't. Last night when I was going through the triple toe loop, in the slow part, I remembered that at Norton Skate Don sat at the end of the rink and made me line it up, right towards him. Putting his arm out front, saying, "Line it up. Line it up!" Because I used to have a really weird triple toe loop. My feet were side by side. One hip was out. It was kind of Sunbeam Mixmaster in the air. Last night was nice. After the opening, I thought, "God, I feel good," because all the jumps were going up nice. I landed my double axel in the opening, like I wanted to do. Hit the triple sow, which I was worried about. Everything felt ideal. I was pushing a little hard in the opening. I felt strong. I was kinda tired at the end of the opening, so I knew I had to rest. But, towards the end of the futzy, I was worried about the triple sow at the end. After I hit that, I felt great. I felt really good. I knew I couldn't have skated better. Yeah, it was nice last night. Except the week before was the pits. Nothing could make up for the week before, no matter what. What's good about it now is that I got this thing for another year. That's great. That's one thing about figure skating. You get your title in January, and you get to keep it for eleven months.

*What was so bad about the week before long?*

It's been the worst Nationals I've ever been to. Transportation was lousy, the rinks were awful, the press was obnoxious. Did you hear what they put in the paper that day? After short? "Hamilton falls. Judges ignore fall. Give perfect score." It's like, hey, I can't do anything to lose here, right? Nobody can sit there and say maybe I'm better at this certain thing, or maybe I'm cleaner or something. Maybe I have something over another skater. No, all they want to say is, "No, he's gonna win anyway, it doesn't matter. He doesn't have to be good here. He doesn't have to be the best. All he has to do is show up and he'll win." That's why this year has been the toughest.

*You feel like you deserve the title now?*
Yeah.

# Oberstdorf, West Germany

*February 19–28, 1982*

# Copenhagen

*March 2–15, 1982*

1982 World Figure Skating Championships

# 27

# *Liebchenland*

The plane came out of the fuzzy late winter sky on the afternoon of Friday, February 19, 1982, bringing skater and coach and absolutely nobody else who had anything to do with them or their sport to Munich.

"Hello, ugly," the Champ said. "Boy, they let anybody come over here, don't they?"

We pushed out of the terminal into the wet concrete dusk where buses and cabs were waiting for people who wanted to go to Munich. You could tell, right there at the airport, that getting away from Sweetheartland was working healing magic on Scott and Don. Even the deepening stupor of jet lag was not going to kill their harmony and happiness.

The good cheer became giddiness at the big Munich *Bahnhof*, which on Friday night had a festival atmosphere. A little group in folk costume made music, and Scott and Don howled like coyotes, making fun of the yodeling. Scott bought film at a kiosk and made the lady who sold him the film pose for a picture. The ragtag locals in the depot cafeteria were much funnier than the yodelers. Scott and Don were carried away with hilarity. The food and beer were good, too. Then it was time to catch the train that would take us southwest, to the mountains.

Each platform showed more snow than the one before. Daylight would have displayed the Alps shark-toothing the horizon, looming higher and higher. Finally the train jinked to the end of its line, and three dazed Americans were met at the station by the manager of athletic facilities for the town of Oberstdorf and his wife. The car went to a dormitory and skater, coach, and writer collapsed in three little rooms and slept World Championship sleep under down-filled comforters that were thick clouds of motherly warmth. From the first, slumber in Oberstdorf was the best.

On Saturday morning at 7:30 A.M., Scott rose and ate the first of ten consecutive breakfasts in the dining room of the athletes' dormitory attached to the West German *Bundeseislaufzentrum* (Federal Skating Center in Oberstdorf, the southernmost municipality in West Germany, a town of about twelve thousand inhabitants at the top of a tiny wedge of the *Bundesrepublik* pushing south into Austria).

The dining room commanded, through picture windows, a view of the reason why Scott was there. Below Scott's table slumbered a medium-sized arena and an oblong of beautiful ice. In the low light of early morning the ice had a subdued metallic sheen, like pewter. In brighter lighting it puddled white, like milk spilled on the concrete floor. It looked like what Scott and Don later said it was, the best ice in the world. The ice was almost always in sight from that dorm. The building could have been designed to look outward, at the Alpine surroundings, but it looked inward, eyes turned to its particular purpose, like a monk under a special vow. You ate looking at the ice. The dorm's lounge and conference room looked at the ice. One of the floors of dorm rooms had windows that showed the ice. Coming and going, even on the way to the shower, you had that ice in view.

Scott had been finding it hard, if not impossible, to concentrate on skating and nothing but skating, as he needed to concentrate to get ready for the World Championships, in his own country. So he was going to concentrate on skating in somebody else's country, at the rink in Oberstdorf. Don had earlier asked officials of West German Sweetheartland *(Liebchenland)* if he and Scott could hide out and train at Germany's skating center. The idea was to give Scott a respite from the dreadful craziness of being himself at home and also give him two weeks before the arrival of the U.S. Figure Skating Team in Denmark to make the complex physiological and cultural-emotional adjustments to being in Europe. The *Liebchenländeren* had been happy to extend their hospitality. The use of rinks in other countries, Don later explained, was a standard courtesy, something you could expect. You could particularly expect such courtesy if you were the World Champion.

And so the morning of Saturday, February 20, found Scott in Germany. The man at the table telling Scott about the ice-time schedule was Erich Zeller, West German National Figure Skating Coach. Herr Zeller was a quiet, serious character of indeterminate middle-age. He was short and muscular, the years having thickened his skating physique so that he now looked like a well-to-do farmer. Like virtually everybody with some years in the international figure skating community, Herr Zeller spoke good English.

Scott had patch after breakfast, then another patch, freeskating at noon, and another freeskating session in the later afternoon. This was about the same as his practice schedule back home. The Champ would be skating with Norbert Schramm, a West German up-and-comer whose star had risen precipitously with his recent first place at the 1982 European Championships. The other notable singles skater on Scott's ice was Manuela Ruben, West German Ladies Champion.

They were not in evidence at breakfast, but Oberstdorf was also the temporary training home of British ultraskaters Jayne Torvill and Christopher Dean, reigning World Champions, future Olympic Champions, and arguably the greatest ice dancers of all time. Jayne and Chris were, probably, already on their ice, which in the morning was another full-sized rink adjacent to the one visible from the dining room. That rink had high windows, with a glorious view.

The British ice dancers and Scott would do a great deal of socializing during Scott's ten days at Oberstdorf. Jayne and Chris had been particular friends of Scott since the tour after 1981 Worlds, their first extended exposure to each other. Not only did Scott like the British dance team, he had the deepest respect for their seriousness and training discipline, his final measure of other skate people. They in turn recognized a fellow true believer. Scott kids around a lot, they later told the tape recorder, but he's really a completely serious competitor, who takes every minute on skates, even exhibitions, very seriously. "He doesn't mess about on the ice," said Jayne.

Those two absolutely did not mess about on the ice. Practice for them had an intensity that burned every second of ice time in the cleanest and most efficient conceivable training flame. Torvill and Dean doing run-throughs made what most of us call work look hopelessly undirected. Their seriousness was phenomenal. Off the ice they were more dignified and undemonstrative than most of their American counterparts, but the reserve was not unfriendly.

The evening meal at Oberstdorf would be taken every day by Scott and Don and me while Jayne and Chris worked below us on their original set pattern dance, which that year was performed to a particularly steamy version of Gershwin's "Summertime." The harmonica howled all alone and the orchestra breathed heavily and the ex-secretary and the former policeman from Nottingham performed slow-motion embraces while traveling at absurd speeds across their piece of ice. The effect was sublime, particularly when Jayne hooked her leg around Chris, her face melting in a very convincing counterfeit of the humid desire described by the music. "Yes, I guess we're acting," Chris said. "All skaters should be actors."

It was very difficult to put together Jayne the ice vamp with Jayne in person, who evoked, in presence, in a distant fashion, the late Winston Churchill. Jayne's cheeks nudged downward in a pretty imitation of the face of the heroic bulldog. This is not to say that Jayne was unattractive. She was adorable, but adorable in a bulldoggian manner. She was, more or less, Kitty's size and weight, five feet tall and a hundred pounds, with a trace of bottom-heaviness and a shadow at the belly that may have been a consequence of her adoration of the local pastries. An afternoon off for Chris and Jayne was apt to include a trip to one of Oberstdorf's dozen-odd *Konditerei* for what she called "sweeties."

Jayne seemed to be the more stolid, and forceful, of the team, an impression that the two of them confirmed. She was the emotional anchor of the pair. Chris was dreamier and more vulnerable, the supplier of choreographic ideas, whose contact with the skating muses seemed to make him more susceptible to emotional upset. Chris was about ten inches taller than his partner, handsome and trim. He conducted himself off the ice with constabular earnestness, a bright and disciplined peace officer, which was, of course, his role in life before skating took all his time. Jayne and Chris had both quit working in August 1980, to train for the 1981 Worlds.

In his press conference after the win that was going to happen at Copenhagen, Scott talked about the benefits that came from sharing the skating center at Oberstdorf with the British ice dancers: "What really helped me was to watch Torvill and Dean. To watch their training habits and to watch their relationship was unbelievable."

Besides Torvill and Dean there were a handful of lesser skaters getting ready for Worlds at Oberstdorf, a German pair of dancers and a Finnish dance team. The Finns were teenagers, flawlessly matched, white-blond and blue-eyed and both six-footers. The rink complement included some kids. Most of the youngest *Liebchenländeren* were gone, as their ranking competitions were over, but a few remained, under the instruction of a handful of coaches that included a German dubbed "Cricket" by Scott, the wife of the town's athletics manager, who lived in and administered the *Bundeseislaufzentrum*. Cricket had a vivid recollection of Scott in the summer of 1976, wild with excitement after winning a silver medal at the competition in Oberstdorf. He was so excited, she said, and so funny, the tiny seventeen-year-old shouting into the telephone, wearing the Alpine hat that was a gift from official Oberstdorf. Immediately after the triumph he had to shout the news back to his mother in Bowling Green.

On the morning of Saturday, February 20, Scott was a good deal less energetic. The gnomish features were blue-gray and the face pulled downward in a manner that said the day was a victim of terrible jet lag. But Scott was going to all his practices. He wasn't going to push himself that Saturday, but he was going to skate.

How do you feel, Scott?

"I feel," he said, "like a foreigner."

# 28

# Mystery Man

The *Liebchenländeren* were, it seemed, all talking about Scott, even though Scott was at a table in the dining room, easily within hearing distance of everybody else.

Sssscott, they were saying at Tuesday's breakfast. Every time somebody said it, you'd look up from the cheese, cold cuts, rye bread and butter, and the headless empty egg in its little cup, to see who was saying something about Scott Hamilton, who was across the table and next to the picture window that looked out on the ice arena. Scott worked on the same sort of breakfast, which was really more like a Mudlands light lunch than breakfast. Initially he had found the *Bundeseislaufzentrum* breakfasts alarmingly unfamiliar, but after a few days he was saying sausage and cheese and soft-boiled eggs made an ideal morning meal, even better than breakfast back home.

So Scott ate, paying no attention to the Germans hissing Sssscott to each other. Sssscott had nothing to do with him, anyway. It was the more audible syllable of the Bavarian salutation *Grüss Gott*, which meant, more or less, Praise God. *Grüss Gott* was a traditional way of saying hello. Everybody in the immaculate little dining room said it to everybody else, giving that false impression that the *Liebchenländeren* were talking to—or about —Scott.

Scott finished his coffee in implosive, quiet thought, eyes drawn to the window and the oblong of ice that puddled below like fresh-poured lead. He stirred and watched the currently deserted arena as if something were happening.

"The ice," Scott said. "It's saying, 'Scratch me.' It's making me guilty to be down there." It seemed by the quietly convincing way he spoke—he wasn't self-consciously using a figure of speech—that the ice really had said something to Scott Hamilton.

Very shortly after the ice called him Scott was breathing its chill breath, pulling supple skate boots over brown knit socks. He stretched and then put blades on the ice. He held in his hand a device made of white metal, with a black rubber handle. The thing simultaneously brought to mind a weapon—it was about the right size and configuration for a small machine gun—and a camera tripod—the part that might have been a gun barrel was a collapsed cylinder of inner-fitting tubes, like a tripod leg. The implement also had short spiky blades, suggesting a giant glass-cutter. Handed to a person unfamiliar with skating, it would have been a complete mystery. But in figure skating, such a tool was as familiar and necessary as ice-making machinery and skates. The thing in Scott's hand was called a scribe. He used it at the beginning of each patch. The scribe filled the same purpose as a tuning fork in the playing of a stringed instrument. Before Scott began practicing his competitive compulsory figures, he tuned up by tracing perfect circles scratched in the ice with his scribe. Each day the scribe set mechanically a standard which Scott endeavored to match with flesh and bone and concentration.

Scott pulled out the tripod leg of his scribe, turning set screws so the inward-fitting tubes would hold their places. When the leg stretched nine feet from the scribe's centering spike, Scott set the last loosened screw and planted the spike. Then, squatting over the spike, he held the scribe's rubber handle and rotated. The stubby, downward-pointing blade at the very end of his scribe's extended leg whipped around Scott, etching a circle eighteen feet in diameter, roughly sixty feet in circumference. The blade scraping the ice made a prolonged concrete sibilance, with metallic singing in the sound. Scratching a sidewalk with a steel chisel would have made the same sound. That first circle was laid down near the board. Scott then scribed another circle, carefully planting the center so the two circles would be tangent, and so their center points and point of touching would lie on a line perpendicular to the boards.

In patch Scott used his scribe just as a drawing compass is used in schoolkids' plane geometry. You could tell he had instinctively mastered the simple geometry of circles in his years of using this giant compass. Actually, experience with the scribe was probably less important in Scott's innate geometry than the fact that after using the scribe, Scott *became* a scribe. For most of each year since his ninth year, six days each week, Scott had been a drafting instrument, solving geometric problems with the blades on his feet. (This business of Scott's innately knowing geometry because of compulsory figures raised a question that his school records in Bowling Green answered. Yes, he had done very well in geometry in school, and showed an early aptitude in spatial relationships. It would be very interesting to see if all fledgling skaters show similarly expanded geometric consciousness.)

The first figure Scott practiced, also the first in competition, the inside rocker, consisted of three tangent eighteen-foot diameter circles, with the center points of the three circles lying on a line. But Scott began the practice session by skating the two touching scribed circles, tracing simple figure eights. This was the tuning-up, a chance to get the feel of ice under him and allow his body parts to remember their diverse roles in making figures. Once the ice was firmly beneath Scott he began an inside rocker, pushing and riding edges through the big figure. Scott's turns, which were rocker turns, came at the points where the uppermost and lowermost circles touched the center circles. Rocker turns were outwardly similar to three turns, instantaneous one-footed switches in direction, but in edge technicalities a rocker turn was quite distinct from a three turn. One difference that became apparent to the nonskater was that rocker turns sounded different. Instead of the delicate two-beat swi-swish of the three turn, a rocker turn scraped. The ice-marks left by a rocker turn also were quite distinct from the print of a three turn.

After tracing the first inside rocker, he studied it briefly. Then Scott moved perhaps a foot farther from the boards, and began a new figure offset evenly from the first one, but intersecting it in many places. He used his ice with the same economy he would have used in a crowded rink, packing a narrow patch with closely spaced figures. Scott slowly created a looping filigree of ice scratches that was very pretty, and very incomprehensible, from the sidelines. It seemed fantastic that concentration allowed him to separate each new figure he skated from the three or four figures with which it intertwined. You would have thought the dead figures would distort the living figure underfoot, or otherwise distract or annoy Scott, but the Champ was absolutely indifferent to the growing clutter. He saw only what he needed to see.

You also might have thought that watching Scott make circles and turns in the ice, for two hours, with no music playing and no talking, would be killingly dull. But those hours, particularly at Oberstdorf, were far from boring. Figures by then were nearly as satisfying to watch as freeskating sessions. Of course the atmosphere and aesthetics were entirely different. Freeskating was a show. Figures allowed you to contemplate, in a monkish hush, the sources of Scott Hamilton's greatness. You could watch the Champ becoming the Champ. This is not to mention Scott's gorgeous physicality. The same perfect body design that made him breathtaking in freeskating worked just as powerfully in figures. You could, without knowing the first thing about figures, know for certain that Scott was making fabulous figures. You would know it because Scott looked so very good doing them. When Scott skated, no part of him, not a proton, was not skating. The concentration of bodily purpose was complete.

Working on his inside rockers, Scott was pressed into the

stylized two-dimensionality of Egyptian tomb paintings. His free leg and arms made slow-motion adjustments, weighting and counterweighting, balancing the bodily apparatus that worked the steel blades beneath him. Out of this deliberation and slowness burst the quick direction-switching turns.

The face was drawn down, serious but not unhappy. Beneath the immobility moved total alertness and the ecstatic concentration of a surgeon. Scott might well have been a surgeon, performing a complex operation with foot scalpels, saving a life. And the sound of Scott working was the sound of orthopedic surgery. A knife was cutting bone.

Scott worked with the sober joy of a person given totally to an endlessly demanding life's work. On several occasions he had tried to tell the tape recorder what exactly he loved, what pleased him, in his hours of scratching the ice. But he faltered, finding it hard to say what he meant. Out of these falterings came the clear and simple idea that working on the ice, particularly when the work was going well, could make Scott deeply happy. On a good day, happiness was there in each particular, even in the noises of steel and ice. "I love the sound of a good turn," Scott said.

The inside rocker, the big three-lobed figure, had two centers, two points where circles met. Scott's points of pushing-off, where his free foot became his skating foot, and his skating foot became his free foot, were at those centers, first one, then the other. Scott pushed and rolled fast around a circle, turned and made a semicircle, his speed constantly diminished by friction. At the point of almost stopping he was at the center that was not the center from which he had just pushed. He pushed again. There were six such pushings. Then, abruptly, Scott stepped out of the inside rocker and began looking at it.

Watching Scott smashed into a human circle-making instrument brought you very close to the heart of the Hamilton skating machine. He seemed from that little distance entirely unlike the turbulent, emotionally volatile kid-becoming-a-man who had all

287

those Scott women aching to take care of him. No, he was some-body else again. He was a mystery. It was never clear which of the voices that talked to the tape recorders was the voice of the absorbed, steady, masterful ice surgeon. It was never clear, for that matter, if that man ever said a word to the tape recorder. Always there is this feeling that the ice-enraptured craftsman in Scott Hamilton said nothing at all to the recorder during all those months on the Hamilton trail.

So Scott was having a great day. He said so while the Zamboni howled and ate the first hour's figures. Figures were almost en-tirely without the psychological vagaries and catches of freeskat-ing. If you worked, Scott said, they got better. He had been working, and his figures at Oberstdorf were making him very happy indeed.

# 29

# Norbert: Strange Beings
# Haunt the Ice

Scott, who for ten days shared the ice with Norbert Schramm six hours daily, ate where Norbert ate, often at the same table, and knocked around in the evenings with Norbert, was blind to something that became apparent to most other observers in Oberstdorf. Behind those friendly piano teeth lurked a skater who was preparing to mount an all-out attack on Scott Hamilton. Norbert Schramm, the 1982 European Champion, on-again, off-again West German Champion, was beginning an assault on the World Championship that would, in Copenhagen, fail, but still scare the hell out of Scott. The attack was so grandiose and noisy and surprising, particularly to the Champ, that he would be temporarily demoralized and thrown into psychic confusion.

If you asked Scott during his days at Oberstdorf which skaters he had to beat at Worlds, he'd name a Canadian or a Japanese or a Frenchman. He didn't perceive at all that his most serious rival was Norbert.

It may have been that Scott blinkered himself on purpose because he needed a rest from the skating wars. Oberstdorf was meant to be a haven from craziness, so maybe the Champ kept his days there as craziness-free as possible by deliberately ignoring Norbert's challenges. Scott refused to return fire for the first five days or so. Then he returned fire, and conducted small psychological offensives. The great majority of Scott's mental forces stayed within the sanctuary, given over to fine-tuning his skating. The fighting with Norbert was miles from the core of Scott's consciousness. So, Oberstdorf remained for Scott and his coach an island of peace, in the year of bad craziness.

That Scott deliberately overlooked Norbert's war preparations in Oberstdorf explains in part why Norbert's achievements at Worlds were such a devastating surprise. Another contributing reason was that the features of Norbert's skating that would cause such a stir in Copenhagen were not apparent in practice. Without a few thousand people screaming and with just a few people watching and his programs dismantled for practice, Norbert Schramm did not look like a skater who could shake up Scott Hamilton, not in a million years.

It may be that Norbert's skating was so radically different from Scott's that Scott was unable to perceive what others would find so potent and exciting. Scott and Norbert were absolutely unalike. They differed in general and in detail, on and off the ice. Their only binding similarity was that they both skated on ice under the rules of the International Skating Union. They were both competitive figure skaters, but their skating was so opposite it seemed like stretching a point to say that they were in the same sport.

Norbert's win at 1982 Europeans had made him a national hero in West Germany, a country that—in contrast to its hypersuccessful Communist sisterland, East Germany—was having slim victory pickings in international sports. Nobody from the *Bundesrepublik* in the winter of 1982 had won much of anything. Nobody but Norbert. And there was more to the craze for Norbert Schramm than that year's medal starvation. One of the coaches at Oberstdorf pointed out that it had been more than eighty years since a German had won the European Figure Skating Championship. Even the great Manfred Schnelldorfer, who had won the 1964 World and Olympic Championships, failed to become *Europameister.* In 1982 the top West German pair had been put out of action by an injury. Christina Riegel and Andreas Nischwitz, who won bronze at 1981 Worlds, were a national sports sob story, just as Americans Tai Babilonia and Randy Gardner had been when an injury ruined their hopes for a medal in the 1980 Olympics. Chris and Andy would be back in 1983. But, in the meantime, all of West Germany's hopes of winning something really big were vested in Norbert. It stood to reason that all of *Liebchenland,* skating officialdom, the sports press, and the public, were mobilized behind Norbert, giving what Scott called "the big push."

Looking at Norbert's record, you wouldn't have guessed any of this was in the offing. Norbert was as inconsistent as Scott had been consistent in recent competition. His win in Europeans had been preceded by a loss in his own national championships to a skater named Heiko Fischer. Fischer subsequently placed too low at Europeans to be one of the two West Germans who would compete at Worlds. The other countryman of Norbert's who would skate at Worlds in Senior men's division was Rudi Cerne, who trained under Carlo Fassi at the Broadmor. Cerne had been West German Champion in 1978 and 1980, Norbert in 1979 and 1981.

Norbert was seventh at 1981 Worlds. The judges placed him seventh in figures, in short program, and in long program. The five skaters who had placed above Norbert and below Scott in Hartford were all going to be at Copenhagen. Given this background, it's not surprising that Scott was worrying about Igor Bobrin, Fumio Igarashi, Jean-Christophe Simonde, and Brian Orser a good deal more than he was worrying about Norbert.

On paper, Norbert didn't look dangerous. In person, to Scott Hamilton, he looked quite harmless. Scott had been expecting much more. To a tape recorder on Tuesday, February 23, Scott said: "I came in thinking he's doing all these wonderful things. But he's the same as he was last year. And he was seventh at

Worlds last year. I just thought with all the talk that's going on about him that he'd improved immensely. I expected something else."

I asked Scott later if he was planning to shoot for anybody in particular at Worlds. He said he'd see when he got there. Would it be Norbert? Scott dismissed the idea. "He's not skating well enough. He's good, but he's too inconsistent."

So there was Norbert Schramm, Oberstdorf's number-one son. He was a corporal in his nation's army, doing required service time as a reservist attached to a post at nearby Sonthofen. The base at Sonthofen, the town where Norbert's parents lived, was for German competitive sportsmen, and the army seemed to serve as a means of giving money to competitors. In spite of his weekend warriorhood, Norbert, like a lot of young Germans, was a fervent pacifist. Norbert was tall for a singles skater at about five feet eight inches, slight in the upper body but with long thighbones sheathed in heavy, flat muscles. His face was a stylized assemblage of oversized features, an art face like the faces on the idols carved out of lava on Easter Island. The effigy face was topped with a neat helmet of brown hair, something like the Beatle mops of yesteryear. Milky blue eyes looked out from under Norbert's arching high brows. Norbert was twenty-two that year. He spoke very good English.

Norbert's stylized physiognomy was just right for his skating, which was intensely stylized. On the ice Norbert performed what looked like weird rituals to lost gods. He used a system of choreography invented and perfected by himself to express his own deep thoughts. The result was uniquely Schrammian. Of course he spun and jumped and did more or less what everybody else did in competitive performances, and he did it very well, but the technical elements were overwhelmed. What you saw was a message in bodily hieroglyphics. Strange beings haunted the ice.

"I think, yes, I'm different from other skaters," said Norbert. "In which way, I don't know. The basics, I think, are my feelings.

I try to put my feelings of the music, I try to put them in movements. And I want to improve in this. Put more in my program, put more of myself."

You could begin to sense the profound differences between Norbert Schramm and Scott Hamilton if you went into Norbert's room at the *Bundeseislaufzentrum* dorm. The room was like that of a certain kind of college kid, a sophomore with an artistic bent who was heavy into the old counterculture. Norbert, who wanted to study art when he was done skating, had painted a naked, dark-skinned woman, bent over backward and rendered in profile, on the wall. His bed was curtained with gauzy fabric, threaded with gold. Other self-consciously artistic touches abounded.

You could go upstairs and look at Scott Hamilton's temporary quarters and know right off that you were dealing with a diametrically dissimilar sort of guy. You saw the room of a man who had come to do the job, with the things he needed to do the job arranged in paramilitary neatness. Nothing more. No frou-frou. Of course this was only a temporary bivouac for Scott. But you could go back to his room at the Landises' and see the same spareness and restraint. You had a machine for making rock and roll noises (a necessity for Scott), a few pictures, and that was about it. Scott's surroundings did not proclaim a great deal about Scott. The walls made no statements about his soul.

Scott Hamilton would not, under any circumstances—not on a bet, not on a dare—have painted things or made gauze hangings for his bed. Such decorative self-expression would have been foreign, and silly, to him, as strange and irrelevant to the Hamilton world view as were Norbert's choreographic eccentricities on the ice. No way would Scott have weirded up his competitive programs by flapping his arms like a pterodactyl or turning his hands into little Pac-Man things that chased each other in front of his face or striking bizarre, unbalanced-looking positions. To Scott Hamilton, Norbert's expressive experimentation and self-indulgence on the ice were entirely beside the point.

"He wants to be different, all right?" said Scott. "He wants to do something that nobody else is going to do. With me, I want to do something that everybody else can do, but I want to do it better. Everything. Spinning, jumping, programs, figures, consistency. I don't want to go so far off into left field that I can't be compared with anybody. I *want* to be compared with everybody. All Norbert's doing is making funny hand gestures. It's nice showy stuff. But it's not skating. It's stuff you need to do in the 'Ice Capades,' but it really isn't competitive."

The differing emphases and characters of these two skaters included completely different styles of practicing. Scott, the technician, pilot of the ultimate skating machine, had technical practices. He'd warm up each part of his machine, do a program run-through, and then work on the parts that seemed to need work. The process was orderly and quite formal, like checking out a jet airplane. And Scott never held back, no matter who was watching. He did everything he was going to do in competition, every day, unless some particular problem kept him from doing everything.

Norbert had artistic practices. He seemed to daub a little on an ice canvas, stand back and look, and then daub again. Norbert, characteristically, gave a lot of practice time to his choreography. He worked intensely on the things that went between his program elements. His strange beings, the personal ice fetishes that swam and flew and crawled through Norbert's programs, were thoroughly exercised every day in Oberstdorf.

The stuff was a scream to watch. A living pageant of sixty years of German avant-gardism, from turn-of-the-century Expressionism to Dada to Max Ernst's surrealism, performed to contemporary electronic machine noises. The closing anthem in Norbert's long program sounded just like woodworking tools singing "Carry Me Back To Ole Virginny." At one point there was thunderous slow booming, and Norbert lunged down the rink like an Olympic fencer having a bad reaction to medication. Everything he did was lurid and twisted out of shape. He reached for things that weren't there. He transformed himself into things from other dimensions. Like Scott, he had a final scratch spin. But instead of blurring with his arms in a graceful over-the-head Gothic arch, Norbert gave his spin the Schramm touch by hanging his forearms vertically, elbows bent, from his horizontal upper arms and spreading the fingers of his long hands wide. Norbert's taste was sometimes execrable, but he wasn't afraid to put his ideas out where everybody could see them. His conceptual rear end was on the line. You had to give him that.

But Scott wasn't giving Norbert anything. The German's rather unusual way of practicing his really unusual material didn't impress Scott one bit. He told the tape recorder so on a number of occasions. The stuff that was going to count, the technical stuff, wasn't there—just look at Norbert's jumps. Everything is wacko and hazardous, Scott would say. And he was right. Norbert's elements had none of Scott's razor edge and surgical precision. Norbert was an exciting, powerful jumper, with triples in his repertoire that Scott didn't do in 1982. But everything looked off-kilter and uncontrolled. He was more daredevil than technician.

Scott's final word on Norbert's skating aesthetic was that it was camouflage, a disguise to make bad technique look artistic.

But Scott was heading for a rude awakening. The Norbert who fiddled around in practice and could be so dreadfully unlucky in competition—the guy who every so often skated into the boards —could also be dreadfully lucky. And the hallucinatory skating that Scott found so insubstantial at Oberstdorf was going to drive people in Copenhagen wild. The Worlds judges were going to go crazy for Norbert.

But that was two weeks away. Scott didn't see a thing to worry about in Oberstdorf. And Norbert himself fostered Scott's underestimation by going to pieces when Scott started working out at the *Eislaufzentrum.* The consequence of Scott's day-in, day-out excellence, his seemingly unbreakable concentration, was the temporary collapse of Norbert's skating. On Monday he fell hard and bruised his seat and lost a day and a half of freeskating practice. After that he bounced back, but remained somewhat furtive on the ice.

Scott made note of this: "He's pulled in his guns, considerably. He's not skating hard. I mean he's not showing his wares. It's almost like he's waiting for me to leave before he starts training. I'm doing fine. He's the one who's a mess."

It must have been frustrating, indeed, to be Norbert Schramm just then, absolutely unable to get the opposing skater to take you seriously.

At midweek, we three Americans and Herr Zeller and Norbert went to the home of Norbert's parents in Sonthofen for afternoon coffee and pastries. Norbert's father, who was in insurance, was gone, so Frau Schramm presided, serving great coffee and wonderful whipped-cream creations from a local bakery. We sat around a massive table in the Schramm's new house, which had been given a native country-home look by heavy wooden furniture. Pleasantries went around, lame jokes, translated for Frau Schramm, and indulgent laughter.

Norbert hooked up a video recorder that he'd gotten while at a competition in Japan and pulled the television around so we could watch tapes of Europeans, and tapes of exhibitions and a television special from Switzerland in which Norbert had starred. Then there were albums of articles and fan mail, saved and bound by Norbert's mother. We looked at those things, too.

All the while an oblivious Scott Hamilton was being regarded by Frau Schramm, in a level, quizzical gaze that brought to mind Mrs. Santee on the buses in Indianapolis. Another skater's mother was looking at the nightmare of other skaters' mothers, Scott Hamilton. It was being asked in another language, but still you could tell the silent skating mom's question reverberated behind the eyes looking at Scott. "Why you?" the question asked. "Why you and not my son?"

Meanwhile Norbert was showing Scott, in black and white, everything Scott was going to find out in Copenhagen. He was showing Scott things he couldn't show him on the ice in Oberstdorf. The video and newsprint and letters said that Norbert, in the right circumstances, could skate credibly, that the judges were buying his style, and that Germany and Europe were very excited about Norbert Schramm.

The boldness of the message-sending in the Schramm house that afternoon was astounding. An afternoon spent similarly with one of Scott's established ice enemies—David Santee, for instance—would have driven Scott wild. He would have fumed and done everything possible to mete out ice humiliation. The afternoon at Schramm's house got only the most feeble rise out of Scott. He said it psyched him up to do a good evening practice. But he refused to acknowledge that Norbert might have been trying to say something scary with the video and albums. And Don, uncharacteristically, failed to see the Schramms' challenge. Aww, the coach said, he's got a new tape machine, a novelty, and he's excited about his skating, and he wanted to show it all off. Perfectly innocent . . .

So there they sat, with coffee and astronomically high-calorie delights, cheerfully oblivious to the not-very-secret writing on Mrs. Schramm's walls.

Boy, the writing said, have we got a surprise for you.

# 30

# The Miracle of Oberstdorf

Maybe the *Bundeseislaufzentrum* was built on holy ground. For reasons wonderful and mysterious, Scott Hamilton was possessed for ten days by a saintly and entirely un-Scottlike forbearance. Having Norbert Schramm in his face was only one of the temptations to wrath that came up in Germany. But Scott resisted all temptations to anger. This was not the Scott of Morristown and Indianapolis, who never passed up a chance to rage like a wolverine possessed by demons; who seemed, indeed, to need and even enjoy such fits. No, this was Scott under the protection of invisible ice angels, or sanctified by the miraculous mountains. Or something.

With or without Norbert Schramm, it might have been more than Scott could stand to practice long program every day in front of paying audiences of up to two hundred people. He had to do just that at Oberstdorf. The national skating center was a tourist attraction with a big draw that year because of Norbert. On the days when it snowed, the seats on the side of the arena opposite the dorm were filled with people looking and clapping. Sunny days drew fewer skate watchers at the noon freeskating session. But every day at least a few dozen people sat and watched. An audience every day was bad enough, but the audience at Oberstdorf was unabashedly pro-Norbert, and, of course, their preference was obvious because their national skating wonder was there on the ice in front of them.

The noon freeskating could well have been a disaster. But disaster never threatened. Scott forwent entirely whatever trouble all the Germans watching might have caused. He had been saying that what he needed just then was privacy, him and his coach and an ice rink, and nobody to screw everything up. Miraculously, those were the conditions that prevailed, in spite of the other skater who wanted to beat him and the hundreds of people clapping for the other skater. Everybody but Scott and Don disappeared. Scott got exactly what he required, which was ten days of peace and privacy and unbroken concentration. That was the miracle of Oberstdorf. Scott Hamilton, by sheer power of spirit, transformed what could have been one more nervous catastrophe in 1982 into ten days of paradise.

In those ten days, Scott never once complained about the lack of privacy during the noon freeskating. He said nothing at all about his audience. The *Damen und Herren* were so much wallpaper to the Champ. The rare instances when Scott showed awareness of his tourist audience had nothing to do with the people; it had to do with their dogs. Scott thought dogs barking when he and Norbert did doubles and triples was funny.

The dogs were particularly comic at noon on a day when an ashen overcast blotted out the mountains and shook out a foot or so of new snow. The storm brought in the week's biggest crowd of skate watchers and at least three dogs—two dachshunds and a poodle. There may have been another *Hund* or two hunkered under his owner's seat. You couldn't see the dogs, except when the people filed in, or left when practice was over.

The audience that filled the stands on the Day of the Dachshunds were mostly post-middle-aged men and women who conducted themselves with discipline and absorption that suggested everybody was going to be tested afterward on what the skaters did. The eyes of two hundred glowing and fit-looking Germans in Alpine costume were absolutely glued to Scott and Norbert and Manuela Ruben. Rink crowds back in Sweetheartland, except in the most riveting moments, evinced pre-adolescent inattention, eyes going everywhere and voices talking. But the Oberstdorf skate watchers never quit looking, not for a second, and they acknowledged each jump and spin with polite clapping—no hollering or Sweetheart-jeering like back home, just hands coming together, like the applause at a chamber music recital held in church. The clapping caused the dogs to lose their otherwise flawless self-control. They barked for as long as the people clapped, four or five sharp vocalizations from each dog before the clapping and barking stopped. The canine voices carried over the restrained applause, so on our side of the arena the effect was that the three skaters were performing for a small group of dogs who knew and appreciated skating. Single jumps earned only the briefest woofs. Triples and other spectacular skating feats got full-throated barking.

So the day had a joke. The skating people shared the mirth by showing each other teeth. Herr Zeller grinned at Don, who in turn bared a slice of wolf ivory. Scott skated away from his jumps in his characteristic hands-on-kidneys contemplation of what he'd just done, but he smiled at the dying echoes from the dachshunds. The smile was a novel addition to a pose that normally included an inward-looking scowl. Scott was his own drill sergeant on the ice. Besides Scott skating, there was another Scott who followed the first, finding everything the skater did beneath approval, mouth drawn down in silent disgust. That inner taskmaster was not the sort of guy who wanted smiles, except of course cruel smiles, on his ice. But the barking was, temporarily, too much, even for a guy like that.

That transient smile on Scott's normally harsh and disapproving face during the moments after he completed his long-program elements was the extent of his reaction to his large audience of German general public. The dogs kept barking, but for Scott Hamilton they passed into the same invisible and soundless dimension that held the dogs' people. Then nothing sent sensory signals to Scott Hamilton but his skates and his coach. He had passed into the miraculous other state of Oberstdorf, the hushed skating cathedral where Scott and Don held daily ice devotions, far from worldly distractions. The hour's drill stretched, uncoupling into actions performed with the cadence and significance of the rituals in High Mass. It was always rewarding to watch Scott practice, but at Oberstdorf, practices expanded overwhelmingly, into one-hour recapitulations of everything Scott Hamilton knew and believed about figure skating.

Scott started practice the way he had started on the ice when he was nine: skating, just skating fast. He jigged and shook his legs briefly, all the off-ice warming-up he ever did before practice, and then put skates on the ice and catapulted into floor-level flying. He swooped raptor fast, but the pumping that pushed him around the rink so quickly was moderate and measured. Forward crossovers rocked him as a small boat rocks at anchor in a harbor, upper body swaying left and rightward as his legs pushed out to the sides. The most marked motion of his legs and skates was sideward. Speed was squeezed out of a machine made of ice and steel, just as speed can be squeezed from slow-pumping a bicycle in high gear. Scott's arms went winglike out to his sides, somewhat relaxed and below the vertical. His face went blank to us, reading inner gauges.

Scott pumped forward, and he pumped backward, following hard little haunches around the rink, watching over a shoulder. It took some hours of skate watching to figure this out—nonskaters always think of ice performers flying forward—but Scott's competitive freeskating had a great deal more backward motion than forward. The reason, Don explained, was that stability and balance were greatly enhanced when a skater traveled contrariwise. All but one of Scott's jumps went up with Scott facing away from the jump, and all jumps landed backward.

With Scott warmed-up and sculling backward, a disconnection of the man and what he was doing manifested itself to the Scott watcher. Of course that was Scott skating out there, absolutely alone. But the perception showed something else. It showed a man operating a machine. The machine was the man skating. Scott handled his machine with all the means by which men control vehicles and steeds. He rode it, flew it, rowed it, pedaled it, climbed it, dove it, reined it, and spurred it. The control of man over machine, even in the simplest maneuvers, was thrilling to see.

The skating machine. The machine was more than an observer's conception. Don and Scott acknowledged the distinction between Scott and what he did in the way they talked, the way they trained. Scott was always uncoupled from something not Scott, an "it." Scott didn't lean on a jump landing. No, skater and coach would say "it" was crooked in the air, so "it" came down badly. Their skating talk was full of machine-operators' detachment, and passivity. Between skater and everything that went wrong or right stood the "it," which you could see while watching Scott on the ice, but which defied precise definition. Sometimes the "it" was a jump, which would be discussed as if it still sat out on the ice while Scott and Don talked about it at the boards. Scott coming down out of a blur wasn't Scott coming down. No, he was "landing a jump," as if the jump were something other than him blurring through the air, something he had to land just as an airplane that is airborne needs to be landed.

That "it" detachment between Scott and Scott skating made possible a process of examination and rehearsal and perfection that might not have worked without detachment. Scott and Don labored like a two-man team of race-car mechanics. They regarded and discussed Scott's skating as if it really were a thing that Scott drove, that they could start and stop, dismantle and put back together. If something was wrong, they considered the malfunction just as they would have considered an automotive malfunction. They'd make adjustments, then start it up and see if it worked better. If it didn't work, they'd knock it down again, trial and error, over and over, until the thing was right. The "it," the skating machine, made possible an egoless dual effort that never would have operated if you had a coach telling a skater *you* did such-and-such wrong, and *you* didn't do what I said, and on and on, and the skater making equally ungenial assaults on his own *I*. Don and Scott, of course, got on each other's nerves, but the acrimony was the forgivable, quick hostility between two men too closely linked to avoid fighting. It came and it went, and when it went they'd work on their competitive skating machine, which, for them, was not an "I" or a "You" but a complexly engineered "it," the gorgeous machine that never could have been built with I's and You's.

At Oberstdorf, once Scott was pumping backward around the rink and the cleavage of him and "it" created the skating machine, Scott and Don were lost to everything else. The two hundred robust, not-quite-senior citizens could have sung ribald songs, in English, or the dogs could have had a noisy fight. Norbert could have done things even more outlandish and troubling to Scott's skating sensibilities than his hallucinatory ice vaudeville. It didn't matter what happened, because in miraculous Oberstdorf, by the grace of the miracle that may have been induced by Scott himself, Scott was in a place where nothing in the world could get between him and his skating machine.

# 31

# The Thing

That day, as every day—twice a day, really, at both long- and short-program practices—Scott Hamilton's skating was born again. Scott progressed from crossovers to slightly more complex maneuvers to elementary jumps that in turn became triples. The complex working parts of each program were redeveloped separately before Scott nodded to Don, who caused Scott's program music to sound out of the rink speakers. That was the birthing, when we saw Scott's miraculous ice organism emerge in all its intricacy and life. Its existence was brief, lasting only as long as the music played. Afterward, Scott and Don conducted an elaborate dissection. What had come together so slowly was taken completely apart.

Each long-program practice would begin the same, with Scott skating laps of the rink to refamiliarize his muscles and nerves with basic skating. He then went into one-legged airplane position, coasting backward around the curved rink ends. He rode his right outside edge, the edge carrying him in a long counterclockwise arc. Left leg reaching backward, Scott balanced on his flexed right leg, arms winging out from his shoulders. The upheld limbs went down and came up again, and the raising and relaxing was like a fledgling bird experimenting with wings, preparing to fly. Scott was, indeed, getting ready to fly, but the winging pose was a rehearsal not of flying but of landing. Most of Scott's jumps brought him down to the ice in that backward airplane position, on his right outside edge. He didn't jump until his landing stance had been thoroughly warmed up. Then he launched himself, skating forward, into the session's first escape from the ice, from forward left outside edge, to a stiff-legged half turn in the air, to the backward right outside edge and his airplane position. The airborne half turn was called the waltz jump. Elementary as it was, the waltz jump provided one of the grandest moments of Scott watching. Instead of exploding into blur smoke, as he did in triple jumps, Scott rose and flew in sharp focus. The jump, probably because of Scott's relative idleness in the air, seemed to go higher and farther than Scott's more complicated jumps. The illusion was an impossibly long trajectory, with Scott hanging arrogantly independent of gravity for an impossibly long time. Airborne in the waltz jump, Scott evoked the rigid bravura you see in turn-of-the-century photographs of men skating. For a long moment he was Ulrich Salchow in 1905. The audience clapped. The dogs barked.

With waltz jumps in good order, Scott added a rotation to the same forward-edge half turn. He did a single axel, an elaboration of the waltz jump that nevertheless maintained that same Edwardian poise. Single axel, which was really a half turn more than a single jump, with one and a half rotations in the air, was upped to double axel, which took Scott out of skating's vanished age of stiff grandeur into the late twentieth century. Double axel was his first jump beyond mere leaping and landing. It went up on a classic-looking forward spring. You saw, for a fraction of a second, the same tintype from skating's attic that you saw at the outset of the waltz jump. But then Scott pulled in his long-leaping limbs and blurred.

Thus, Scott entered skating's atomic age. The statement is not entirely figurative. Man learned to harness the atom and high-revolution skating jumps at about the same time. Skating's first uses of blur-dimension in competition came just three years after the first use in warfare of atomic weapons.

As were the A-bombs, the premier blur-jumps were American. Dick Button fathered the Blur Age. He performed his first double axel in Switzerland in 1948, and then exploded the world's first competitive triple toe loop in 1952, an advancement closely parallel to the development of the H-bomb at about the same time. In the years following Dick Button's pioneering feats, blur-jumps proliferated and skating, for better or worse, was irreversibly transformed. International Sweetheartland in 1982 heard a widely voiced yearning for triples control or even reduction. The idea was that skaters had overarmed themselves with competitive triples, to the point that skating's beauty and flow was compromised, and the sport was in danger of becoming a barren contest of who could execute the most triples in long program. The plan to save skating included multilateral jumping deemphasis, and a worldwide recommitment to balance and aesthetics in competitive performance. This sort of peacenik talk was heard behind the scenes at each of Scott's 1982 competitions. People spoke with the same sort of sincere but patently make-believe hope you hear when people talk about world disarmament.

After his double axels, Scott's warm-up continued briefly to be a reenactment of skating history. He went to double toe loop, a sub-blur rehearsal for triple toe loop, the leap into three revolution modernity first taken by Dick Button thirty years earlier. Triple toe loop had a look unlike anything he had done to that point. The axels, even the blurry double axel, give the Scott watcher an understandable picture of a man jumping up from the ice. He sprung upward as a running person would spring, off one foot, the launching leg straightening and shooting, the free leg held upward and bent in front of him. Toe loop was the result of ice mechanics entirely mysterious to the nonskater. Going backward, Scott simply exploded and smeared into an airborne smoke that flew momentarily and then became Scott Hamilton coasting backward on his right outside edge in airplane position.

Triple toe loop seemed to mark the end of his formal warming-up. By that time he had shed his warm-up jacket, revealing bare arms tomatoed by the workout, as if it were too warm in the rink, belying the refrigerator chill against which the spectators shivered. On the Day of the Dachshunds, Scott wore a BMW T-shirt, which emblemized his fondness for the great German automaker. Scott at that time dreamed of owning his own BMW, a newer, racier version of Don's. At that noon freeskating session Norbert had on a New York City T-shirt, and Manuela was wearing a blue U.S.A. sweatshirt.

After triple toe loop, Scott began a rehearsal of long-program elements. He tried out the program's moving parts, more or less in the order in which they occurred, performing choreographic snippets with jumps and spins, starting and stopping abruptly, and then brooding on what he'd just done in his hands-on-kidneys pout. Scott possessed a memorized schematic of his program, which seemed to be much like the mental sheet music of a pianist with a performance piece committed to memory. He could have counted out for you every step and change of edge and gesture in his long program, but on the ice he worked according to a deeper, nonverbal memory. He *became* his long program, and then became himself mulling, or talking to his coach. In such a manner Scott went from kidney-handed cogitation to a line of bellicose gestures from his program's opening section. He crouched and exploded into a toe-pick triple, after which he skated, with one hand on his lower back, to his coach. Scott voiced vague dissatisfactions with the jump. Don said it looked fine. Scott jumped again, and then made a face saying how absolutely bad that one had been.

Don scolded the approaching Champ: "Whether you like it or not, it's a damned good jump."

Scott did a piece of exasperation shtick for me. "I make a face," he said, "and *he* goes on for five minutes." Then he talked to Don. "That one did come out better, but I feel tight. It's kind of like I'm stuck."

Scott sounded like a lady with no mechanical vocabulary trying to explain a car problem. Don acted like a mechanic who thought the lady was imagining things. Scott was commonly much more critical than Don about his skating, and their talk at the boards, particularly at the *Bundeseislaufzentrum,* featured many minutes of Don telling Scott that he couldn't see what was supposed to be wrong with things that Scott found substandard. Sometimes such exchanges were clearly fishing on Scott's part for reassurance from his coach. And sometimes Scott meant what he said. The problem, Scott later explained, was that he could sense difficulties invisible to his coach. Everything might look fine, but Scott could tell that something had almost gone wrong. He could feel trouble even when it didn't happen.

Norbert by that time had loosed his skating creatures. People applauded and dogs barked for him, too. Scott was at the boards when one of Norbert's triples went up and came down, and he absentmindedly joined in the clapping for the European Champion. Then he skated. Up to that point the sounds coming out of the rink speakers had been background tapes put on by the skaters, first a medley of Spike Jones' musical slapstick from which Scott and Don were planning to cut music for a funny exhibition program, then some of Norbert's stuff, German high-brow pop, one hundred percent electronic synthesized, which sounded like round-singing by porpoises and high-speed dental drills. Neither Spike Jones' hilarity nor Norbert's microchip glee club threw Scott off the rhythms of his program snippets. He skated as if he heard clearly the music that went with what he rehearsed, apparently deaf to the racket coming out of the speakers, just as he was deaf to the tourists clapping and the dachshunds barking.

But then it was time to skate to long-program music we all could hear. Scott raised eyebrows to Don, who asked him if he was ready. "Let's do it," Scott said. Norbert's singing electrons were stilled. Dead air followed, and then the hiss and popping that was the beginning of Scott's long-program tape. The Champ had assumed man-of-war position out at center ice.

What followed looked like a great run-through, with just one minor bobble. The triple in the slow section, where Scott's octopus swam to underwater-celeste music, popped into a double. Everything else hit hard. The futzy section, which had always cracked up the practice audiences at Indianapolis, failed utterly to amuse the stolid Oberstdorf skate watchers. But the futzy flopped like that every day in Germany. It was unnerving to watch Scott caper through a section clearly meant to be droll—against that backdrop of unbendingly serious burghers. But Scott seemed not to care at all whether his thirty-second ice comedy played well in Oberstdorf. The audience stiffness may have been a matter of national loyalty to Norbert. The people were always highly responsive to the hometown boy's attempts to be amusing.

Besides the popped triple in the slow section, the long-program run-through was a success, sufficiently successful, you would have thought, to make Scott happy. But Scott was clearly unhappy. Consternation showed on top of the usual post-run-through agony at the boards. When he could talk between wrenching breaths, he hissed, "Dammit, I wanted to land that thing."

"You'll get it," Don said.

"Triple flip. Darn that!" Scott slapped his thigh. "That's the only thing."

"We'll work on it," Don said.

Norbert's program music had come on. He did a demi-run-through, skating parts of the program, coasting briefly, and then going back into the program. Scott turned around and propped his elbows on the boards, watching peripherally. "Those dogs," Scott said, chuckling when they barked for Norbert. The Champ remained at the boards until Norbert's run-through was done. When the final chorus of table saws concluded, he shook out his legs and said to Don, "Here goes absolutely nothing."

And there went another shot at triple flip. The routine in practice was to give first attention after the run-through to whatever had gone wrong. Scott's long program, like any other over-reaching and complex human enterprise, was subject to perpetual, unpredictable, though usually minor, trouble. It seemed that the four-and-a-half-minute performance was too demanding and vast for all of it to be perfectly controlled by one man in one practice run-through. Perfection could be approached only in competition, when extraordinary pressure gave Scott Hamilton extraordinary powers.

Scott had days when double axel wobbled and scraped on landing. So he'd work on it, and the next day everything would be fine with double axel. But then triple Lutz would go. Triple Lutz was cake for Scott Hamilton, the first jump in long program, and absolutely the last jump you'd expect to give him trouble. When the jumps were all great, spins previously centered and stationary would creep, toy toplike, across the ice. Coach and skater then had to spend time after run-through fixing the spin. If it wasn't one thing, it was another. They fretted over every detail, tinkering and tuning, never satisfied. Probably Scott owed his consistent success to that perpetual dissatisfaction. Practice, Scott said, never gave you absolute mastery. Bad luck and trouble were always around. You were going to miss once in a while. But practice improved the odds, the odds of nailing everything when it counted.

Effective freeskating practice was, for Scott Hamilton, a far more subtle and complex business than doing everything over and over. The wrong kind of practice for a program element could be worse than no practice at all. He had to know when, and how, to work on something. Certain jumps got no warm-up before run-through. Others absolutely had to be warmed up. Scott and Don said it was counterproductive to give attention after run-through to whatever worked well. Scott said: "If something's good, you don't sit there and force it down your own throat. That's dumb, because you start getting sloppy on it. Wait until you have trouble before you start repeating."

So it didn't pay to fix skating that wasn't broken. There were times, too, when it didn't pay to fix skating that *was* broken, because repetitions and attention to an element's trouble might cement the trouble, making it much more resistant to correction. Scott and Don were very cautious with difficulties that seemed to be ephemeral. If the wrongness didn't remit quickly, you'd often see them let the problem go, passing on to something else. Leave it alone, their judgment dictated, and the problem will go away. Scott particularly wanted to avoid getting what he called a "Thing" about a program element. A Thing was a very potent, tenacious form of trouble. If something went wrong too many times, a powerful wrongness-association set up permanent housekeeping among Scott's ideas about the offending element. His big Things all seemed to involve jumps. The very idea of wrongness virtually assured that the jump in question was going to come out wrong. Trouble on the mind was harder by far to get rid of than over-rotation, leaning in the air, a low hip, or other merely physical jump malfunctions. To remove a Thing, you had to consistently nail the jump, but consistently nailing a jump with a Thing on it was next to impossible. So a Thing was very heavy voodoo, indeed; the principle behind it says that if you believe in something, it's real. And right then, after run-through on the Day of the Dachshunds, Scott was beginning to believe that triple flip was the new home of a very nasty Thing.

Scott's first attempt after run-through to do triple flip, the "Here goes absolutely nothing," popped, not a pretty pop, or an almost-made-it pop, but a pop beyond salvage. No way was it going around three times. He was lucky to get out of it on his feet.

Scott skated away from the wreckage, all business, much too serious to make faces at us. Then he shot backward, riding his left inside edge, right leg reaching back for the toe-pick explosion. Triple flip was a three-revolution version of the double jump that went up first in short program's two-jump combination. Double flip, triple toe loop had, of course, been a big, bad Thing, dating all the way back to 1978. It was the worst Thing of all until Scott broke the spell in Morristown. The obvious connection between the two Things, the one dead and the other newborn, was the flip jump. But Scott had no difficulties with double flip. The problem in combination had been triple toe loop, the change of technique Scott had to make in triple toe loop so it would work in combination. Scott had no general problems with flip jumps. He did not, for that matter, have a history of trouble with triple flip. In 1981 he had a perfectly good consistent triple flip.

But that was 1981. This was 1982, and Scott's second attempt died in mid-blur, suspending Scott splayed and looking down between his feet before his right foot scraped the ice. He looked over the scratches from takeoff and landing, and then circuited the rink to compose himself.

The next triple flip disintegrated, absolutely blew to pieces, dumping Scott on his rear end. You could hear and feel the fleshy slam of Scott hitting the ice.

"Ouch!" Don said. Scott made no sound whatsoever. He was beyond the overacted rage he gave failures in practice. He sat on the ice for some seconds, legs flat in front of him and opened to a wide angle. Scott had a mild, thoughtful look as he sat there.

Number four popped, not a hideous pop but a quiet loss of power, like a single-engine plane coughing into silence, except for the wind whistling, at three thousand feet. Without enough oomph to rotate three times, Scott stalled and glided down to the ice.

He was beginning to show anger. But since we were in Oberstdorf, and two hundred people and three dogs were looking, he showed discretion. He poked iceward the middle fingers of both hands. The gesture was made as if it were perfectly natural to skate with both hands fisted except for the two tallest digits. It would have been easy to miss Scott's message to the ice, or the jump, or whatever he was silently cursing.

Number five popped. But Scott was not giving up. This was the day to have it out with triple flip, once and for all.

And number six was fine. Boom. Three times around. Clean-edge landing. Don relaxed and blew out air. The Champ's face showed relief, but he looked no happier for having landed triple flip. The grim face was coming over to tell Don something. "That's fine," Scott said. "It's a Thing." The voice was quiet. That's all he said.

And so Scott met on the ice at Oberstdorf the second great adversary of his 1982 World Title defense. The triple flip Thing. He was fifty feet just then from the first, and by far more danger-ous, enemy—Norbert Schramm. But of course he had yet to acknowledge the threat from the German ice sorcerer. Scott was still blissfully ignorant on that score, whistling and walking un-aware into Norbert's long-program ambush in Copenhagen; but he did not similarly overlook his new Thing. He knew from that day on that the Thing had a death grip on triple flip, a jump not used by Scott at Easterns or Nationals, which he wanted very much to have for Worlds.

A few of the men who were going to skate at Worlds out-tripled Scott. The plan had been to close the gap by doing triple flip in the slow section of long program, at the point where he had done triple toe loop at Easterns and Nationals. The substitution should have been easy. The only difference in preparation was that triple flip went up on the left foot, triple toe loop on the right. Changing feet was simple, Scott said. Relearning a jump that had previously given him no trouble should have been simple, too. With a Thing, though, nothing about triple flip was going to be simple.

Once the Thing showed itself, Scott and his people began scoring triple flips attempted and landed. We counted just as we once had counted combinations in practice, back before Easterns. Practices with bad triple flips didn't bury a day in gloom in the manner of bad combination days, probably because triple flip was not an absolute requirement for victory, as was the combination. But nevertheless, triple flip became the big question in every

313

long-program run-through and practice. Scott started working on triple flip during short-program practices. He kept a mental data bank on his bedeviled jump that included cumulative and daily tallies going back to his first day at Oberstdorf. By the end of the ten days in *Liebchenland,* he had a daily success rate of fifty percent. Not nearly sufficient statistical confidence for competition, but a great deal better than the Day of the Dachshunds, when his failure rate pushed eighty-five percent. The trend was encouraging. But, as it developed, the encouraging Oberstdorf numbers were wrong. Triple flip stayed shaky at Worlds. The Thing hung on. At Copenhagen poor Scott would have to skate his long program with that old demon Thing messing around with all the brain cells that knew how to do triple flip. Bad trouble, particularly when he had just been bushwhacked by Norbert Schramm.

Back in Denver the advent of that Thing would have wrecked the rest of the practice and probably the rest of the day, for sure. Who knows what Scott would have done? At the least he would have purpled and gargled out the most awful words in the English language. Maybe he would have lost control altogether and chewed the bang boards. But Scott was in Oberstdorf when the Thing introduced itself, his psyche saved by the amazing grace of the *Bundeseislaufzentrum.* Blowing six out of seven triple flips didn't even blight the rest of the hour. Scott passed on to other elements, and worked through the last ten minutes as if nothing had particularly gone wrong.

The session ended as most of the sessions in Germany ended. A thoroughly skated-out Scott Hamilton came toward his coach, the falcon coming back to the falconer's leathered wrist. No more skating, no more flying left in him. But it wasn't time to land just yet.

The tomato flush had faded from Scott's face and arms. The hour of work had Scott pumping air like a bellows, the metallic inhalations and exhalations less frantic and wracking than right after run-through, but still deep and fast. He skated like an old man then, somebody's grandfather who used to be terrific on the ice.

"Let's do some spins," Don said.

So the old guy with his tired grin ceased to be a man and became a tall smear making noise like a surgeon's skull drill boring down into the ice, a wet steely cutting that was strangely satisfying to hear. The sound of Scott spinning would have gone well with one of Norbert's electronic choirs. Then the smear was a man again, talking and smiling, with no sign of dizziness. He smeared and unsmeared once more.

"Good," Don said.

The directed attention of coach and skater dissipated. You knew without being told that the practice was over. Just as Scott had been drained of skating, both were now drained of work, all done.

Scott said what he said after every noon freeskating session in Oberstdorf. "*Essen?*" Which meant in German, "Shall we eat?" Eating was our standing joke at Oberstdorf. In that monkish hush meals were the biggest off-ice events of the day. They were also big events because they were unbelievably good, and the food seemed to get better as the ten days wore on. Scott didn't lose weight as he normally would have in a week of intense training. He actually put on weight.

"*Essen?*" Scott asked, stepping off the ice. And it wasn't possible to be hungrier, or happier, with nothing in the world to think of than what a fabulous dinner we were about to eat.

# 32

# *Auf Wiedersehen, Liebchenland*

Saturday, February 27, 1982, was an afternoon that, in a movie version of that frightful competitive year, would have a song and happy fadings-in and -out of Scott Hamilton and the other global ice Sweethearts amusing themselves some thousands of vertical feet above the *Bundeseislaufzentrum.* That Saturday Scott relaxed and broke his monkish training regimen, which hitherto had featured only the most sedate and simple interruptions. On Saturday after lunch Scott and the skating-center Sweethearts and adult ice people rode into the sky on one of the cable-slung gondolas that swung every few minutes out of a building neighboring the skating center. The gondolas had been going up the mountain all week, hauling skiers and sightseers to a peak called the Feldhorn.

The bus doors shut and the group, pushed into friendly proximity, thrilled and exchanged smiles when the gondola swooped and the windows showed trees and houses marching down the mountain beneath. Milky light flooded Scott's face as he took pictures of the town shrinking to a road-map depiction of itself. He looked good that day, rested and robust. The blue-gray of the previous Saturday was gone, supplanted by a fine translucency. In sunlight Scott was like a man fashioned of flesh-toned porcelain. Seemingly suffused with dreamy joy, he smiled, his face assuming a lanternlike image of unfeigned happiness. All the skaters, Germans and Finns and Brits and Scots, faced the windows and told each other how beautiful it all was. The gondola discharged the group at a station above the trees. Another car went higher, ascending into a vast stage with distant backdrops of snow and ice and naked mountain rock. Skiers came down the distant drapings and past the lodge on trails that went into a ski-out ending just laughing distance from the dormitory where Scott slept. All week we had been hearing the whoops of skiers finishing their long runs down from the mountaintop. Norbert Schramm was among the skiers that Saturday, which irritated Scott. The idea of a competitor putting flesh and bones in jeopardy on the eve of the World Championships flew in the face of Scott's seriousness about skating. A passing snideness about Schramm on skis was the only shadow in that otherwise bright afternoon. The shadow passed quickly.

Scott and the ice Sweethearts trooped from the gondola station onto an expanse of trampled and wind-hardened snow. They walked along a ridge to a patch of bare rock from which the snow field fell away, giving a grand view of the surrounding peaks. The skaters lined up so Scott could take a picture and then he handed his camera to a volunteer and joined the group for more pictures. There he was, larger than the others by virtue of his smallness and his expansive good cheer.

They left the rock patch and started toward the lodge, where skaters and ice adults were to meet for coffee and pastries. Scott chased Jayne, who ran and emitted a prolonged laughing squeal. At bay, she batted at him and he wrestled her to the snow, pulling her down a slope. Jayne skidded on the hard-packed snow, sliding as easily as if she were sled-borne and not on her back with Scott hauling her by the legs. Jayne's off-ice aplomb was gone entirely. She blushed vividly, face glowing red in the stark glare. All the while she skidded Jayne made the girlish scream. Then she was up again. There was more nonsense with snow throwing and face rubbing.

The final picture of Scott on the Feldhorn is a gnome face

stretched downward with eyes closed and lips clamped on a fork being pulled out of his mouth. The face was registering delight because of the sensory messages sent by a superb piece of cake. Next to Scott was the British ice-dancing coach and Cricket, with Don Laws across the table, and other ice people populating one side of the dining room on the mountain. The sun outside was still high and the sky still cloudless, but the light was yellowing, aging. The wristwatches said that the time for romping on the Feldhorn was passing, almost past.

The gondola floated downward over the *Bundeseislaufzentrum* to its final stop. The bus doors opened and Scott stepped onto concrete at ice level. That step ended forever the protective enchantment of Oberstdorf.

That Saturday night Scott said, "You know, Worlds is in less than two weeks. It really hasn't hit me yet." The statement, of course, indicated that the fact of Worlds *had* hit him. It broke the mental calm that, until then, had been mirror smooth. Once again the mental weather was unstable. Like a storm approaching from a long distance, the emotional squalls of Worlds came first as puffs of nerve wind and distant rumblings. Scott was traveling once more from the here-and-now to his worry dimension, where he would watch Worlds unfold in the worst possible ways. He was harassed by people who weren't around him yet, whom he wouldn't see until he got to Copenhagen.

Sunday featured an exhibition with all the Oberstdorf Sweethearts, including Scott and Chris and Jayne, and a few German skaters from other cities. Scott skated "New York, New York," to a crowd that saved its loudest approbation for its hometown hero, Norbert Schramm. Schramm was brilliant that night, performing his comic pantomime for every decibel of noise that the two thousand skate watchers could make. Scott, who skated very well, was unperturbed that Norbert's ovations were somewhat noisier than his own, which were noisy enough. Scott seemed to find the situation rather funny.

"I feel," he said on his way to the ice, "like I was in Park Ridge, Illinois." Park Ridge, of course, was the hometown of his erstwhile competitor, David Santee.

Scott made a little joke at the expense of the Oberstdorf tourists, who had been halting him here and there all week so they could take snapshots. He took his instant camera out on the ice with him when he made his final bow. Scott faced the crowd and hand-motioned them to get together. He flashed his camera. Then he turned and made the same motions to the other side of the little arena. Everybody was very amused. The camera flashed again.

The souvenirs of Oberstdorf include two prints of happy people stacked in rows, smiling and waving to Scott Hamilton, who had one more training day at Oberstdorf and then a day of travel to take him to Copenhagen, where he would try to win, for the second time, the World Figure Skating Championship.

# 33

## *Scotterdämmerung*

It is strange to watch the moving image of Scott's long program at the 1982 World Championships, stored in a videocassette owned by Mrs. O, and reflect on the post-victory collapse suffered by Scott and his followers. The screen shows a solid victory; not a beginning-to-end nailing of long program, as in Indianapolis, but a job well done, performed under the most frightful pressure.

The one glitch in an otherwise good performance had to do with triple flip, the blur-jump that Scott had tried to introduce into long program at Oberstdorf and which should have been manageable but for the malevolent Thing that got hold of it and would not let go. The Thing went to Copenhagen, teasing Scott and Don by letting the Champ land just enough triple flips to give the cruelly false hope that the Thing had gone away. But of course it was there, playing a nasty game of peekaboo that went on until the early afternoon of Thursday, March 11, 1982, the last practice on long-program day.

In a partial run-through, the landing scraped. Scott skated away from the scrape with an index finger pressed to the side of his nose.

He went up again and the jump popped into a clumsy double.

"Out!" The gargling voice purpled with rage, but the rage was whitened with bloodless fear.

Walking away from practice, Scott amended the "Out!" "I'll plan on it tonight," he said, "I'm not going to warm it up, though."

The one glitch shown by the tape had to do with Scott's last-second substitution of triple toe wally, a jump he had considered for just such a contingency, even though he hadn't practiced it all season. The jump blurred and brought the booming glee that blur-jumps bring from excited skate people, but the landing wobbled. Otherwise, long program was highly workmanlike. The performance seemed a trifle cautious, but, the videotape shows, it was really a complete success, down to the stirring moment when Scott stood, hand on heart, on top of the medalists' podium and watched the flag of the United States rising at the end of the arena, speakers playing "The Star-Spangled Banner." The cameras caught the Champ with tears in his eyes, overflowing with some sweet emotion.

Scott won with a second in figures, first in short program, and first in long program. His across-the-board excellence made him a shoo-in by the time he skated long program. And the tape shows that the long-program victory was earned. Scott outskated his competition, no question about it.

But this video says nothing about the emotional atmosphere of the 1982 Worlds. As Scott successfully defended the World Championship, a defense made to look easy by Scott's powerful skating, the psychological moment was such that winning was less important than the possibility of losing.

Scott's long program followed that of Norbert Schramm, whose skating planets were in perfect alignment; 1982 was the Year of Norbert. He burned through his long program, combusting each jump and spin and bizarre body position in the flames of his glaring red costume. The people went wild, absolutely carried away with the surprise of Norbert and his choreographic ice menagerie. He was a creature of the moment, and the audience, which loved such moments, was with him. The videotape shows a messy landing and a technical performance not up to that of Scott Hamilton, but international Sweetheartland was a captive of Norbert's fabulous moment. For those minutes he was *it.*

When Scott took the ice, and Norbert was collecting his bushels of rose bouquets, Scott was skating without *it*ness. The psychological moment was particularly disadvantageous to Scott because the challenge from Norbert, which was really an illusion of the moment, should have been answered with a ringingly victorious performance. But nailin' it to the wall was beyond Scott, because the challenge was an illusion. Scott could have been third in long program and still have won overall. Norbert's second place was numerically far behind Scott's first place, because of Scott's performance in figures. Scott couldn't lose, so he couldn't win either. He could win Worlds, but he couldn't win the moment.

This is not to say that Scott failed to capture the crowd. He conquered the skate watchers at Copenhagen as he always conquers the thousands looking down at his ice. The wild animal noises came, booming at each jump and program element, and going up into continuous exultation at the end. Roses rained as thickly on Scott's ice as they had on Norbert's. But somehow, for Scott, it was all inadequate.

"That stunk," he kept telling Don as he signed autographs for kids crowding around the chute that led to the ice. "That really stunk. That was the worst I've skated all year."

It would be some time before Scott accepted that difficult victory and gave himself the credit that he deserved, that everyone else was giving him.

Thursday was the second final events night. Wednesday had been pairs, a night made very happy for the United States ice people when Kitty and Peter placed third. A medal in pairs for Americans was momentous, as the event traditionally belonged to the Eastern bloc. The week went on to grand, crashing success when Elaine Zayak won ladies overall. The victory was a spectacular upset. Elaine was in eighth place after short. But unlikelihood made a mess of long-program night, as it had on the night Elaine lost her National Championship in Indianapolis. This time the perverse skating fates were on Elaine's side.

But while the United States Sweethearts showed the World

what for, Scott was lost in frantic partying, which was so good and prolonged it was terrible. All was disarray among the Champ and his people, each of whom seemed angry about something. The great detoxification began the night Scott won, and we all swam in the accumulated nerve poisons of the most noxious year of all. Scott raged on, dancing and drinking. His exhaustion showed in a disastrous performance at the post-competition exhibition on Sunday. He bombed "New York, New York," wobbling and even falling in front of the Queen of Denmark and a sellout crowd. But people still went wild for him. He was, after all, Scott Hamilton, with ice magic even when he was too tired to skate.

"It was my first queen," he said lamely to Dick Button as he came off the ice.

The following morning Don and the Scott people abandoned Copenhagen. The skaters who did not win medals went home, and those who had medals, along with a few who wanted to sight-see in Europe, stayed another night in a steel-and-glass skyscraper hotel that was no longer the temporary home of Sweetheartland. The magical place was gone, vanished like the mythical village of Brigadoon.

And so we come to the twilight of Scott's season, *Scotterdämmerung*, with the Champion of the World in one last implosive hour of post-competitive suffering. A Promethean late afternoon, with Scott chained to the rocks high on the ninth-floor cliff of the Scandinavia Hotel; mind demons in the shape of ice enemies and members of his own entourage materialized and tore at him. Before letting the bad season go, the Champ spent this final dark afternoon as Scott Bound.

Dusk was falling, and Scott became a silhouette in his hotel room. There was no choice but to be pulled into the darkness of the moment. For the last time Scott Hamilton turned on the tape recorder and spoke:

I hope it gets better. Every year I win this thing I get more and more depressed. This year has been a bad year. Ever since I've been done I've felt people looking at me to make mistakes, to be stupid. And I've been stupid. I haven't been smart at all.

*Seems as if Schramm shook you up.*

I didn't have any respect for Norbert. But I do now. I can't be the minority of one who doesn't like what he's doing. It's always the same. When Toller Cranston was doing that, people thought he was just the most incredible thing. He was winning Worlds freestyle, but he was always low in figures. And now Norbert's got a European push behind him. I said to some people I just couldn't understand the big push behind Norbert, because I didn't really think he was that good. I thought there were a lot better skaters. But I'm thinking about it now, and there really aren't. The Canadian Brian Orser's better, but he didn't deliver this time. Other than that, Norbert's the best one. Igor Bobrin is good for what he does. Christophe Simonde never put it together. Norbert has got a push now. He was eleventh on the first figure here. From then on it was straight up. He ended up sixth in figures. He'll never be that low in figures again.

*The writing is on the wall. The world sees him as your big challenger.*

No, I think they see him as the champion. Last year it was the same thing. Except they saw David Santee as the champion. At Worlds last year, David got more applause at every practice. He got more applause for stepping on the ice. It was like people wanted him to win because they felt bad for him, because he's been second all his life. With Norbert, he's entertaining, and he's fun to watch, and he's scary. His landings aren't all secure. So it's exciting to watch. And it looks like he's really doing neat things. I never took him as a serious threat until the day after long. Remember at Oberstdorf? We looked at him and said, "God, he's awful! He doesn't train. He lands one out of four jumps. He lands everything on an inside edge. . . ." Remember that? I was talking to Peter Carruthers about it because I was really depressed last night. He told me Luddy compared it like this: You go to the zoo.

Senior men's event is the zoo. You go to the zoo, and what do you look at? You look at the tigers and you look at the monkeys. Monkeys are the most fun to watch because they're the most animated. Norbert's a monkey. I'm a Bengal tiger. See the difference? And that made me feel a lot better. Because I know I'm better than he is. I watched him the other night do the exhibition in his zebra pants. His legs were bent. He had no clear distinct line. His arms were all over the place. But what he did is just do something nobody else would do. Because they don't want to make a fool out of themselves. You see, all this talk and all these people just make me wonder if I'm good enough to win anymore. You know, it's weird. The way I've been thinking the last couple days, and the way they're talking here, it's like he was second, but now I'm trying to catch up to him.

*Why is that?*

It's something I think he and the German association and the German press have tried to plant in everybody's mind. Did I tell you what happened the other night? I went into the reception for Dortmund Europeans next year. Europeans are going to be in Dortmund next year. And I came in and a lot of people looked at me like, "What are you doing here?" Then the press people started coming up and asking me to take pictures with Norbert. But he was sooo busy. I had to wait for him to get done talking to people. And then this German guy says, "Get together, get together!" He wanted Norbert to pick me up in his arms and hold me like this. I told him *No way!* I was really angry and I really looked at him. *No way!* I was furious. The nerve of that guy! Pick me up and carry me like a baby . . . And some man from German television came up to me and said, "You're going to quit." He had this big smile on his face. I said no, I am staying in. He looked at me like he was thinking, "You poor fool, get out while the getting's good." The German federation was telling Peter that he ought to quit, too. I told Peter that if the Germans were really that confident that Tina and Andy [Christina Riegel and Andreas

325

Nischwitz, West German pairs team, bronze medalists at 1981 Worlds, who did not compete at 1982 Worlds due to an injury] were going to beat the Carrutherses, they wouldn't be shoving them to get out. . . . Next year if I beat Norbert, I'm going to give the German press everything they don't want to hear.

Next year I'm going to have to be so cool to the press, so cool it'll have to be incredible. Because they're going to ask me about Norbert. I'll have things to say like, "Oh, I think he's very entertaining."

*Your long program looked a little flat.*

It was. It wasn't pretty, but it was good enough to keep me in there. I was sitting there going, "You know, it doesn't really matter how I skate because I'll be in the top three in freestyle." That's how I was thinking. I was all ready to go out and do a substandard performance, and then I saw Norbert get a standing ovation. And I said, "Now, I've got to be good." And that was, like, massive turn-the-act-around.

*Sorry about it now?*

Yeah, I should have known that something like that with Norbert was going to happen. Had I known, I would have thought more about winning the freestyle medal. I knew I was going to win overall, after short.

*You did beat him in freestyle. You won five out of seven judges.*

Not according to the German press. They're already calling him the world's freestyle champion. I thought, if I win this year I'm in great shape because I'll improve a little each year, and I'll be in great shape going into the Olympic year. Now I'm thinking, "God, it isn't going to let up!" Unless Norbert does a real wazoo next year.

*He seems dangerous because he's unpredictable. He's so inspired by the crowds.*

How long's that going to go on, though? Is it something chemical that makes him skate clean in front of people? He's still blue collar. What scares me is if he goes white collar. If he goes white collar, I'm in trouble. A blue-collar skater has something electric, but it's kind of low-budget. It's good, but it's not elitist yet. It's not great. If he goes white collar, if he does his New Wave thing with class, and does it right, then I'm in trouble. But then again he has got to deliver short and figures, too.

*Is Orser another threat?*

You see, you take a balance between what you've got in presentation and choreography and what you've got in technical merit. That's a balance. He's got so much technically and so little in style that it's unbalanced. It's not easy to watch. You don't notice anything else—like he's a smooth skater or a classy skater or he's got a good line. All you notice is that he's got a lot of jumps. Orser's a good one, though. Maybe he and Norbert will screw each other, and I can stay in there. You know what Dick Button was telling me? He said Norbert's fresh now. Dick told me, "Hey, you could lose, you could skate as well as you skate now and go all the way to Olympics and lose." He told me that somebody else doesn't really have to improve to beat me. He just has to get closer to me, and it'll be exciting. Just through maturity and competitive experience, somebody can give the illusion of improving. And he can beat me if I don't stay fresh somehow. I think the best thing I can do for next year is get a new look in my long program, not anything bizarre or different, just a brand-new long, a fresh look. And improve technically. I'm gonna be a little bit different, a little more bizarre, but I am not gonna be New Wave. What Norbert does is all fine and good for him and his look. But for me if I tried doing that stuff, I'd look foolish. I've got to improve. But, I don't really have to improve. I've got to be different.

This whole year is going to be hard. Don and I are going back to the way we trained in 1979. In 1979 I went through four months, five months, of solid character adjustment. I'd never worked so hard. I'd never changed so fast. Don took me from blue collar to white collar that year. I'm gonna stay white collar. And like I told Dick Button, for every one good performance of Norbert's this year, I'll do three. I want to put my head on the chopping block, because I want to put any claims to rest. I'll do two international competitions, and Easterns, and Nationals, and Worlds. And I have a feeling this year Norbert will get serious because he's got a shot at Olympics. [Rallying, feisty] I shouldn't be letting him get to me. Rodnina and Zaitsev have been out-skated. But they were never beaten because they never let anybody get to them. They just did their stuff. You know, I think I can do it next year, as much as it's going to be hard. [Sudden switch back to long program] I still didn't see how he skated. Was he really, really on, or was he just good?

*So-so. He wasn't too clean, but he was so hot emotionally. The place went berserk.*

Everybody was waiting for me to fall apart after he skated so well. I don't think I could skate that well after a mediocre per-formance. I haven't done it in four years. . . . I don't know. You know, after I screwed up in exhibition, I started wondering, "Is this what it's going to be like next year? Am I gonna get my underwear tied up in knots every time this guy skates?" It's all so stupid! I mean I won Worlds with second in figures and first in short and long program. How many times has that been done in the last ten years? It was too easy. I won with a two-point-six at Worlds. And you know what's really sick, and I hate myself for it? When Elaine won, I was so happy. And then a second after it happened, I said, "My God, I'm no longer the champion anymore. I'm second now." Isn't that sick? That's the way I've been ever since I won this damned title. I've been paranoid about losing, about not being a star.

*But you won!*

But I lost everything. I won and I lost everything. Every year, I'm losing more and more by winning. It's only human nature for everybody to want Norbert to do really well. And I in my own way am happy for him.

*You and Don had some trouble here.*

It started at the beginning of the week. Remember how I told you I thought he was hounding me a little bit, how he was hovering? Well, I corrected that, and not very nicely. I told him I was a big boy and I could take care of myself. "Just take it easy —you're making me nervous." It was a dumb thing to say. And it really upset him. That's when he started getting mad. He thought I was shutting him out. But, you know, Don is all right. I didn't understand him before. Remember how I told you I thought he was living his skating fantasies through my career? I don't think that anymore. And you know how I said that he could walk away from this? I don't think he can. This isn't only me skating and him trying to help. This is a personal commitment on his part. And he can walk away from it when I'm done. But not before I'm done. He's not in this for laughs.

*Don seemed to be mad at you because you weren't working with him after your final event.*

Oh, Don and I talked about that. I partied two nights, but that was after events were done. During the day, I was always available. I wasn't sleeping till noon. I was always up and over to the rink.

*Still in all, you did some hard partying. How come?*

I don't know. I was just so caught up and fed up. It built up. This has not been one of my better weeks. Why can't people just let me live my own life?

*You're in such a bizarre position, caught between these people, and everybody thinks he or she knows what you need.*

Last night I sat down on my bed and my dad was hounding me about getting things ready. "Hurry up, I'll wait for you!" He said he was going to wait for me to go down and get my ticket, because he knew what I needed to do to get it. I said, "Dad, I'm twenty-three years old. I've done this before. I've gone to Worlds before. I've handled my own life. I've come this far. Please don't ride me. Don't hound me. Enjoy yourself here. Have a good time, but leave me alone. I'll do what you want, but don't tell me what to do. I don't tell you how to teach biology, right?" But he was sitting there, and he kept on, kept on. "I'm just trying to help!" And he is and I love him for it. They're all just trying to help. I see my dad at competitions. I go home to the Bowling Green ice show. I'm never home long enough to just spend time with him. The time we get together is when we're at competitions. . . . I couldn't believe the stuff he was saying to me.

*Come on, Scott, parents and their children always get on each other's nerves.*

I was sitting on the bed the other night, and I told him I hate my life. I hate it so much. At times it's great, but the down times are so bad. The times when I have to go out and bust my ass when I'm still exhausted from doing a show for somebody where I didn't get a cent, where I didn't get anything at all out of it. . . . When you came to see me the first time, in December, in Denver, I had nothing to give to skating. I hated that rink. I didn't want to be anywhere near it. I hated it. I wish my mother was still alive. She was so great, and she was so cool. Nothing was more important than just being right about things. Doing things properly. She was great. She was so great. And I've got all these people that are so —I don't know. It would be so great if I could have all these people, Mrs. O, Mrs. Camp, and my dad, in a place that wasn't just a competition.

*Couldn't you put a little distance between you and the entourage people? Maybe tell them you need to have more time to yourself?*

I don't know. I've tried here. I just mainly said I've got a job to do and I want to do it. And they thought I was unreasonable. No, I don't know how I'm gonna handle it. Here, I said, "Look, go enjoy yourself. I've got my thing to do. And you're here having a good time. It's a vacation and a wonderful trip to Europe. So, sight-see. Do things, just please . . ." I just don't know. Guilt trip after guilt trip after guilt trip. [An hour and a quarter pass. Peter Carruthers arrives. Peter, like Scott, is deeply reflective. Scott charges up and brightens. Eventually, Peter too will become festive. We drink as we talk, working toward the critical beer-and-whiskey dosage for one last Worlds-end party.]

Scott: Oh good, more beer.

Peter: Oh, you got the awful stuff. I brought the good stuff. Sure I'm not interrupting? [Reassurance that he isn't interrupting] Well, I got all finished. Did all my laundry.... [Sits, ponders] A jellyfish, that's what I feel like right now. Just floating around in the ocean, doing nothing. You know, your day is so planned out before a competition. Every day from July has been well planned-out as to what I was gonna do. Now I'm finished. I don't know what I'm doing. I live from one minute to the next. I can't believe I'm depressed.

*Has this been tough on you, Peter?*

Peter: More than I ever expected it to be.

Scott: It's been tough on him because everybody has been telling him to turn pro.

Peter: The only thing I can say is you don't realize what it's like until it happens to you. You know what I mean? You can watch people make it around you. You can always imagine and speculate what it's like, until you do it. It is probably one of the best highs, and the most depressing lows you can get—four days after you've accomplished one of your goals. A goal you've been striving for all year and the last twelve years. So you get that high. And that night nobody could have touched me. Then I woke up the next morning and everything was fine. Then somebody made a comment to me on the elevator. I forget who it was. I can't remember who. Somebody said, "So, what are you going to do now?" I said, "What?"

Scott: You see, this is the thinning-out year, the second year, between Olympics. A lot of skaters look at turning pro at this point.

Peter: I said, "Well, I'm going to continue. Hopefully, we'll go for it." Then at twenty-minute intervals all day someone would ask the same thing, "You're going to stay in, aren't you?" That bothers me. And I'm just a little scared because I don't want to ever go below the bronze medal. I think I'd kill myself. [Laughs] I sat there in bed last night and every night before that and said, "What am I going to feel like next year if I go up to the results sheet and I'm in fourth or fifth place." I said to myself, "I couldn't cope." And then I said to myself, "Well, you've got to take the good with the bad." All that stuff has been bothering me.

*You people have such an extreme value system. If anybody in the rest of the world was told he was third best in the world at what he does, or fifth, or tenth, he'd be ecstatic. If it happened just one year, he might be happy for the rest of his life. And the television, the travel you guys get. What do you want?*

Scott: Yeah, but wouldn't you feel like you were going backwards or you were falling if you were third one year and you weren't third the next year? Let's say one of your goals was to be the third-best writer in the world. . . .

Peter: In writing you can't compete, it's like—

Scott: It's an art. A dancer, a writer, an actor. No such thing as the best, everybody's got his niche. But when you're an athlete, it's different.

Peter: It's material, it's a little more materialistic. You know, the Olympics was a funny thing for me. I think I got a little lost in the medal stuff. The gold medal, any medal. And from then on, I pushed this thing, "Oh God, how badly I want a medal." I still do, and now I've got a Worlds medal. But if you don't balance it out—you have to one hundred percent love what you do—if you don't balance it, it won't happen.

*To win you have to forget winning and skate for something else?*

Peter: I understand it now. One thing got me through this competition. Luddy, my coach, said to me, "If you go to Worlds, and if you're an artist, you'll come out fine. But if you go to win a medal, you're going to lose."

*David seemed unable to set aside the idea of winning. It's as if he couldn't skate for himself.*

Scott: No, he couldn't.

Peter: You know when I knew David was going to lose? At Worlds last year, he was second, and I said, "David, congratulations." And he said, "For what?" And I told him if he didn't know, then he wouldn't ever know.

Scott: He considered himself like this: like this other guy told me about medals. When you get gold, you're a winner, right? When you're a silver medalist, you're a loser. With bronze, it's, "Hey, I'm up there with the big guys!" I thought, when I heard that, it's got a place, that sort of thinking has got a point, but at the same time it's sick!

Peter: I saw something pretty neat when I left home. "Winning is being totally prepared."

Scott: [Dismissive laughter] That's something you see on a locker-room wall.

Peter: No, it's not that way at all! I was a scatterbrain before this. I didn't think about winning. I just wanted to skate well. You know, I'm very insecure with myself. Not as a person, but as a skater. Sometimes, I'll stroke around the ice, and I'll say to myself, "Oh my God! It doesn't feel like I should even be skating." And then I'll go out and do the performance of my life. I can't take anything for granted. My ambition exceeds my talent by a mile. I have to work so hard to get everything. Don't ever let anybody fool you that you can ride on talent. I don't believe you can do it.

*It never lets up for you guys, does it?*

Peter: The thing that bothers me about skating, it's the only thing in the world besides gymnastics that's subjective. And I don't understand gymnastics enough to make a comparison. Everything else comes right down to a line. You can understand what you have to do. But skating is so vast—it's like the universe. And all the people are telling you, "This is what you need." The judges come to your practice and say, "Your footwork steps should start in the corner more." And another judge will tell you your footwork's fine, but something else needs fixing. It's not a finish

333

line when you attain a goal in this sport. It's not a finish line at all. Do you feel that, Scott?

Scott: Three hundred million Chinese don't give a damn. How's that?

Peter: [Maundering now, under the influence of beer and exhaustion] And I can honestly say that I'm in love with what I do. Practicing with Kitty and skating in competitions.

Scott: [Giggling, pushing into uproariousness] It beats the hell out of working and going to school.

It's happening again. The tape runs on, but the noises the machine plays back are not reproducible. Peter launches into more monologue, but Scott is far too hilarious to listen. Peter tries to compare the expectation and the fact of medal winning to sweet desire and the letdown of love. But this leads into obscene repartee from which a return to seriousness is absolutely impossible. Peter doesn't even try. Instead he announces, "I could really heavily get into partying with you tonight, boy. . . ." The deadly solemn anthems from *Chariots of Fire* are long gone. Scott's boom box is giving us electro-ferrous primal scream.

"I'd better stop the tape," I said.

"Yeah," Scott said. "It's getting really bad, isn't it?"

So the little recorder stopped listening to Scott for the last time, forever. The Champ, of course, in his final sentence meant that things were getting really good, not bad. They were better than good. They were *gurre*at, getting *gurre*ater by the minute. The long lonely gray Sunday of suffering after victory was dead. And we were at the dawning of a new night, excellent and fair.

The Champ wanted to play now. And we were going to play on his screen. He put his finger on the button that would send us shooting out of the Scandinavia Hotel into the night. Into Scott's party hyperspace, that mad dimension beyond Hamilton's Planet. But Scott didn't push the big button just then. He waited, and there was a moment of delicious, crazy hush. The silver blaster was shut off. We suited up into shoes and coats and stood, taking a last comradely look at each other before the big jump. Then Scott pushed the button.

Our cab bore down a dark street at warp speed, apartment blocks smearing by, the driver wild with the urgency radiating from his passengers, inches and microseconds from a smashup so we could get to the night's most delicious places before anybody else. Scott cackled, firing bolts of white manic laughter into the darkness.

*Turn out the lights!*

# Afterword

That wild night in Copenhagen closed the 1982 World Championships, Scott's moment of greatest peril on the road to Sarajevo and the Olympic gold medal. By repeating his World Championship, Scott established a hegemony that was never seriously challenged. What could have been anyone's became *his*. Each win thereafter—and there were only wins—consolidated a position that seemed unassailable by the time he took the ice on Thursday, February 16, 1984, the day of long program at the Olympics.

Each competitive season after Copenhagen included new pressures and difficulties, but none was as cruel as 1982, Scott says. What was the hardest year for him was also, for a variety of reasons, the hardest year for his people. The Scott people all carried personal difficulties to the competitions that were so harrowing for the Champ himself. Scott, when I last saw him, in February 1985, was anxious that the reader know that 1982 was extraordinary, and that he, his people, and his sport should not be judged solely on the basis of what had happened in 1982. It got better, he said. And it got happier.

February 1983 saw Scott win another National Championship in Pittsburgh, Pennsylvania. He won figures, short program, and long program. He popped two triples in long, but those omissions failed to tarnish the program's overall shine. All nine judges gave Scott 5.9s for presentation and style. At the 1983 World Championships, Scott was second to Frenchman Jean-Christophe Simonde in figures. He took the lead, as in 1982, by winning short program. After his overall win at Helsinki, Scott spoke to reporters about the extraordinary pressures of that year. What really helped, he said, was talking to Dr. David Jenkins, the United States team physician. Dr. Jenkins once won three consecutive world skating titles, 1957 to 1959. Twenty-four years before Scott's triumph in Sarajevo, David Jenkins had won an Olympic gold medal. At Helsinki, Scott wore for the first time a type of costume that he and Don invented. The new outfit was a modified speed-skating costume, one-piece, dark, with bold stripes at the sides and no other adornment. The suit, a prototype for others Scott wore at the Olympics and still wears, was part of Scott's campaign to masculinize his sport, to make the world see it as a sport.

In November 1983, Scott competed in an obscure international meet in Zagreb, Yugoslavia. The Zagreb Golden Spin would not normally have merited the World Champion's participation, but Scott and other top competitors went to Zagreb to make an acquaintance with the host country of the upcoming Winter Olympics. After his win at the Golden Spin—over Norbert Schramm, among other Olympic hopefuls—Scott paid a visit to Sarajevo, to see what would be his most momentous ice.

Scott's last ranking competition before the Olympics was the United States National Championships in Salt Lake City, Utah. Looking back, he called this competition a dream. It was, indeed, near perfection. He won each event resoundingly, earning four 6.0s in long program. After winning this fourth National Championship, Scott said that those 6.0s, the most earned by a singles skater at Nationals in recent memory, would send signals across the Atlantic. Europe would take note of the fabulous numbers.

On the eve of the 1984 Olympics, Scott was proclaimed to be the heavy favorite. It seemed inconceivable that he could lose, after more than three years of winning. His grip on the gold medal seemed even more unbreakable after figures, which he won. The Olympics was the first major international competition in which he placed first in figures. Norbert Schramm virtually removed himself from contention in those compulsories by placing ninth.

Victory at that point should have been easy, but Scott placed second in short program to Brian Orser. The Canadian, who had beaten Scott in the St. Ivel International Competition in London in 1980, giving Scott his last taste of losing, was suddenly very hot. Scott was suddenly cold. Orser was fabulous again in long program, and Scott was a good deal less than fabulous. Scott had counted nine solid long-program run-throughs in practices before the Olympics. But solidity would not come to him when he most needed it. The world viewing audience could see the Champ's tension and terror as he started long program. This time he couldn't skate away from those inner enemies. The performance was tentative and off-center. Triple flip went bad on Scott, as it had in 1982 Worlds. He landed only three of his five planned triples. His first words coming off the ice were spoken to Don Laws. "I'm sorry," he said. He remained apologetic about that long program for weeks.

The world, of course, saw nothing to apologize for. Scott had won, under the most frightful pressure imaginable. Scott-mania reached a new pitch. He had made himself a bona fide national hero.

The following month, Scott competed at the 1984 World Championships. Worlds were in Ottawa, Canada, the site of the first World Championships in which he had competed. In 1978 Scott was eleventh at Worlds. In 1984 he was first, in a victory much more convincing than the perilous win at Sarajevo.

At the end of March 1984, Scott announced that he was leaving amateur figure skating competition. "Now it is time to go on to the adult part of my life," he told a press conference in Atlantic City, New Jersey. It was a highly emotional moment for the Champ. He told reporters that he was considering offers from several professional shows. Later, he signed with "Ice Capades." As he turned professional, Scott hired the management firm represented by the pilot fish at the Park Lane Hotel in New York City in 1982. His first year as a pro included a professional competition, which he won; exhibitions on TV; and commentary on the 1985 World Championships in Tokyo, Japan. In 1984, Scott, it seemed, was at the beginning of a long and profitable career as a sports personality, fulfilling a promise apparent to his followers for years.

Scott has met President Reagan, he has been feted and paraded, he has won awards. Wherever he goes he is the subject of attention and adulation. But the most booming triumph came in May 1984, when he came home to Bowling Green. He skated, as he has since 1968, in the Bowling Green Skating Club's annual show, which for years has been a High Mass of hometown Scott-worship. It has also been, because of Scott, a memorial to Dorothy Hamilton. Money is raised at each annual show to support cancer research.

The Bowling Green crowd, for its size, is the wildest in all of Sweetheartland. The wildness is unbelievable when Scott Hamilton skates. The ears hurt from all the screaming, the hands hurt from the furious and prolonged clapping that Scott compels. Sitting in that crowd, there is no choice but to join the mad, noisy adulation.

At the end of his numbers at the last of the three Bowling Green shows in May 1984, Scott stood at center ice, smiling and shaking from too many encores. "Thank you. Thank you," he mouthed to his adorers. He might have been saying it loudly, but all sound was lost in the pandemonium.

Scott's next move was one of those bits of ice theater at which he is so good. He drew down the zipper of his skating costume, from collar to heart level, and fished up a ribbon from which hung a shining disk of gold. He was showing the people the Olympic gold wrought from the ice in front of them, where a little boy, supposedly dying, had started skating eighteen years earlier. The gold medal trick, of course, went over just right, and the crowd boomed louder than ever.

But it seemed to me just then, as it seemed to other Scott people, that Scott Hamilton was not showing the medal to us. No, he was showing it to Dorothy Hamilton, who had always known that that gold medal belonged to her son.

# Index

United States Figure Skating Association (USFSA), 25, 70, 140, 178
United States Figure Skating Team (1980) ("Dream Team"), 117–118
United States Figure Skating Team (1981) ("Wazoo World Team"), 118
USFSA Memorial Fund, 125

Wagenhoffer, Robert, 189, 237, 247, 248, 257, 260, 262–263, 269, 271
Wagon Wheel (Rockton, Ill.), 35–37, 39, 40
Wakeman, Rick, 82, 83, 84, 91–93
wally, triple toe, 253, 321
waltz jumps, 25, 305
*Washington Post, The* 228
Weymouth, Mass., 3
Whitaker, Jack, 182, 183–184, 187
White, Jim, 152, 154, 155
"Wide World of Sports," 240, 246, 250, 251–252, 260–261
William G. Mennen Arena (Morristown, N.J.), 99–100, 122, 149, 151, 160, 161
*Wizard of Oz, The,* 222–223, 224

World Championships (1978) (Ottawa), 50, 225, 238
  Senior men's long program in, 218
World Championships (1979) (Vienna), 51, 142
World Championships (1981) (Hartford), 52, 69–70, 214, 326
World Championships (1982) (Copenhagen), 67, 69, 257, 320–340
  compulsory figures in, 321
  Senior men's long program in, 82–87, 88–96, 320–321, 326
World Championships (1983) (Helsinki), 336–337
World Championships (1984) (Ottawa), 338
World Championships (1985) (Tokyo), 339

Zagreb Golden Spin, 337
Zaitser, Aleksandr, 328
Zamboni, 130–131, 160, 197, 236, 288
Zayak, Elaine, 165, 237, 253–254, 255, 322, 328
Zeller, Erich, 279, 296, 300